POPULAR CINEMAS OF EUROPE

Also available from Continuum International

Will Brooker
Batman Unmasked

Sue Harper
Women in British Cinema

Chris Jones and Genevieve Jolliffe
The Guerrilla Film Makers' Handbook, Second Edition

Geoffrey Macnab
*Searching for Stars: Stardom and
Screen Acting in British Cinema*

Robert Murphy
British Cinema and the Second World War

Ulrike Sieglor (ed.)
*Heroines without Heroes: Reconstructing Female
and National Identities in European Cinema 1945–51*

Ginette Vincendeau
Stars and Stardom in French Cinema

POPULAR CINEMAS OF EUROPE

Studies of Texts, Contexts and Frameworks

Dimitris Eleftheriotis

Continuum
NEW YORK   LONDON

2001

The Continuum International Publishing Group Inc
370 Lexington Avenue, New York, NY 10017

The Continuum International Publishing Group Ltd
The Tower Building, 11 York Road, London SE1 7NX

Printed in the United States of America

Library of Congress Cataloging-in-Publication Data

Eleftheriotis, Dimitris.
    Popular cinemas of Europe : studies of texts, contexts, and frame
works / Dimitris Eleftheriotis.
        p. cm.
    Includes bibliographical references and index.
    ISBN 0-8264-5592-1 (alk. paper) -- ISBN 0-8264-5593-X (pbk. : alk.
paper)
        1. Motion pictures--Europe. I. Title.

  PN1993.5.E8 E52 2002
  791.43'094--dc21

                                                        2001056190

To
Lindsay, Ruby
and Emil

CONTENTS

Acknowledgments

A N EARLY VERSION of Chapter 1 has appeared in *Futures*, vol. 30, no. 10, in 1998, and under the title "Euro-visions: technologies of vision in *Until the End of the World*." A shorter version of Chapter 3 was published in *Screen*, vol. 41, no. 1, in 2000, under the title "Cultural difference and exchange: a future for European film" and as part of the "Millennial debates."

Many people have contributed to the completion of this project. I wish to thank all my colleagues at the University of Glasgow for their help and support throughout the project: John Caughie, Ian Craven, Ian Garwood, Ian Goode, Suzy Gordon, Karen Lury and Tony Pearson. Sean Cubitt and Julianne Pidduck for their encouragement and support. Special thanks to friends who have generously helped me to trace sources: Akis Georgopoulos, Rania Eleftheriotou, Yiannis Leventis, Nicos Maratos and most of all Gary Needham who provided me with hundreds of tapes of popular Italian films. Finally, many thanks to Lindsay Pratt for the many discussions which have helped enormously to give this book its shape and identity.

Introduction

THE STORY OF this project begins at the last chapter of the book. A bit like Toto's experience in *Nuovo Cinema Paradiso*, my fascination with cinema has a clearly defined time and place of origin. It was in the open-air venues of Greece in the 1960s that I discovered the fun and (again like Toto) the "magic" of the movies and formed an understanding of what cinema is all about. And while the last chapter of this book describes in neutral, objective terms certain aspects of that experience, it necessarily fails to communicate the extent to which that particular understanding became (as childhood things usually become) the unquestionable norm and a completely naturalized definition of cinema. That definition included not only an interruptive viewing experience that this book explores but also a genuinely international menu of films, stars and genres: the comedies of Louis de Funés and of Ciccio and Franco, spaghetti westerns and Greek melodramas, peplum and *policier*, but also Hollywood blockbusters, *Godzilla* and *Mother India*. My film universe was impure but hierarchized and one in which all these different kinds of cinema had a place.

Obviously Hollywood was exceptionally polished, but Greek films were really much more enjoyable and closer to me, whereas European and "other" films had a glamour and style that was absent from both of the first two. The difference between art and popular/commercial films had not occurred to me yet: *La dolce vita* was just a film (a bit weird admittedly) with Mastroianni in it.

But the present book is not an exercise in nostalgia that tries to recapture a lost plenitude that transcends cultural hegemonies and national borders, but an attempt to come to terms with the uncomfortable interface between the naturalized norm of my childhood and the discursive practices of Anglo-US film theory and criticism.

Significant parts of my experience and understanding of cinema remained either outside the scope or firmly in the margins of the discourse within which I operated as a student and teacher of film studies in Britain. It is the frustration in that experience that motivates the book's attempt to interrogate the appropriateness of the Anglo-US theoretical/critical frameworks for the study of popular European cinemas and, through an identification of the limitations of such frameworks, to propose more effective revised, expanded or alternative models.

Such a process involves a necessary initial consideration of definitions as well as an exploration of the discursive positionality and effects of such key terms as "Europe," "European film," "popular cinema" and "national cinema." The objective behind such questioning is not to provide accurate designations but to indicate how these terms are implicated in complex and interconnected clusters of meanings, connotations and discursive functions that inform not only critical evaluations but also theoretical and historical models. The first four chapters of this book are directly concerned with the conceptual revision of the theoretical frameworks that have traditionally informed the study of popular European cinemas. This revision, however, is not motivated by the desire to offer new precise definitions but by the need to challenge the authority of the existing ones and to disengage the study of popular European films and cinemas from sterile, exclusive and ultimately misleading binaries such as art/popular, political/commercial, European/American, national/global. Necessarily, many of the arguments that this book promotes are initially based on working definitions of the key terms "popular" and "European," which are subsequently challenged and expanded. Readers are asked to see the inability (and in this case unwillingness) to offer definitions not as a profound methodological weakness that undermines the validity of the argument, but, on the contrary, as a necessary frustration of certainty that takes the argument into new (and hopefully interesting) territories.

Indeed, the project of this book is not to fix meanings and positions but to suggest ways in which more inclusive, fluid and interactive approaches can be employed. This is one of the principles that informs the undeniably eclectic choice of case studies. The texts examined here are in most cases examples that challenge hegemonic definitions of the "popular" and the "European." In addition, and given the normative position that Hollywood occupies in Anglo-US film studies, an important concern of this book is to offer extensive considerations of specific historical and cultural contexts in which the case studies operate. In that respect, the challenge has been to acknowledge the relevance of national context while at the same time identifying ways in which such contexts are implicated in complex processes of interaction with broader cultural and historical forces. The case studies examined here are located in national and transnational contexts, are often examined as informed by processes of transculturation, and test the limits of totalizing and universalizing theoretical and critical paradigms.

It is important to realize that the case studies are to some extent arbitrary but not unmotivated choices. This book does not claim to offer a picture of popular European cinema that represents adequately the wealth of traditions, histories and styles that make up the object of study. It is important to note the geographical and historical eclecticism of the project: it covers only the post-World War II period and omits from the studies a great number of national European cinemas (nothing from "Eastern" Europe and Scandinavia, for example). As outlined above, the objective has been the methodological questioning of frameworks and the placing of texts in relevant contexts—the latter demands the in-depth study of a limited number of cases.

However, an effort has been made to use case studies that complement each other and work towards offering detailed knowledge of certain areas. The consideration of the *Gendarme* series in Chapter 4 offers a counterpoint to the discussion of the *Nouvelle Vague* in Chapter 2, and in that sense the two case studies capture something of the dynamism of French cinema in the 1960s. The analysis of spaghetti westerns in Chapter 5, the examination of the films of Lina Wertmüller in Chapter 6 and of cinéphilia in Chapter 8 offer an outline of Italian cinema in the 1960–1990 period. Similarly, the studies of Melina Mercouri's star image in Chapter 7 and of open-air cinemas in Chapter 8 provide useful insights into the Greek context in the 1950s and 60s. The three case studies in Chapter 7 aim to offer a diachronic and transcultural examination of the function of the family in Mediterranean cinemas. Finally, the analysis of *Until the End of the World* in Chapter 1, *Mediterraneo*, *Bhaji on the Beach*, and *Underground* in Chapter 3 and of *Nuovo Cinema Paradiso* in Chapter 8 raise different but interrelated issues of European film policy in the 1980s and 90s.

This book aims to facilitate research as well as teaching and learning about popular European cinema. The case studies were chosen with pragmatic pedagogic needs in mind, based as they are on some of the better known texts that are also (relatively speaking) easily accessible. At the same time, an effort has been made to treat the conceptual/theoretical considerations of the book in autonomous sections so that they can be flexibly adapted to function in relation to different texts and contexts.

This book appears at a time when the study of popular European cinemas is rapidly becoming an established and credible object of academic scholarship and is making an impact on curriculum design and research projects. It is important to acknowledge the efforts and achievements of academics such as Thomas Elsaesser, Christopher Frayling, Christopher Wagstaff, Ginette Vincendeau, Andrew Higson and Richard Dyer (the list is by no means exhaustive), whose formative and pioneering work in the 1980s and 90s has laid the foundations for the legitimization of popular European cinema as an object of study and research. Without their contributions the present book would appear even more eccentric and eclectic.

1 "EUROPE" AND THE "EUROPEAN FILM"

"Europe" is a slippery term. With every effort made to pin down its meaning(s), new sets of excluded concepts, overlooked relations and forgotten histories surface. This book adopts a *prima facie* pragmatic view of Europe: "Europe" as an encyclopaedic entity and a geographical term (a mass of land and islands extending from the Atlantic to the Urals, from the North Sea to the Mediterranean). In this sense "European" is a tag attached to a film merely because it was produced within these geographical boundaries and not a signifier of a fundamental European essence. This is a necessary simplification if anything at all is to be written about this under-researched area. But this pragmatic approach must be seen as the opening move, as a hesitant and admittedly reductive initial attempt to define the parameters of the object of study. The purpose of the current study is to explore the variety of ways in which the popular films and cinemas of Europe challenge unproblematic definitions and uses of the terms Europe and European. This first chapter is exclusively devoted to such elaboration but throughout the book conceptual, methodological and theoretical questions are raised in more specific contexts.

I shall first explore the positions that the terms "Europe" and "European film" occupy in relevant political, historical and cultural discourses and identify some of the contradictory meanings attributed to them. I shall also examine more specifically how some of these are articulated in the film *Until the End of the World* (original title *Bis ans Ende der Welt*, dir. Wim Wenders, Australia/Germany/France, 1991)

EUROPE

As BARRY SMART explains,[1] "Europe" as a geographical term originates with Herodotus, and it describes "one of two 'continents' that set limits to their [the ancient Greeks] northward sea passage, the other 'continent' being named Asia."[2] Not only does Herodotus's Europe bear no similarity to current geographical perception, it also indicates that the ancient Greeks had a clear sense of Europe as being outside their territory. Etymologically, Europe has its origins in the Greek myth of Europa, the daughter of the king of Tyre who was carried off by Zeus, but it is uncertain how the mythological figure of Europa came to represent what was erroneously believed to be a continent.[3]

A different account of the origins of the word places it in opposition to Asia in the Semitic Assyrian-Phoenician binarism *ereb/acu* (sunset/sunrise).[4] In either case, within mythology and etymology Europa/Europe is located outside Greece and outside what we now understand as Europe. This is ironic for two reasons: During the Renaissance (a historical period that produced a powerful and still influential definition of Europe), it was the Greek term that was used to define Europe as a geographical entity radically different from its original designation; and the revival and re-appraisal of ancient Greek civilization gave Europe its first unified project and constructed a sense of Europeanness as shared past and destiny.

This digression into the depths of history is only useful as a reminder that the search for European origins of a historical, cultural or even geographical nature is a more or less futile exercise. It also indicates that "Europe" is a term used in many varied and often contradictory ways in different periods and contexts. Furthermore, and in a positive way, it demonstrates that although the search for origin and essence is intellectually doomed, the meanings attributed to "Europe" and "Europeanness" can be traced and analyzed. Indeed, what passes as "Europe" and "European" has now become a major stake in a complex field of power relations. Current political discourses define "Europe" primarily as an "idea," or a "culture," shaped by historical processes and events and imagining itself in terms of certain "emblems that constitute the time and space of the Europeans."[5] At the same time they acknowledge and even celebrate the existence of a diversity of cultures.

Within these parameters, recent publications of pan-European organizations (such as the Council of Europe or the European Union) debating and making European cultural policy are very anxious to offer definitions invested with intellectual and political legitimacy. It is important to note the overwhelmingly anxious tone of such reports, as they try to reconcile the desire to discover unifying concepts with the need to avoid essentialism, both of which appear to be fundamental conditions in claiming the right to make policy in the name of Europe.

The 1997 report *In from the Margins: A Contribution to the Debate on Culture and Development in Europe* attempts to define "Europe." After declaring that "there are many Europes, whether viewed from a historical perspective or in terms of contemporary practicalities," the report proceeds to discover a unity in the realm of ideas:

> As well as ideas of Europe, there is too a Europe of ideas, transcending geography. From its Graeco-Judaic origins, transmitted through the Roman Empire, it persisted in the Renaissance of the fifteenth and twentieth centuries. It was accompanied by revolutionary technological advances, among them the invention of the compass and the printing machine. In the age of Reason during the eighteenth century, this culminated in a set of scientific and philosophical concepts (democracy, a progressive theory of history, human rights) and methods (rational enquiry, the industrial revolution). Although Europe has its roots in Christendom, its modern characteristics are predominantly pragmatic, materialist and secular."[6]

The European definition offered here is a selective reading of the history of the last 2,500 years that pays particular attention to the post-Renaissance period. It is in many ways a typical definition that constructs a unity and identity by privileging a specific and endlessly repeated set of historical events and processes:

– *The Renaissance*, which placed enormous emphasis on the humanistic traditions of Greece and Rome. More importantly the Renaissance introduced a system of representation that through perspectival systems established an individual and unified point of view. As Martin Heidegger has pointed out[7] this is crucial for understanding Europe's relationship with the world, as the techno-scientific aesthetics of perspective enabled artists, cartographers and scientists to objectify and master the world through the production of a "world picture."

– *The Enlightenment*, which introduced Reason as the epistemological mode through which Europeans make sense of the world. Reason was also seen as a guiding principle in the process of the reorganization of society. The epistemological and organizational models, as well as the ethical and cultural values that the Enlightenment produced, were (and in many ways still are) perceived as essentially European. Significantly, they were also perceived as fundamentally and unconditionally superior to any other alternative models and values originating inside or outside Europe.

- *The French Revolution* was the political process that embodied and materialized the values of the Enlightenment. As Michel Foucault notes[8], the death of King/God as a source of absolute personal political power is the essential requirement for the birth of the modern European as a subject who rationally deliberates in democratic institutions and is committed to the material, moral and cultural improvement of society.
- *The Industrial Revolution*, which materialized the faith in the positive effects of scientific progress and technological development, and the political and economic ambitions of capitalism.
- *Finally, modernism*, in which European experience found a concrete aesthetic expression and one that foregrounds doubt and uncertainty as fundamental components of European modernity.[9]

The European identity that emerges through this eclectic (and overwhelmingly hegemonic) re-working of history is celebrated in the humanist rhetoric of the *European Declaration on Cultural Objectives*, which affirms that

> the main aim of our societies is to enable everyone to achieve personal fulfilment, in an atmosphere of freedom and respect for human rights; such fulfilment is linked to culture which, together with other social, technological and economic influences, is an essential factor in the harmonious development of society; human resources—spiritual, intellectual and physical— provide both the object and the mainspring of development; these resources take the form of aspirations and values, of ways of thinking, being and acting, and they represent the fruits of historical experience and the seeds of the future.[10]

Skeptics like Sven Papcke, on the other hand, question the very necessity and political desirability of European identity. Papcke, while hostile to the project of discovering a unified essence of "Europe," is still able to assert

> the individual and his or her free will is a European discovery— if not a European invention, like the notion of political liberty. From it grew a *civil society* in Europe. Nowhere else have the ideas of personality, democracy, social justice, liberty, human rights and so on been defined.[11]

The key question that needs to be addressed here is the practical and political usefulness of such descriptions of Europeanness. Agnes Heller is one of the critics rejecting the possibility of pinning down a meaning to the word, even if this is guided by the will to deconstruct it:

> Modernity cannot be buried for it never died; rather, it simply worked out its own determinations. Europe, European culture, the European tradition and the like cannot be buried because they were never in existence. Mythological heroes and demigods are not buried.[12]

The resistance to pinning down a meaning for Europe is, nevertheless, enhancing its God-like ability to be "present everywhere and yet invisible."[13] Offering a definition based on the reading of modern history as discussed earlier has certain advantages. It makes obvious the fact that this understanding of Europe occupies a hegemonic position in national, transnational and pan-European political and cultural discourses and policies. It also offers a point of reference for mapping difference and diversity within Europe and for exploring the numerous contradictions inherent in such definition. Finally, it represents a rallying point, something tangible that we can engage with and deconstruct. Importantly, this hegemonic definition of Europe has become the target of post-colonial criticism, whose critique of Eurocentrism[14] has provided extremely invigorating and groundbreaking theoretical work. To dissolve Europe into an incoherent multitude of diversities is to make it immune to such criticism.

It is indeed postcolonial criticism that has sharply brought to attention some important historical processes and events that hegemonic definitions of Europeanness exclude:

- The so called "journeys of discovery" that led to the colonization of the rest of the world, as well as the crucial military role that cultural achievements such as cartography played in the process.
- The ruthless exploitation of the human, natural, economic and cultural resources of the planet, of which the slave trade represents the most obvious and shameful example.
- The various pseudo-scientific discourses of racism that were produced in the name of Reason and objectivity in order to support oppressive European practices.

- The systematic destruction of the planet in the name of technological progress.
- The blood baths of the last two centuries that were carried out
  in the name of democracy and/or nationalism.
- The systematic dismissal of the cultural production of the rest of
  the world as inferior and insignificant.

These processes and events are clearly as exclusively European as
the ones that the dominant definition foregrounds. They form an historically and culturally repressed in European identity that resurfaces
again and again as a strong sentiment of collective guilt. Antoigne
Compagnon notes that European identity is founded on doubt,

> not only Descartes' hyperbolic doubt, that is, the strength to
> make a *tabula rasa* of one's own reason, as has been achieved
> repeatedly in the history of Western thought and science, but
> also the doubt which I would call, with Hegel, the moment of
> "unhappy consciousness."[15]

It is indeed this "unhappy consciousness," this collective guilt
usually disguised as philosophical doubt, intellectual liberalism or
political self-criticism, that is expressed in Europe's commitment to
cultural diversity under the banner of multiculturalism. This usually takes the form of a re-working of European values in order to
accommodate diversity and difference.[16] As a result, diversity in the
form of multiculturalism is celebrated as an expression of cultural
democracy, while difference is endorsed in terms of the fundamental
human right to self-expression. The following passage from another
Council of Europe resolution is revealing.

> Policy for society as a whole should have a cultural dimension
> stressing the development of human values, equality, democracy
> and the improvement of the human condition, in particular by
> guaranteeing freedom of expression and creating real possibilities
> for making use of this freedom . . . Cultural policy can no longer
> limit itself exclusively to taking measures for the development,
> promotion and popularisation of the arts; an additional dimension
> is now needed which, by recognising the plurality of our societies,
> reinforces respect for individual dignity, spiritual values and the
> rights of minority groups and their cultural expressions. In such a
> cultural democracy, special efforts must be made on behalf of dis-
> advantaged and hitherto unprivileged groups in society.[17]

Despite the humanist (and patronizing) rhetoric, the contradiction between essential "unifying concepts" and "cultural diversity" is impossible to resolve in any meaningful way except through ad hoc political pragmatism. European unity in the sphere of culture, then, becomes an objective rather than a given, and it is to be achieved through the measures and policies introduced.[18]

It is important to consider briefly other contradictions inherent in dominant definitions of Europe, the first of which revolves around the universal character of European values. This privileged identity depends on an intellectual heritage of a European historical origin that, nevertheless, negates its geographical and cultural specificity[19] because European values are transformed into "universal principles," to be European means to be nothing in particular.

In a different but highly pertinent context, Richard Dyer has noted that "there is no more powerful position than that of being 'just' human. The claim to power is the claim to speak for the communality of humanity."[20] The ability of the European identity to dissolve itself as a particular position echoes Foucault's analysis of modern subjectivity as demonstrated within representation in Velazquez's *Las Meninas*.[21] The fact that the self-effacing subjectivity described there is defined as modern rather than European is not an analytical oversight but reflects this constitutive aspect of European identity on the level of philosophical meta-language. The structural similarity and the conceptual overlap between Europeanness, modern subjectivity and whiteness (as both Dyer and Foucault demonstrate) have powerful effects on discourse and politics. At a historical moment when all three categories are under attack, nevertheless, this powerful construction becomes an insurmountable weakness in attempts to answer questions about the specificity and distinctiveness of contemporary European identity.

Another aspect of the dissolution of Europeanness into universality is the "planetary consciousness" that characterizes Europe's historical relationship with the rest of the world since the Renaissance.[22] This originates with the first perception of the world as a planet and the representational and political activities that accompanied it. Europe sees itself as part of a whole but from a privileged position and with a specific role to fulfil. In the course of history the role and the position may change (for instance, from exploring to exploiting to civilizing to raising ecological awareness), but the perception, dictated by Europe's planetary consciousness, remains fundamentally the same. The disastrous results of centuries of European interventions have led to the recent crisis around the impossibility of discovering a meaningful role for Europe in the world, a position that cannot go beyond simply expressing its guilty or unhappy consciousness. It is not paradoxical, then, that Europeans have intensified their efforts to reclaim a position and a role in the world by waving the flag of enlightened multiculturalism and through the exploration of their self-inflicted colonial traumas.

This is clearly linked to yet another problem in the formation of contemporary European identity. As the definition offered earlier outlines, Europe understands itself in terms of a past carefully chosen from the mixed bag of history. But the need of heritage or tradition for the establishment of a common cultural identity goes against the modern impulse to break with tradition and the past. Indeed, in many contemporary discourses the past emerges as a nightmare that still haunts Europe. The recent wars in the former Yugoslavia were very much interpreted in terms of a regression to a past that is best forgotten rather than as a conflict with understandable (albeit horrific) motives and objectives. From his position as president of the European Bank for Reconstruction and Development, Jacques Attali wrote in September 1992:

> We take pride that western Europe, which travelled the sad road of disintegration before, has been able to put in place structures to combat our oldest, most shameful vice, that of racial repression, which taints our history from the expulsion of the Muslims in 1492 to the concentration camps of the second world war . . . Without action to stop wholesale disintegration, the basic political unit in the East will become tribal. The normal state will be one of war with other tribes, each fighting for a position of dominance that it can only hold temporarily, each feeling insecure and threatened by its neighbors and each seeking alliances to pursue its narrow ends. Life for the individual will become like that described by Thomas Hobbes in *Leviathan*: solitary, poor, nasty, brutish and short.[23]

This is a perfect example of the attempts made to reconcile the impossible contradictions of Europeanness: the present conflict is exorcised as something belonging to the past whose resurgence threatens the political and cultural achievements of the present. The circularity of the argument goes hand in hand with an understanding of history repeating itself, running in perpetual circles, which in itself shatters any belief in progress and development. Attali also divides Europe (in the most banal and reactionary way) into East and West in terms of their different forms of political and social organization.

This is only one of the ways in which differences within Europe can be mapped in relation to the defining historical processes discussed earlier. Other differentiations include the distinction between North and South (in terms of industrialization), the distinction between nations actively involved in the "journeys of discovery" and colonization and those who did not, the questioning and sometimes rejection of Enlightenment values in South-eastern Europe,[24] and, crucially for this book, the distinction between high forms of art of the modernist tradition and popular forms of mass entertainment.

The European Film

AT THE BEGINNING of this chapter it was stressed that this book defines "European films" in a very pragmatic way. It is now the time to consider the meanings and connotations attached to the term, the positions from which they are coming from and what specific power effects they have.

An obvious starting point is the exploration of differences and contradictions of Europeanness in the specific context of film culture. The European "difficulty" around unity/diversity becomes crucial here: should we understand European films as expressions of a shared set of aesthetic, moral, philosophical and cultural values and attitudes or, conversely, as expressions of the diversity of such values across Europe? On the level of policy making this is often articulated as a conflict between a commitment to develop national film production (especially in the smaller countries) and the desire to encourage the production and distribution of films which can cross national borders.

To privilege unity, in this context, is to ignore the historical contradictions and differentiations within European identity; it also demonstrates a reductive understanding of the interaction between culture and society which assumes that shared values somehow find expression in the various national and regional cultures of Europe and their films. Richard Dyer and Ginette Vincendeau outline some of the ways in which a fragile unity can be established around the "heritage" genre and various projections of a shared European history, or around the important aesthetic movements of European modernity: realism and modernism.[25] A theme that combines the two is the understanding of cinema as an essentially European invention, which constitutes in this sense an essential cultural component of a common European heritage and represents in its simplest form a technological and scientific apparatus firmly embedded in European modernity. The recent celebrations across Europe of the one hundred years of cinema offered a clear manifestation of this theme.

To privilege diversity, on the other hand, entails an understanding of European film as simply one that happened to be produced within the national culture (in itself fragmented) of a particular country in Europe. Despite the rhetoric of "shared cultural values" and the commitment to various forms of transnational cooperation, this appears to be the *modus operandi* of the policy-making bodies in Europe. Such an understanding invites the obvious and cynical question of what gives to these films their Europeanness. The various responses to this question take us back to arguments around unity, but they also map a number of important positions in relation to European cinemas.

A very common (and very old, as Dyer and Vincendeau point out[26]) response is to define the European film in opposition to Hollywood. This binary operates on two levels: on the level of the industry, it surfaces in the familiar arguments around the challenges of globalization (and American dominance) and strategies for the survival of European cinema. On the level of cultural policy it is often raised in debates around cultural imperialism, resistance, quality and identity. There are several important problems with the Europe/Hollywood binarism. Firstly, and fundamentally, it tends to establish European identity in a negative way, as a negation of America. Secondly, it imposes essential qualities on both European and Hollywood films that oversimplify and reduce the complexity of both. Stephen Cleary, of British Screen Finance, offers one of many examples of the latter:

> We should recognize that European cinema is in no way similar to American cinema. It does not *explain* the world to its audience, it comments on it. In Europe, we used art to explain the world to ourselves during the Renaissance, we're older, more tired, a little more frightened than America, but we've seen more.[27]

Thirdly, the Europe/Hollywood distinction is usually translated as an opposition between art cinema (perceived as essentially European) and entertainment/popular/commercial cinema (seen as American), which is counterproductive for the study of both Hollywood and European films.

Finally, this distinction implies that the only meaningful comparison for European cinema is Hollywood, and in this sense relegates the rest of the world's film production into epistemological otherness.

Another way of discovering European unity is by equating Europeanness with universality, very much in the manner discussed in the previous section. From this perspective the challenge for European filmmakers is to discover and tell stories that, although local and European in origin, have a universal appeal. This rather worn out argument about the nature of "true art" is used repeatedly in debates around European film policy. For example, Jean-Claude Carriere (President of the Foundation for Audiovisual Professions, FEMIS, France) in the Third Plenary Meeting of the European Television and Film Forum, argued:

> A local story can become a world-wide one, if it is true, if it goes into depth. The main thing is to respect the truth, the reality of the story: if human nature is felt to be infinitely true and profound, the story will become known to all even if it is set in remote or forgotten surroundings. Contrary to "Middle Ocean Pictures" of the 60s, a story with true meaning will interest everyone and will not get lost in the middle of the Atlantic Ocean like these films which sought to be both European and American at the same time, and which ultimately were neither, but just good for throwing "into the middle of the ocean."[28]

This rhetoric demonstrates a number of profoundly Eurocentric assumptions. It is based on the belief that truth and "great art" are universal and that Europeans have a privileged access to both. It suggests that a successful film is one that negotiates the trans-Atlantic journey—yet another journey of discovery/conquest. It takes for granted that everyone is interested in the great European stories. And finally, it assumes that commercial or popular films (the "middle ocean pictures of the 60s") have no place and no aesthetic value within European culture.

It is particularly alarming that such banality informs the discussions and the decisions of the policy-makers on a pan-European level. It must come as no surprise at all, then, that ambitious pan-European programmes (such as the two MEDIA initiatives) can only deal with the fundamental unity/diversity contradiction by resorting to criteria that resolve nothing. For example, the European Script Fund of MEDIA I identified as a priority the funding of "strong stories that travel across one or more European borders." This already vague general principle is implemented in a very simplistic and mechanistic fashion: "Preference is given to those projects with interest from co-development partners in countries other than those from which a project is submitted."[29] It is this logic that has led to the creation of the notorious category of the "Euro-pudding," a term used to describe a co-production that is determined by the necessities of funding rather than the desire of the makers to work together.

In critical and theoretical discourses the terms "European cinema" and "European film" are equally elusive. A well established canon operates in the UK in terms of the choice of films, directors, historical periods and national cinemas that are usually included in courses on "European cinema." The canon is too well known to be listed here, but Dyer and Vincendeau's comment is highly relevant:

> Part of the existing map of cinema is coloured in quite clearly: there is America, which is Hollywood, which is popular entertainment, and there is Europe, which is art. Critics and historians of film have started to put new shades into the picture: the USA has since the First World War, been massively part of European cinema, above all for audiences; aesthetic developments in European film have time and again found their way into Hollywood production (e.g. expressionism, the horror movie and film noir, the new waves and "New Hollywood Cinema"). Yet one aspect of the equation remained stubbornly unacknowledged: popular entertainment cinema made by Europeans for Europeans.[30]

An additional difficulty is that in the UK almost every European film (with the possible exception of films starring Gerard Depardieu) is exhibited in art house cinemas, thus further reinforcing the identification of European cinema with art cinema. The only area of engagement with popular entertainment cinema is within a culture of so called "Euro-trash" cult films, which has its own lesser known but still well-defined canon. This book, as any book on the subject, will have to challenge the hegemony of both canons and revise the critical approach to them.

Some of the contradictions around definitions of Europeanness and European film and cinema will become clearer in the following section with specific reference to the film *Until the End of the World*.

Europe and the World in *Until the End of the World*

UNTIL THE END of the World tries hard to be a global film. It is an international co-production involving three countries and four production companies: Warner Bros., Argos Films, Village Roadshow Productions and Road Movies Filmproduktion. It was shot on location in many different countries (Australia, Italy, Japan, Portugal, Russia, USA, France and Germany), and relied on local crews for much of the technical support. It boasts a cast of international stars: William Hurt, Sam Neil, Jeanne Moreau, Max von Sydow and Solveig Dommartin, among others. It is not only in terms of the production process that the film appears to be global, but also in terms of its thematic preoccupation with the future of the planet, its narrative mode (a chase around the world), and its potential global appeal (a film relevant to different people across the globe). The latter is a highly contentious issue, however, as the film was very much a failure in box office terms and not particularly popular with the critics. More importantly, I will argue that in its attempt to speculate about our global future the film mobilizes distinctive and definitive European perspectives.

The film's imagining of the near future, as is usually the case with science fiction, focuses on technological development. To its credit, *Until the End of the World* avoids naïve technological determinist views of the future, making clear links between the past, the present and the future, and exploring the social and cultural dimensions of technology. The film is particularly preoccupied with the future of "technologies of vision," the techno-scientific and artistic ways through which we represent the world around us.

These technologies of vision are contrasted with more traditional processes of story telling. I shall examine the narrative structure of the film with particular emphasis on the position and the function ascribed to the narrator. The discursive origins of technologies of vision and the film's critique of them do not occupy antithetical positions, but belong to a singular historical process, sharing a common "destiny" and coming from the same perception of the world. In other words, the film's indictment of technologies of vision offers a futuristic vision of the world that is nothing else but a Euro-vision.

This vision is particularly significant as the film can be also seen as a contradictory, confused but very powerful statement on the future of cinema in Europe. This is further underlined by the fact that the film is directed by Wim Wenders, who

> has committed himself to promoting European film through his chairmanship of the European Film Academy while he also warns of the supreme importance of retaining a specifically European cinema, since without its own images, Europe will lose its identity.[31]

Interestingly, as Stan Jones argues, Wenders perceives his filmmaking as part of a "European way of seeing"[32] that he contrasts with the American view of the world. *Until the End of the World* is particularly important as it can be read not only as an allegorical manifesto on the future of cinema but also as a fiction about the future of technologies of vision and vision itself.

Technologies of vision are systems of organizing and ordering our visual perception of the world. This usually involves sophisticated technology (as in digital imaging, television, cinematography, photography, cartography, map-making and X-rays), but it can also be accomplished by simple applications of scientific principles (as in perspectival systems of representation, the camera obscura, shadow theatre and optical toys) and even very "low tech" embodiments of practical knowledge (as in the structure of lecture theatres, hospitals and prisons, or in the "packaging" of nature as a set of landscapes, panoramas and vistas).

Until the End of the World presents us with a vast array of such technologies ranging from digital cameras, camcorders, computer graphics and videophones to futuristic apparatuses such as machines that enable blind people to see and equipment that records the unconscious process of dreaming. Significantly these technologies are also shown as key communication instruments: the technologies of vision of our past, present and future also define the possibilities and modes of human communication.

Indeed, a way of understanding both communication processes and technologies of vision is in terms of their belonging to the same project of conquering time and distance—a process characteristic of European modernity. This is powerfully expressed in Marshall McLuhan's fantasy of the global village,[33] which connects technological "progress" with an optimization of communication opportunities and democracy.

David Harvey, in his book *The Condition of Postmodernity*, examines time-space articulations in European systems of representation, scientific discourses and political processes, and proposes "time-space compression" as one of the defining characteristics of modernity and postmodernity:

> I use the word "compression" because a strong case can be made that the history of capitalism has been characterised by a speed-up in the pace of life, while so overcoming spatial barriers that the world sometimes seems to collapse inwards upon us . . . As space appears to shrink to a "global village" of telecommunications and a "spaceship earth" of economic and ecological interdependencies—to use just two familiar and everyday images—and as time horizons shorten to the point where the present is all there is (the world of the schizophrenic), so we have to learn how to cope with an overwhelming sense of compression of our spatial and temporal worlds.[34]

Interestingly, in its very title, *Until the End of the World* suggests a coming together of time and space. The "end" of the world is both a moment (the destruction of the planet, the moment the Indian satellite gets shot down by the Americans) and a place (the antipodes, the final destination in the journey of the characters around the world).

The film launches a humanist critique of the myth of the "shrinking world": far from bridging the distance between people, or between individuals and their dreams and desires, modern technologies of vision appear to be alienating and destructive. The film perceptively foregrounds some of the recurring themes of European modernity starting with the primacy accorded to sight. In a detailed analysis of the role of the senses in different cultures and historical periods, Constance Classen traces a long history of European obsession with the visual, an obsession that intensifies with modernity.[35] As Classen argues, this preoccupation with vision stretches across a wide field of disciplines, sciences, artistic practices, everyday life[36] and public imagination.

Until the End of the World indirectly but clearly equates blindness with death, as the restoration of Edith Farber's (Jeanne Moreau) vision becomes a life-absorbing quest for her son Sam (William Hurt) and her husband Henry (Max von Sydow). Equally significant is the fact that the importance of vision is defined negatively, in terms of the tragic consequences of its loss. This kind of negativity is also encountered in the perception of time and space (and even of the world itself), as they can only be perceived at the moment and place of their end. According to Michel Foucault, this is a major (and tragic) paradox of modern European definitions of life. The emergence of secularism and scientific rationalism liberates human beings from the restraints of theology, while at the same time it leaves them unprotected from mortality.[37] As Foucault argues, within the modern discursive regime life is only understood as non-death—this principle underlies the foundation of the human sciences and conventional medicine[38] and is epitomized by anatomy, which seeks to discover the secrets of life in the examination of dead bodies.

Henry and Sam try to define the meaning and purpose of their own lives in a similar fashion in terms of a negativity (in fact a double negativity): the removal of blindness. It is worth noting at this point that Max von Sydow's most memorable role is that of the Knight in Ingmar Bergman's *The Seventh Seal* (Sweden, 1956), where he engages Death in a game of chess with his life as the stake. The Knight comes close to defeating Death but he loses in the end, a striking similarity to Henry's ultimately unsuccessful struggle to defeat blindness in *Until the End of the World*.

Henry's scientific project is criticized by the film as a rational but ultimately inadequate way of perceiving life that reduces experience to a series of visual and neurological data. *Until the End of the World* employs a number of strategies to this effect: fragments of dialogue ("the eye does not see the same as the heart"), narrative incidents (Sam losing his sight in the process of recording "the biochemical event of seeing," and Claire's [Solveig Dommartin] addiction to the "dream-recording machine"), but most powerfully around the character of Edith.

Her relationship to the new technology that will deliver her from blindness is ambiguous. While curious and excited about the possibility of seeing again she also seems to be stoically resigned to the role of the victim assigned by her husband. In a highly emotional sequence she rediscovers vision as her brain replays Claire and Sam's recordings of messages from her relatives. But the sadness of the experience outweighs the fascination of seeing people again.

The visual contact with the image of her daughter (the first person she sees) is marked by sentiments of distance, separation and loss, rather than the pleasures of a reunion. The sequence opens with numerous shots of the hectic preparations for the experiment. This immediately attracts attention to the technological apparatus and the processes of control rather than the emotional implications of the event. Furthermore, the actual experience initiates with Edith's oral description of the material components of the image ("Colours. Blue. Yellow. Red. A person sitting by a window. Blue hair-band. Yellow dress. She's sitting, hands folded."), which is followed by a rather ambiguous moment of recognition ("Can this be our daughter, Henry?"). This drives a wedge in the assumed natural, transparent and self-affirming link between the signifier and the signified of the image, and it foregrounds the basic inadequacy and impossibility of the project: capturing the signifier does not entail the reproduction of the experience.

Furthermore, the overwhelmingly sad mood of the sequence can be understood in terms of Roland Barthes' well known argument that the photographic image is marked by a sense of loss or death, as the presence of the photograph is the ultimate proof of the absence of the person depicted.[39] In this instance, the splitting of the signifier and the signified is caused by the overwhelming reality of life as a continuum and the impossibility to bridge the gap between past and present—in Edith's experience the referent returns with a vengeance. This is further emphasized by the nature of the recorded messages addressed to Edith: they celebrate the technological miracle of the restoration of her vision but they also lament the lack of direct contact with her and emphasize the time that has lapsed: "This is your granddaughter. You went away before she was born" or "I wish Sam had found me home in Lisbon—with the kids."

The voice-over confirms the sadness of the experience: "Edith Eisner had been eight years old when she lost her sight. The experience of seeing the world again was exhilarating but it was also confusing and disorientating and unpredictably sad. Her childhood friends aged fifty years in a minute; the world they moved in was darker and uglier than she could possibly have imagined. It would have been ungracious for her to mention these things. Her grief was there for those with eyes to see it."

To the complete incomprehension of her husband, Edith chooses to die rather than live in a world that has now become meaningless to her. Here again we see the equation of sight with life (formu-
lated negatively): unable to choose blindness, she chooses death.

Until the End of the World proceeds to criticize the implications
of the obsession with the image and technologies of vision: Henry
develops an electronic system of recording and playing-back
dreams. The Mbantua people abandon the camp and Henry, who
is now obsessed with success and fame, continues to work alone
until American agents arrest him. Claire and Sam become dream
addicts wandering in the narcissistic labyrinth of their own unconscious and lose interest in each other and any desire to live outside
the world of images.

At this point the film offers an alternative to the destructive
addictiveness of the culture of the simulacrum.[40] Both Sam and
Claire are cured, the former through the rituals of the Mbantua people and the latter through reading Gene's story, which is at the same
time the narrative of the film.

The importance of narrative in a postmodern world obsessed
with the image and the visual has been emphasised by cultural
theorists and critics. Fredric Jameson's pessimistic diagnosis of a
contemporary culture immersed in a perpetual present, describes
it (in terms that echo the film's critique) as schizophrenic. The
term implies the breaking down of the signifying chain and the
dislocation of the relationship between signifier and signified
which results in a loss of meaning—the dissolution of a continuous temporal structure (a sentence or a story for example) into
numerous fragmented instances in which the present emerges
"overwhelmingly vivid and material." This form of temporality
leads, according to Jameson, to an inability to articulate a coherent historical perspective and to arrange a temporally lived experience or social life.[41]

Eugene Fitzpatrick, the narrator of the film, expresses a similar
conviction in the film as his voice-over explains: "I didn't know the
cure for the disease of images. All I knew was how to write. But I
believed in the magic and healing power of words and of stories."
The film clearly implies that Claire is cured precisely because she
reads the narrative that Gene has written, a chronicle of Claire's
adventures that helps her to get her life in perspective and make
sense of it.

Until the End of the World explores the act of story-telling in a variety of ways. It foregrounds the complexity surrounding the role of the enunciator of the story. The narrator is defined as being a character in the story (Eugene Fitzpatrick the novelist), as performing a function (telling the story of the film) and as a position (from where we can make sense of the diegesis). Furthermore, the film problematizes the relationship between enunciation and enunciated. When Claire tells Gene that she plans to go to Berlin to look for Sam, her utterance "I'm going to Berlin" appears on the screen of his voice-sensitive computer. In this way a tension is created and playfully exploited between the moment of action and the moment of narrating the action, between enunciation and enunciated. Later, the collapse of Gene's computer leads to a return to the beginning of the story: "I'd been trying to write a novel that wouldn't come right . . . so as we run before the fatal winds I began again . . . I wrote: '1999 was the year the Indian nuclear satellite went out of control . . .'" Finally, *Until the End of the World* introduces a model of "depth" (again reminiscent of Jameson's critique of postmodernity) whereby story-telling is shown as closer to capturing the richness and complexity of lived experience than the superficial reproduction of the visual data of this experience through technologies of vision.

On the other hand, the nature of Sam's cure from his image addiction relates to Jean François Lyotard's reappraisal of the function of narrative in postmodern societies.[42] The kind of knowledge that the Mbantua people mobilize in order to cure Sam is described by Lyotard as "narrative," a term that emphasises the fact that this type of knowledge circulates within society almost exclusively by means of story-telling. Significantly, Lyotard suggests that such knowledge has the effect of maintaining the cohesion of society, and it is in this respect radically different from scientific knowledge that develops in relative independence and with little feedback from society.

Until the End of the World, then, offers a comprehensive survey of the role and function of narrative in contemporary culture. At the same time, the film criticizes our society's obsession with the visual. This appears to be a paradox, as Wenders' cinema depends on a combination of the two, on the inter-relationship between audio-visual and narrative modes of representation. Furthermore, it can be argued that the appeal of *Until the End of the World* lies primarily with the audio-visual: not only in terms of the exotic locations, the impressive photography and the beauty of the dream sequences, but also in terms of the carefully selected non-diegetic music (for many the most appealing aspect of the film). It seems that Wenders is trapped within a binarism (surface/depth, image/narrative) that the film fails to resolve. This is not the only binarism that the film relies upon: the old dichotomies mind/body, instinct/science, male/female inform the stereotypical technophobia of the film.

Martin Heidegger and Michel Foucault have identified as a defining characteristic of technologies of vision the unbreakable link between techno-scientific representations of the world and the political project that they help to realize. Heidegger explains how the development of perspectival representation is closely related to a will to objectify and master the world. Heidegger understands the latter as both the "world around us" and the world in the political and economic sense (the planet and its resources).[43] Foucault, on the other hand, makes specific connections between scientific discourses, technological applications and political practices in his analysis of technologies of vision as systems of maintaining social order and control.[44] Furthermore, as postcolonial criticism has demonstrated, these systems of control are closely connected to the European scientific, political and cultural domination of the world.

Until the End of the World's critique of technologies of vision is restricted to a purely individualistic dimension, as the characters' obsession with the image is blamed for the destruction of European sensitivity. It is only in a humorous and rather tokenistic fashion that the film refers to political implications and possible action—in the final sequence of the film Claire is shown orbiting the planet in a "Greenspace" satellite "watching the planet for pollution crimes."

The film represents the world as a set of attractive and exotic locations that provide a commercially appealing and visually stunning background to the action. The engagement with "other" cultures is completely superficial as they are often reduced to orientalist stereotypes. While "depth" is required to recapture Europe's "soul," "surface" is rendered adequate for the representation of Russia, Siberia, China and Japan as the worn out visual clichés demonstrate. Aboriginal and Japanese "traditional" methods are employed in order to cure the effects of Western technology—yet another binarism that the film mobilizes.

The critique of technology offered is not new or original. The film's humanism falls well within the Romantic tradition of European modernity. From Mary Shelley's *Frankenstein* to Fritz

Lang's *Metropolis*, and from Daniel Defoe's *Robinson Crusoe* to Sigmund Freud's reading of the Promethean myth,[45] what we witness again and again is Europe's anxiety with technology. This is often represented as human-made technology out of control, threatening the very existence of humans and throwing Renaissance and Enlightenment definitions of identity into deep crisis, and is undoubtedly symptomatic of Europe's "unhappy consciousness," discussed earlier. Importantly, this anxiety (as is clearly the case in *Until the End of the World*) is expressed in an insular, soul-searching manner, without awareness of its own historical perspective and with no will to address its political implications. The film's critique of technologies of vision is structured around sensibilities treated as universal and eternal instead of arising within the specific context of the crisis of European identity and culture.

The anxiety around the power of images is currently particularly intense in Europe. Characteristic of this tendency is the fact that the two most influential critics of the culture of the simulacrum, Jean Baudrillard and Umberto Eco, not only locate this culture outside Europe, but also assume a European position of distance and superiority. "American intellectuals envy us" claims Baudrillard,[46] while Eco asserts: "When I am in France or Germany I am not conscious of being European. When I am in the United States I am."[47]

While Wenders does not seem to make such a blatant statement in *Until the End of the World*, he clearly employs an "us" and "them" binarism, which places Europeans in situations where they learn from other cultures in order to cure themselves. The film is about Europeans discovering the cure for the "disease of the images," and, if we unravel the metaphor, about the future of European cinema. This is particularly significant because, as already discussed, Wim Wenders is an influential personality whose vision of the future of the European film industry is often evoked in debates around cultural policy.[48] If *Until the End of the World* is a model for the European film of the future, a clear recipe emerges: a self-reflexive narrative, supported by impressive cinematography, a marketable soundtrack and international stars, which offers a balanced combination between anxious European soul-searching and a reassuring demonstration of global sensitivity.

The suggested remedy, nevertheless, is vague and contradictory. The rediscovery of the art of story-telling and the respect for other cultures is a banal and empty suggestion which echoes the equally vague analysis of the policy-maker who in a manner reminiscent of *Until the End of the World*, urges the

> artist to consider Europe, the necessity for it to protect itself, to be a presence and to have a perception of other cultures which are infinitely richer, but which are denied costly technological means, so that other cultures, other stories do not disappear with it.[49]

Ironically, the film's commitment to story-telling is undermined by the fact that the pleasures that it offers have very little to do with the circular and contrived narrative but mainly with the attraction of the images and sounds. The dream sequences, a mixture of film, video and digital technology, are the most memorable and engaging of the whole film. The soundtrack proved to be more successful commercially than the film itself.

Despite its rhetoric, then, *Until the End of the World* imagines and offers a comprehensive example of a future in which cinema's specificity is lost within a general audio-visual sector of convergent media. Remarkably, this is identical to the view of the (not so distant) future expressed by European policy-making bodies: not only in many recent debates and documents the term "audio-visual" replaces specific references to cinema but the audio-visual itself becomes part of a broader framework as blueprints for an "information society"[50] emerge.

Notes

1. Barry Smart, "Europe today and the postmodern paradox," in Brian Nelson et al. (eds), *The Idea of Europe: Problems of National and Transnational Identity* (New York/Oxford: Berg, 1992).
2. Ibid, pp. 26–27.
3. See for example Terry Jordan, *The European Culture Area: A Systematic Geography* (Harper and Row, New York, 1973) which discusses the "misconception of Europe as a continent" in its first chapter entitled "Europe: a culture rather than a continent."
4. Ibid, pp. 2–3.
5. Antoine Compagnon, "Mapping the European mind," in Duncan Petrie (ed), *Screening Europe* (London: BFI, 1992), p. 109.
6. Council of Europe, *In from the Margins: A Contribution to the Debate on Culture and Development in Europe* (Strasbourg: Council of Europe Publishing, 1997).
7. Martin Heidegger, "The age of the world picture," in *The Question*

Concerning Technology (New York: Harper and Row, 1977).

8. Michel Foucault, *The Order of Things* (London: Tavistock, 1970); Michel Foucault, *Discipline and Punish* (London: Penguin, 1977).
9. A. Compagnon, op. cit.
10. *European Declaration on Cultural Objectives*; Appendix to Resolution no. 2 of the 4th Conference of European Ministers responsible for Cultural Affairs, Berlin, 23–25 May 1984.
11. Sven Papcke, "Who needs European identity and what could it be?" in B. Nelson et al, op. cit., p. 72.
12. Agnes Heller. "Europe: an epilogue?" ibid, p. 23.
13. A. Compagnon, op. cit., p. 106.
14. For example Ella Sohat and Robert Stam, *Unthinking Eurocentricism: Multiculturalism and the Media* (London and New York: Routledge, 1994).
15. Compagnon, op. cit., pp. 110–11.
16. For a distinction between cultural diversity and difference see Homi K. Bhabha, *The Location of Culture* (London and New York: Routledge, 1994).
17. Resolution no. 1 on "The challenge to cultural policy in our changing society," 1st Conference of European Ministers responsible for Cultural Affairs, Oslo, June 1974, as quoted in *40 Years of Cultural Co-Operation: 1954–1994* (Strasbourg: Council of Europe Publishing, 1997).
18. Ibid, pp. 125–38.
19. For a discussion of some of the problems arising see *Specificities and Universality: Problems of Identities* (Strasbourg: Council of Europe Press, 1995).
20. Richard Dyer, *White* (London and New York: Routledge, 1997)
21. M. Foucault, *The Order of Things*, op. cit., pp. 3–16.
22. See for example Jose Rabasa, "Allegories of atlas," in *Inventing A-M-E-R-I-C-A: Spanish Historiography and the Formation of Eurocentricism* (Norman, Oklahoma and London: University of Oklahoma Press, 1993).
23. Jacques Attali, "Hope borne on a trade wind," *The Guardian*, 8 September 1992.
24. See for example, Paschalis Kitromilides, *Enlightenment, Nationalism, Orthodoxy: Studies in the Culture and Political Thought of South-eastern Europe* (Brookfield and Aldershot: VARIORUM, 1994).
25. Richard Dyer and Ginette Vincendeau, "Introduction," in Richard Dyer and Ginette Vincendeau (eds), *Popular European Cinema* (London and New York: Routledge, 1992), pp. 5–10.
26. Ibid, pp. 8–9.
27. Stephen Cleary as quoted in Angus Finney, *The State of European Cinema: A New Dose of Reality* (London: Cassell, 1996); John Caughie offers a far more sophisticated argument around the ironic/melodramatic distinction in his "Becoming European: art cinema, irony and identity," in D. Petrie, op. cit.

28. As quoted in translation in *Conflict or Cooperation in European Film and Television* (Manchester: The European Institute for the Media, 1992), p. 25.
29. *Media: Guide for the Audiovisual Industry* (Brussels: Commission of the European Communities, 1991), p. 35. The same ideas guide the other programmes of MEDIA I.
30. R. Dyer and G. Vincendaeu, op. cit., p. 1.
31. Stan Jones, "Wenders' *Paris, Texas* and the 'European way of seeing,'" in Wendy Everett (ed), *European Identity in Cinema* (Exeter: Intellect, 1996), pp. 45–52.
32. Ibid.
33. Marshal McLuhan, *Understanding Media: The Extensions of Man* (London and New York: Ark Paperworks, 1987).
34. David Harvey, *The Condition of Postmodernity: An Enquiry into the Origins of Cultural Change* (Oxford: Blackwell, 1990), p. 240.
35. Constance Classen, *Worlds of Sense: Exploring the Senses in History and across Cultures* (London: Routledge, 1993).
36. For example see Classen's discussion of the changing perception of the role of the rose in the garden, ibid, pp. 15–36.
37. Michel Foucault, *The Order of Things*, op. cit.
38. Ibid and Michel Foucault, *The Birth of the Clinic* (London: Tavistock, 1973).
39. Roland Barthes, *Camera Lucida* (London: Flamingo, 1984).
40. Jean Baudrillard, *Simulations* (New York: Semiotext(e), 1983), and *America* (London: Verso, 1988); see also Umberto Eco, *Travels in Hyperreality* (London: Pelican, 1987).
41. Fredric Jameson, "Postmodernism or the cultural logic of late capitalism," *New Left Review*, no 146.
42. Jean François Lyotard, *The Postmodern Condition: A Report on Knowledge (*Manchester: Manchester University Press, 1984).
43. Martin Heidegger, *The Question Concerning Technology*, op. cit.
44. Michel Foucault, *Discipline and Punish*, op. cit.
45. Sigmund Freud, "The Acquisition and Control of Fire" in *The Origins of Religion* (London: Pelican, 1985).
46. J. Baudrillard, *America,* op. cit., p. 79.
47. Umberto Eco. "All for One, One for All," *The Guardian*, 11 September 1992.
48. Angus Finney, op. cit.
49. Jean-Claude Carriere, op. cit., p. 25.
50. See for instance *European Community Audiovisual Policy* (Luxembourg: Office for Official Publications of the European Communities, 1992); also the *White Paper on Growth, Competitiveness, and Employment* (Brussels, December 1993) and *Europe's Way to the Information Society: An Action Plan* (Brussels, July 1994).

2 NATIONAL CINEMAS

THIS CHAPTER WILL explore some of the contradictions that lie at the heart of the concept of "national cinema" and the ways in which they inform critical discourses as well as political and aesthetic practices. I shall first examine some of the most influential ideas about nation, nationhood and national identity that have become central in film studies since the 1980s. It is clearly beyond the scope of this book to analyze in depth the vast and quickly accumulating body of work on the topic; my exploration will offer an eclectic mapping of the area that identifies the most relevant concepts for the study of national cinemas in the European context. I shall then explore in some detail problems in the critical discourse of national cinemas and propose an approach to the subject that does not perceive the contradictions inherent in the term as destroying its theoretical usefulness. I shall suggest that the analysis of the agonistics[1] of the directly or indirectly competing discourses around nationhood and national cinema offers extremely useful insights into the dynamics, the politics and the history of cinema in European countries. This analysis is also helpful in locating some of the problems around "popular" cinema within a national and European historical context. Finally, I shall illustrate some of these points with reference to a specific period in the history of French cinema, the late 50s and early 60s, the period of the emergence of the *Nouvelle Vague* as a movement that represents both a rejection and a celebration of national cinema.

Nation

THE LAST FIFTEEN years have seen the publication of a number of books and articles challenging essentialist ideas of nationhood, nationalism and national identity. Coming from the different but clearly overlapping perspectives of anti-essentialist and post-colonialist criticism, recent works have shattered the theoretically naïve and politically suspect beliefs in unified, ahistorical nations and national identities.

The influence of these works on the way film studies conceived national cinemas was extensive: Hollywood's position as "universal" (as opposed to national) cinema was debunked, as was the unproblematic acceptance of critical canons as bodies of essential texts constituting national cinemas as objects of study. The anxious re-thinking of the methodology of the study of national cinemas was also forced by the challenge to the established critical/theoretical hegemony in Anglo-US film studies that was launched from the "margins" beginning in the late 1970s. These challenges not only fragmented the unity of Anglo-US film theory but also discredited any attempts to conceptualize national cinemas as unified and singular.

A standard point of reference for many of the anti-essentialist approaches to nationhood[2] is the 1882 lecture "What is a nation?" delivered at the Sorbonne by Ernest Renan.[3] Despite its spiritual mysticism and undisputed essentialism what makes this text pivotal is its systematic demolition of one after another of the conventional points of anchorage of the meaning of "nation." Renan discards dynasty, race, language, religion, community of interest and geography as concepts proven to be inadequate to articulate and express the unity of the nation. Significantly, Renan rejects ahistorical understandings of nationhood ("Nations . . . are something new in history. Antiquity was unfamiliar with them"[4]) and locates the origins of the concept of the nation in the context of European modernity. The lecture concludes with an idealistic definition of nationhood:

> A nation is a soul, a spiritual principle . . . A nation is . . . a large-scale solidarity, constituted by the feeling of the sacrifices that one has made in the past and of those that one is prepared to make in the future . . . A large aggregate of men, healthy in mind and warm of heart, creates the kind of moral conscience which we call a nation.[5]

What is striking about this definition, despite its commitment to unity and coherence, is the conceptualization of the nation as a cultural convention with political implications and as the "spontaneous" but deliberate construction of "a large aggregate of men."

Both of these ideas are crucial for anti-essentialist definitions of nationhood. Ernest Gellner, revisiting Renan's question "what is a nation?" offers a very reserved definition of nationhood as a unity of culture which is politically willed by the citizens. He makes clear, nevertheless, that both the will and the shared culture are the product of specific historical and political conditions:

When general social conditions make for standardised, homo-
geneous, centrally sustained high cultures, pervading entire pop-
ulations and not just elite minorities, a situation arises in which
well-defined educationally sanctioned and unified cultures constitute very nearly the only kind of unit with which men will-
ingly and often ardently identify . . . under these conditions,
though under these conditions *only*, nations can be defined in
terms both of will and of culture, and indeed in terms of the
convergence of them both with political units.[6]

Particularly interesting is that fact that in Gellner's approach culture is placed in the center of nationhood. A crucial contradiction
arises from this. The imposition of the unity of a state-approved and
constructed high culture on the nation goes against the nationalist
rhetoric of acting in the name of the people and the reliance on a
popular or *Volk* culture, which is invariably multiple, fragmented
and local. The implications of this are important for the study of
European national cinemas: legitimate (or official) national cultures
tend to exclude popular forms from their canon. Given the precari-
ous position that cinema occupies within high culture[7] it is only the
nationally (and, ironically, internationally) acknowledged art films
that can potentially become part of the national cultural canon. It is
extremely difficult to accommodate both Shakespeare and *Carry On*
films within an official culture that supposedly meets the universal
approval of the nation. The controversy around Tony Blair's recent
attempt to define contemporary national identity in terms of "cool
Britannia" by mobilizing diverse populist and nationalist aspects of
culture is a testimony to the crucial and yet paradoxical position
that culture occupies within formations of nationhood. The advantage of Gellner's formulation of nationhood is precisely this
foregrounding of the contradictory (or agonistic) ways of viewing
the function of cultural heritage and production within nations.

But if European nationhood is historically synchronous with
the Enlightenment so is the establishment of art as an autonomous,
self-regulated sphere of social activity.[8] This perhaps explains the
remarkable ability of European nation-states to perceive their
national cultures (as well as European culture as a whole, as discussed in the previous chapter) as simultaneously unified and
diverse. The celebration of cultural diversity is carried out in the
name of the autonomy of art that enriches the life of the nation,
whereas the assertion of unity takes the form of a modern

nationhood that can accommodate and even profit from such diversity. Of course this apparently resolves the contradiction only on the level of state rhetoric rather than in material, historical terms. The political project of establishing modern nations and the philosophical aspiration of enriching social life through autonomous culture of universal value co-exist in a fundamentally contradictory mode. The legitimacy of the nation depends on the production and acceptance of a shared "high culture," whereas the "autonomy of art" principle places the latter in a distant, alienated position from the national community.

This is just one dimension of the conflict between "the 'political' power of nationalism vs. their philosophical poverty and even incoherence,"[9] that Benedict Anderson in *Imagined Communities* identifies as one of the paradoxes of modern nationalism. Significantly, the other two (the "objective modernity of nations vs. their subjective antiquity" and the "formal universality of nationality vs. the particularity of its concrete manifestations") can also be understood in terms of the conflict between the philosophical legacy of the Enlightenment and the political project of nationalism.[10]

Anderson's definition of the nation as "an imagined political community—and imagined as both inherently limited and sovereign"[11] is perhaps the most influential idea about nationhood that has emerged recently. Working along similar lines with Gellner, Anderson historically investigates the emergence of modern nations, identifies the different kinds of nationalism that have appeared in the last two centuries, and explores some of the contradictions and paradoxes of nationalist ideologies. According to Anderson, although imagining the nation is an extremely powerful way of constructing a community it is also historically unstable and riddled with paradoxes. Not only various types of nationalism (populist and dynastic or official, for example) are accommodated within conceptualizations of nationhood but the imagining of the community is subject to constant revision and renegotiation, continuously reinterpreting the past and reinventing the present and the future. This dynamic, anti-essentialist model allows for an understanding of national identity based on struggle and change rather than established and accepted orthodoxy.

Importantly, Anderson also considers the different kinds of nationalism. He defines the nationalism of the "last wave" as a reaction against "global imperialism," which in many ways replicates the models of nationhood that the imperialists themselves established.[12] This "defensive" nationalism[13] was a mobilizing and unifying factor in many of the colonial struggles for independence in the nineteenth and twentieth centuries and cannot (and should not) be equated with the aggressive nationalism of the colonial powers. In Frantz Fanon's words:

> To fight for national culture means in the first place to fight for the liberation of the nation, that material keystone which makes the building of culture possible . . . A national culture is the whole body of efforts made by a people in the sphere of thought to describe, justify, and praise the action through which that people has created itself and keeps itself in existence . . .[14]

Interestingly, it is the rhetoric of this defensive nationalism that is currently employed by many ex-colonial European countries in the defense of their national cultures from the advances of American cultural imperialism. In this instance it is the universality of American mass culture (universality based on economic and political power rather than value) that is played against the national uniqueness of "high art."

Postcolonialist critiques of nationhood have utilized the "constructedness" of nationhood (that Gellner, Anderson and Fanon foreground) in order to question the limits of the "imagined communities" and demonstrate the ways in which this imagining functions in a divisive, exclusive way.

There are two main variations of this approach. The first attacks the supposed unity of the nation by asserting diversity and difference as characteristic of national identities. The second sees post-colonial identities in general as essentially "hybrid"—all identities (individual and/or collective) are formed in the interstices, in the "in-between" spaces of complex and fragmented post-colonial cultures.

Stuart Hall is the main exponent of the former. Addressing issues of identity in the specific context of black culture in Britain in his seminal essay "New Ethnicities," Hall identifies a shift in the politics of identity. This involves a move away from an emphasis on the shared nature of the experience of racism and marginalization (expressed by the term "black"), to an emphasis on the diversity of this experience across lines of ethnic, gender, class and sexual difference. He connects this shift to both political changes and the rethinking of the politics and aesthetics of cultural production by "ethnic artists," and he concludes:

> This marks a real shift in the point of contestation, since it is no longer only between antiracism and multiculturalism but *inside* the notion of ethnicity itself. What is involved is the splitting of the notion between, on the one hand the dominant notion which connects it to nation and "race" and on the other hand what I think is the beginning of a positive conception of the ethnicity of the margins, of the periphery. That is to say, a recognition that we all speak from a particular place, out of a particular history, out of a particular experience, a particular culture, without being contained by that position as "ethnic artists" or film-makers. We are all, in that sense, *ethnically* located and our ethnic identities are crucial to our subjective sense of who we are. But this is also a recognition that this is not an ethnicity which is doomed to survive, as Englishness was, only by marginalizing, dispossessing, displacing and forgetting other ethnicities. This precisely is the politics of ethnicity predicated on difference and diversity.[15]

Hall makes clear that the recognition of particularity and positionality is crucial for the understanding of nationhood and national identity, but also that this understanding is politically motivated, forced through years of political struggle over representation and identity.

This is the starting point for Homi Bhabha's influential theorization of postcolonial cultures and identities as hybrid.[16] Bhabha's critique focuses on the impurity of cultural production and cultural products, an "impurity" that has also been a central point of reference for postmodernist and poststructuralist approaches to culture and identity. Furthermore, what makes the "post" of recent theoretical works attractive to Bhabha is not a sequential understanding of the word but a recognition and identification of the politically crucial limits of European philosophical thought:

> If the interest in postmodernism is limited to a celebration of the fragmentation of the "grand narratives" of postenlightenment rationalism, then for all its intellectual excitement, it remains a profoundly parochial enterprise. The wider significance of the postmodern condition lies in the awareness that the epistemological "limits" of those ethnocentric ideas are also the

enunciative boundaries of a range of other dissonant, even dis-
sident histories and voices —women, the colonized, minority
groups, the bearers of policed sexualities.[17]

This kind of criticism is a clear rebuttal to multiculturalist
approaches of nationhood that can easily be assimilated within an
"enlightened" European tradition of valuing cultural diversity, as
discussed in the previous chapter. Both Bhabha[18] and Hall[19] make a
sharp distinction between cultural diversity and difference, asserting
the latter as a dynamic process of producing and signifying new
positions and identities. The constructedness and impurity of
nationhood and the politics of a cultural/national identity based on
an agonistic assertion of difference are key conceptual tools for the
study of national cinemas.

National Cinemas

IN RECENT YEARS the study of national cinemas has changed. What
used to be self-evident and obvious in the constitution of the
history, the texts and the "national" of a country's cinema, is now
extensively questioned and challenged. This crisis is the effect of
a number of developments in different spheres of political, critical and cultural activity: the questioning of the unity of the
nation-state, the deconstruction of the "center" of
cultural/national identity, the foregrounding of the
margins/periphery, the production of audio-visual work which
directly or indirectly acknowledges and asserts positions and
identities traditionally excluded from the canon of national culture. Any contemporary study of national cinema(s) has to face
questions around methodology, the constitution of the object of
study and even the usefulness of the enterprise. In what follows I
shall identify and explore specific problems around the study of
national cinemas that are particularly relevant for the project of
this book.

The obvious point of departure is the text: the films that make
up the body of study, the texts of a national cinema. The absence of
commercial or popular films has been widely acknowledged in
recent works[20] that foreground the bias of the critical canon towards
"art" or "quality" productions (with the occasional blockbuster
included for sociological purposes). It seems to me that the construction of the canon of a national cinema involves an act of

violence, a forceful forgetting, that Renan identifies as characteristic of modern nations:

> Forgetting . . . is a crucial factor in the creation of a nation, which is why progress in historical studies often constitutes a danger for nationality. Indeed, historical enquiry brings to light deeds of violence which took place at the origin of all political formations . . . Unity is always effected by means of brutality.[21]

In the worst cases this brutality involves the drawing of a strict and exclusive high art boundary around the texts worth considering under the rubric of national cinema. In the best cases it dictates the consideration only of films which, in one way or another, are seen as expressions of the assumed characteristics (aesthetic, cultural, economic, historical) of a national cinema. In this sense the texts selected are *de facto* endowed with specific critical and/or cultural values.

Related to this is the question of what films actually qualify as part of a nation's cinema and of the criteria employed in such classifications. This involves trivial but illuminating considerations of whether the finance, the production base, the language or the creative talent are the determining factors of a film's "nationality." It is practically impossible to discover films which are completely "pure" in terms of their national origin: even if all the crew share the same nationality, what about the nationality of the equipment, the film stock, the aesthetics of editing, the style of the clothes? The critical drive, nevertheless, has been to establish as an object of study films grouped together according to nationality rather than, for example, themes or aesthetics or genres. This is particularly the case with European cinemas, as Ginette Vincendeau has noted: "Many of the seminal film histories were studies of national European cinemas or of world cinema organized along nationalist lines . . ."[22] An interesting case here is the almost universal dislike for co-productions, a dislike which is very rarely based on close consideration of the films themselves.[23] In Susan Hayward's study of French national cinema, for example, co-productions are unambiguously condemned:

> It is in this murky area of co-productions, especially when they are the predominant production practice, that the identity of a national cinema becomes confused—as was the case in the

1920s and in the 1960s . . . It is not just the loss of the specificity of a national identity that such practices can entail . . . the
pursuance of these practices also caused a loss of small- to medi-
um-budget films which are the mainstay and hallmark of the
French national cinema.[24]

Here the lack of "purity" in the co-production is not only the
source of classificatory confusion but also a serious threat to a national mode of production that in turn "results in a lack of renovation and
innovation." Despite the best intentions of the author this appears to
be a very nationalistic and elitist approach to cinema that is, nevertheless, typical of the critical reaction to the nationally and aesthetically impure cultural phenomenon of film co-productions.

Critics have reacted to this difficulty in the identification and the
purity of the "national" aspect of a country's cinema by expanding
the object of study and by challenging the geographical limits
imposed on it. Notable in this respect is the work of Andrew
Higson[25] and Stephen Crofts,[26] among others.

Higson, arguing in the context of British national cinema, suggests that "it is inadequate to reduce the study of national cinemas
only to consideration of the films produced by and within a particular nation state."[27] He identifies three areas of study: the whole
range of films in circulation in a country including foreign films, the
audiences of different types of films and the discourses about film
that emerge and circulate in the culture. Simplifying the argument,
we can say that Higson's formulation proposes the study of a
national *film culture* rather than the study of a national *cinema*.

Crofts identifies a lack of emphasis on "textual and generic
questions" in Higson's arguments, and proposes a mode of analysis
of national cinema that takes into consideration a broader spectrum
of practices: production, distribution and exhibition, audiences, discourses, textuality, national-cultural specificity, the cultural
specificity of genres and nation-state cinema movements, the role of
the state and the global range of nation-state cinemas.[28]

Both Higson and Crofts, nevertheless, offer a particularly useful revision of the object of study, by opening it up to include popular texts, by placing the study of films in a wider cultural context and by defining this context as fundamentally trans-cultural
and trans-national.

Another set of problems revolves around some of the contradictions of the very concept of "national cinema." I am referring here

to the tension between the two contributing terms of the compound, "national" and "cinema." This is a tension that surfaces in most critical discourses around national cinemas and takes the form of a conflict between, on the one hand, a search for locality, specificity and difference that the construction of the "national" demands, and, on the other, an understanding of cinema as a "universal language" beyond and above national specificity. One way of understanding this is by considering the paradox (perceptively identified by Thomas Elsaesser[29]) of films becoming part of the national canon only after they have proved their artistic merits in international festivals or through international critical recognition. In this sense, the national canon is determined by judgements based on universal values and often pronounced outside the geographical boundaries of the nation.

Illuminating from this point of view is Michael Cacoyannis' (one of the two or three Greek film directors known outside Greece) assertion that "cinema has no country; and it's not the form of the film that betrays its nationality. It is the director's medium . . . and it is the director's outlook which colours the film rather than any national outlook."[30] This enthusiastic endorsement of auteurism demonstrates the idealist and romantic belief that cinema is the sole creation of a gifted individual but it also proposes a rather crude form/content dichotomy that underlies a certain type of critical discourse on national cinema. Is the national to be discovered in the stories and the themes of the films or in the mode of representation? Clearly, this is a binarism that film theory has successfully dealt with, but one that resurfaces in the specific context of national cinemas. So, Jean-Luc Godard, filmmaker and critic, while paying lip-service to the form/content dialectic, asserts:

> I think there is no French cinema, but there have been French film-makers and the French are so good at talking about themselves that everybody thought that there was a French cinema. There have been four cinemas which have shown reality in a new way through a new form: a Russian cinema, a German cinema, an Italian cinema and an American cinema.[31]

Obviously, this raises a number of methodological questions, such as what is particularly Russian about montage, or whether neorealism is equivalent to Italian cinema. On the other hand, Soila,

Söderbergh and Iversen seek the national aspects of Scandinavian cinemas not in form but in content:

> Nationality in the area of film thereby implies a relation to the topical and the specific for the culture. A certain country's national film is determined by the separate life values, in relation to other countries, which have been worked in the form of fictions, rather than from any singularly demonstrable difference in stylistic measures between different countries' productions. The concept of national cinema in other words both presupposes and relates to a context.[32]

The Cacoyannis/Godard and the Soila, Söderbergh and Inversen approaches seem to occupy opposite poles of the form/content dichotomy. However, they share a very similar conceptualization of national cinema. This is based on the belief that a national cinema can be defined on the basis of a fundamental unity, seen as characteristic or expressive of the nation and its culture, a unity that the critic can derive from the form or the content of the films in relation to their national context. Clearly Higson's and Crofts's critiques discussed earlier problematize and challenge this belief. I think it is useful, nevertheless, to further explore the tension between the "national" and the "cinematic" because it seems to indicate a way in which cinema and national identity can be approached that does not depend on unity and purity but on diversity, contradiction and struggle.

It is clear that the tension exists on the level of discourse as a conflict between statements made about the "national" and conceptualizations of the "cinematic." Here the term discourse is used in its Foucauldian sense,[33] as ". . . the historically and logically apposite frame of reference within which something may be discussed, considered and acted upon within a given period in the social development of such ideas."[34] One way of studying national cinemas without reducing the complex and contradictory nature of the object of study is the investigation of statements made about nationhood, national identity and national cinema in specific historical moments and in specific nation-states. These statements (whose patterns, regularities and conflicts constitute the discourse) emanate from a variety of sources with different and often diametrically opposing philosophies, world-views and material and ideological interests. Clearly, the discourse that these statements constitute cannot be understood as a unified, consensual formation, but as one riddled with conflict and even incompatibility.[35]

The study of the discursive formation around a national cinema, then, will not strive to discover and impose a coherence and unity where none exists, but to expose both the contradictory aspects of the discourse and how it achieves its apparent unity. This approach is consistent with (and draws upon) Lyotard's theorization of the nature of the social bond as the agonistics of conflicting language games.[36] It is also in accord with recent theories of nationhood that have placed great emphasis on the role of narrative in the construction of the imagined community of the nation. This is clearly reflected by Anderson's particular attention to the ability of the novel and the newspaper to represent the nation,[37] Brennan's understanding of his field of study as the "myths of the nation"[38] and Bhabha's explicit definition of his project as the study of "the nation through its narrative address."[39]

Statements on nationhood can be usefully played against those on national cinema capitalizing on the structural conceptual tension between the terms as discussed above, as well as the different positions that the enunciators of such statements occupy within the structure of the nation-state. Finally, these statements must be placed within the context of what the films that circulate within a nation say about both nationhood and national cinema.

The films themselves need to be addressed not as monosemic and culturally insular products that reiterate and/or articulate fixed and permanent national identities. This is a temptation to which many studies of national cinemas succumb and one that must be rigorously and decisively resisted. A clear example of this tempting reductionism can be found in the opening dedication of Joao Benard de Costa's history of Portuguese cinema: "To Luis de Pina; with whom I learnt to enjoy the Portuguese cinema and who taught me to see in its stories, always the same story. After all, our story."[40]

Although the present book is not a study of popular European cinemas in terms of national cinemas, and is in effect a critique of such narrow nationalistic approaches to the subject, it is important to stress the usefulness of the "national" as *one* of the contexts within which popular films and cinemas can be analyzed. The following discussion of the French *Nouvelle Vague* will give a concrete example of the analysis of national cinema as a discursive formation in the way outlined above and demonstrate the possibility of overcoming the strictly national as the frame of reference in the study of European cinemas.

The Nouvelle Vague

THE FOLLOWING BRIEF discussion of the French New Wave must be understood not as a comprehensive analysis of the movement, its films, directors and stars, but as a case study with a limited function. I am using the Nouvelle Vague as an example of the way in which statements about nationhood, national identity and national cinema, emanating from politicians/policy makers, film directors and/or critics and the films themselves, relate to each other in contradictory and agonistic ways.

It is important to note that these different classes of statements do not only exist in conflict with each other (the politicians vs. the directors, the films in opposition to both) but they are also marked by internal contradictions (politicians, directors, critics and films say different things about the nation at different times). The nature of the statements is fundamentally diverse: What a politician says about national identity might be more or less explicit and direct, but what a law on cultural policy says about national cinema needs to be analyzed and interpreted. Furthermore both types of statement are profoundly different from the way in which a film makes statements about the nation.[41] Bearing all these difficulties in mind, I shall focus primarily on the critical discourse around the Nouvelle Vague as expressed in certain key articles of Cahiers du cinéma, as well as in more recent works on French cinema. The critical discourse will be contextualized with brief references to the cultural formation and the political climate of the period (in particular the peculiar nationalist rhetoric of the de Gaulle government) and the ways in which the films produced by the New Wave have been analyzed by critics.

Two initial and rather banal observations on the nature of the critical discourse are necessary at this point. Firstly, that many (but not all) of the directors associated with the New Wave were also the producers of work of critical and theoretical nature in Cahiers du cinéma. A number of the contradictions of the discourse and the inconsistencies between the writing and the film-making of the directors of the Nouvelle Vague have been identified by critics,[42] but it is worth noting here the more general potential incommensurability between the polemics of critical discourse (usually expressed in manifestos) and the aesthetics and politics of film practice. Second, that in the critical and cinematic work of the movement there are both national and transnational dimensions—the place that the New Wave claims within French cinema is as important to the critics/directors as its place within international film aesthetics and history.

The best manifestation of the first contradiction is the divided opinion of the directors about the possibility or even the desirability of the commercial success of the movement. As Jim Hillier notes:

> Godard and Rivette realised increasingly that the nouvelle vague—or their own conception and development of it—was not going to be the new "popular" French cinema. While, ultimately, Truffaut, Chabrol and Rohmer could be said to have achieved some kind of serious "popular" success, Godard and Rivette came to understand that their new cinema would be "oppositional," avant-garde, almost necessarily condemned to marginalisation and misunderstanding by the press and by the general public.[43]

The view of the *Cahiers* critics in the 1950s, however, seemed to be unanimous in its rejection of commercialism, of a "cinema based on supply and demand."[44] The model of national cinema that the critical discourse of the 50s seems to emulate is that of Italian neorealism. As Rivette put it: ". . . what is most lacking in French cinema is a *spirit of poverty*."[45] On the other hand, interviews with directors such as Rohmer and Truffaut in the 60s reveal their profound indifference to the material conditions and politics of production, distribution and exhibition of films.[46]

But what is more interesting for the current discussion is the ambivalent placing of the *Nouvelle Vague* within film making traditions which are simultaneously national and trans-national. As Hillier has observed,[47] although *Cahiers du cinéma* appeared to be preoccupied with American and Italian cinema, the real concern of the journal was the future of French cinema. In many ways the *Nouvelle Vague* was the cinematic expression of a critical polemic that places French cinema firmly within the context of international aesthetic paradigms. While, in their attempt to create links between the past, present and future of French cinema, the *Cahiers* critics were mobilizing French cultural traditions (e.g., the Paris School in painting, French novels), film *auteurs* (Becker, Renoir, Tati, et al.) and cinematic styles (pre-war film noir, poetic realism), they were also placing these national traditions in direct comparison to American and European trends. So, in a celebrated 1957 discussion, the participants repeatedly make comments like the following from Rohmer: "French cinema doesn't depict French society, while American cinema, like Italian cinema, is able to raise society to a level of aesthetic dignity."[48]

Significantly, in another debate (the 1963 discussion of Alain Resnais' film *Muriel*) the context shifts in order to place the New Wave firmly within European aesthetic traditions (a shift that is characteristic of the declining position of Hollywood, both aesthetically and politically, in the columns of *Cahiers* in the 1960s):

> And because in Europe there has for a long time been a lack of any correspondence between society and the individual, that has given rise to a particular artistic tradition. It has produced a cinema which deals solely with that dislocation, and as a result also deals with the whole, since it deals with society in its relation to the individual.[49]

It is clear that the *Cahiers* critics and the directors of the *Nouvelle Vague* are demonstrating the tension explored earlier in this chapter, between the national and the cinematic components of "national cinema." This is particularly evident in Truffault's vitriolic attack against the "tradition of quality" of French cinema which he juxtaposed with the universal category of the "men of cinema."[50] In that programmatic essay, as in many critical writings of the *Cahiers* group, the fundamental pre-condition for a distinct identity of the New Wave is for the movement to break free from the hegemonic national forms, looking for inspiration outside the nation in the cinematic traditions of Europe and Hollywood.

Ginette Vincendaeu has pointed out that the critical discourse on the New Wave (with the *Cahiers* group a significant contributor) has consistently (and in many cases deliberately) downplayed the dependency of the *Nouvelle Vague* on mainstream cinema, fetishising instead the influences of the American B movie:

> It has become almost a cliché to state that the New Wave "would not have existed without the American B movie." Like all clichés, this is partly true. But there would have been no New

Wave either without the mainstream French cinema, the "tradition of quality" so despised by New Wave critics and pretty much everybody after them.[51]

Furthermore, Vincendeau notes that there is nothing new or oppositional in the New Wave's fascination with Hollywood: ". . . manifestations of French resistance or hostility to Hollywood cinema have consistently taken place against a background of both popular success and high-brow cultural embracing of American products."[52]

The critical discourse, then, seems to problematize the pure Frenchness of this, most widely recognised as French film movement. The outward look of the critics/filmmakers of the *Cahiers* group, combined with the rejection of the national mainstream cinema of the time, make it extremely difficult to construct a discourse that places the New Wave in the continuum of an insular, purely French national cinema. Furthermore, the critical discourse around the New Wave had a significant impact on the way other (mainly European) national cinemas imagined themselves and their histories. A struggle between old and new, in the model offered by the *Cahiers*, is a recurring story in histories of post-1960 European cinemas.

Apart from the transnationalism of the critical discourse around the New Wave, another of its defining characteristic is the importance of what is perceived to be an almost revolutionary "newness" that challenges the national hegemony and fragments in this sense the unity of the national discourse. The latter is divided along lines of old and young (the New Wave vs. *le cinéma de papa*), conservative and progressive, commercial and art, and so on.

This becomes even more problematic and ambiguous in the context of the Fifth Republic established by de Gaulle in 1958. The Gaullist period of the Fifth Republic was marked by a clear redefinition of French nationhood and national identity. As a number of historians indicate, de Gaulle's perception of France was one of a modern, dynamic, unified, independent country with a distinct role in the world. As Brian Jenkins and Nigel Copsey argue, in their essay "Nation, nationalism and national identity in France":

The various "nationalist" positions adopted in the 1950s thus confirmed the existence of a common core of beliefs which transcended the differences between nationalisms of Right and Left—namely the conviction that France was an exemplary nation with a world role. It was on this basis that with the advent of the Fifth Republic, de Gaulle was able to construct a synthesis which neutralised many of the classic contradictions between Left and Right views of the nation . . . his pursuit of an independent foreign and defence policy within the broad framework of the Western Alliance and the EEC gave a measure of satisfaction both to convinced Atlanticists and Europeanists, and to those like the communists who welcomed de Gaulle's occasional flourishes of anti-Americanism . . . With the consolidation of the Fifth Republic, therefore, it seemed that French national identity had become more consensual and less problematic than ever before.[53]

While the emphasis on dynamism and modernity in the Gaullist redefinition of the nation can be clearly seen as compatible (to say the least) with the ground-breaking newness of the *Nouvelle Vague*, the internationalism of the film movement and, more importantly, the divisive, polemic tone of the critical discourse, not only fall outside the limits of the Gaullist discourse, but seem to stand in opposition to it. How can we explain then the warm endorsement of the *Nouvelle Vague* by de Gaulle's government and the eventual elevation of the (initially iconoclastic and rebellious) movement to the position of a genuine representative of French national culture?[54]

Firstly, we must note that the Gaullist discourse (like any other discourse emanating from government) is a selective one as it is the synthesis of majority views articulated into a unified notion of nationhood, national culture and identity. The selective reworking of the critical discourse of the *Nouvelle Vague* belongs to the same discursive modality: certain aspects of it are adopted and heralded, some others conveniently forgotten or repressed.

But what makes this eclectic appropriation of the *Nouvelle Vague* possible is the profound ambiguity of the nature of the films of the movement. Indeed, critical opinion since the 1960s has been divided in terms of the evaluation of the cinema of the *Nouvelle Vague*: For some critics the films of the movement demonstrate a stylistic and thematic revolution and they are (in their majority) deeply political; for others, they are primarily personal films, encapsulating idealistic and romantic notions of art and creativity. It is not my intention to take sides in this debate or to overlook what is critically and politically at stake in the disagreement, but just to point out that the difference of opinion suggests that there are at least two possible ways (even if they are not of equal critical value) of interpreting the films of the New Wave. This critical ambiguity offers the possibility to the Gaullist political discourse to read the films of the *Nouvelle Vague* not as texts informed by radical politics but as personal artistic expressions of a group of young and exceptionally talented French directors.

The interpretation of the films of the New Wave as personal and innovative masterpieces that radicalize film language offers a point of coherence for the various discourses on nationhood, national identity and national cinema. This is not only compatible with the modern (and fundamentally European) commitment to the autonomy of art (symbolically emphasised by the establishment of an autonomous sector, the Ministry of Culture, under de Gaulle), but also with both the critical and the political discourse of the period. In the critical discourse it enables the conceptualization of the New Wave as part of the cinematic rather than the national of a national cinema, as discussed earlier. In the Gaullist discourse the Frenchness of the *Nouvelle Vague* comes from the universal value of the films made by French filmmakers, offering a distinct and privileged position for French culture in the new post-war world, a recurring theme in de Gaulle's rhetoric. Furthermore, the critical value placed on the director as author of and creative force in the text is very much in accord with the bourgeois rhetoric of the all-powerful, unified, dynamic individual in control of his/her destiny, a rhetoric that echoes the renewed faith in the destiny of the French nation under de Gaull.

This schematic discussion of the French New Wave has been used here as a reminder of the many contradictions of discursive formations of national cinema but also of the uncanny ability of the nationalist discourse to discover and mobilize points of coherence. In the two following chapters, I shall first explore the possibility of conceptualizing identity and cinema in a more fluid and dynamic way that takes account of both national and transnational contexts. Following that I shall examine the contradictions and ambiguities of the term "popular" and, through the study of films of Louis de Funés, revisit France in the 1960s by considering the role that these popular/commercial films play in definitions of national cinema and identity.

Notes

1. The term is used here in the way that it was introduced by Jean François Lyotard in *The Postmodern Condition: A Report on Knowledge* (Manchester: Manchester University Press, 1984).

2. See for example Ernest Gellner, *Nations and Nationalism* (Oxford: Blackwell, 1983); Eric Hobsbowm, *Nations and Nationalism since 1780: Programme, Myth, Reality* (Cambridge: Cambridge University Press, 1990); Benedict Anderson, *Imagined Communities: Reflections on the Spread of Nationalism* (London and New York: Verso, 1991).

3. Original title "Qu'est-ce qu'une nation," published with translation and annotation by Martin Thom in Homi K. Bhabha (ed), *Nation and Narration* (Routledge: London and New York, 1990).

4. Ibid, p. 9.

5. Ibid, pp. 19–20.

6. Gellner, op. cit., p. 55.

7. Industrial, mass produced cultural artefacts are very rarely seen as belonging to the national cultural heritage of a country.

8. See Jürgen Habermas "The project of modernity" in Hal Foster (ed), *Postmodern Culture* (London: Pluto, 1985) .

9. Anderson, op. cit., p. 5.

10. A point that Gellner makes explicit: "Kant's identification of man with that which is rational and universal in him, his fastidious and persistent, highly characteristic distaste for basing anything of importance on that which is merely contingent, historical or specific, makes Kant a very model for that allegedly bloodless, cosmopolitan, emaciated ethic of the enlightenment, which romantic nationalists spurned and detested so much and which they so joyously repudiated in favour of a more earthy, shamelessly specific and partial commitment to kin or territory or culture," Gellner, op. cit., p. 131.

11. Anderson, op. cit., p. 6.

12. Ibid, pp. 113–40; see also Partha Chatterjee, *Nationalist Thought and the Colonial World: A Derivative Discourse* (London: Zed Books for United Nations, 1986).

13. See Timothy Brennan, "The national longing for form" in Bhabha (ed), op. cit., esp. pp. 45–46, 57–60.

14. Frantz Fanon, *The Wretched of the Earth* (London: Penguin, 1976), pp. 187–88.

15. Stuart Hall, "New ethnicities," in *Black Film, British Cinema*, ICA Documents, 7 (London: Institute of Contemporary Arts, 1989), reprinted in Bill Ashcroft, Gareth Griffiths and Helen Tiffin (eds), *The Post-Colonial Studies Reader* (London and New York: Routledge, 1995), p. 227.

16. Homi K. Bhabha, *The Location of Culture* (London and New York: Routledge, 1994).

17. Ibid, pp. 4–5.
18. Ibid, especially in the essay "The commitment to theory," pp. 19–39.
19. Hall, op. cit.
20. See for example Andrew Higson, "The concept of national cinema," *Screen*, vol. 30, no. 4 (1989); Susan Hayward, *French National Cinema* (London and New York: Routledge, 1993), esp. "Introduction," pp. 1–17; Pierre Sorlin, *Italian National Cinema 1896–1996* (London and New York: Routledge, 1996); Tytti Soila, Astrid Söderberg Widding and Gunnar Iversen, *Nordic National Cinemas* (London and New York: Routledge, 1998).
21. Renan, op. cit., p. 11.
22. Ginette Vincendeau, "Issues in European cinema," in John Hill and Pamela Church Gibson (eds), *The Oxford Guide to Film Studies* (Oxford: Oxford University Press, 1998).
23. See for instance Angus Finley, *The State of European Cinema* (London: Cassell, 1996); and Susan Hayward, op. cit.
24. Susan Hayward, op. cit., p. 37.
25. Andrew Higson, op. cit.
26. Stephen Crofts, "Reconceptualising national cinema/s," *Quarterly Review of Film and Video*, vol. 14, no. 3, 1993 and "Concepts of national cinema" in Hill and Gibson (eds), op. cit.
27. Higson, op. cit., p. 44.
28. Crofts, 1998, op. cit., pp. 386–89.
29. Thomas Elsaesser, *New German Cinema: A History* (London: BFI/Macmillan, 1989).
30. "A sense of belonging: an interview with Michael Cacoyannis," *Educational Broadcasting International*, vol. 11, no. 3, September 1978, p. 150.
31. "Jean-Luc Godard in conversation with Colin MacCabe," in Duncan Petrie (ed), *Screening Europe* (London: BFI, 1992), p. 101.
32. Soila et al., op. cit., p. 4.
33. Michel Foucault, *The Archaeology of Knowledge* (London: Tavistock, 1982), esp. pp. 21–76.
34. David Boswell, "Health, the self and social interaction," in Robert Bocock and Kenneth Thompson, *Social and Cultural Forms of Modernity* (Cambridge: Polity Press, 1992).
35. Foucault, op. cit., pp. 34–35.
36. Lyotard, op. cit., esp. pp. 9–11.
37. Anderson, op. cit., pp. 24–26.
38. Brennan, op. cit., pp. 44–45.
39. Homi Bhabha, "Introduction," in his *Nation and Narration*, op. cit., p. 3.
40. Joao Benard da Costa, *Stories of the Cinema* (Lisbon: Imprensa Nacional—Casa da Moeda, 1991).

41. Clearly what a film "says" about the nation is not something that can be determined in a simple and unambiguous way. Films "say" things to specific audiences, using historically and culturally specific codes that are in themselves subject to semiotic ambiguity and struggle. What I am suggesting here is the examination of some of the "statements" about nationhood that the critics have extrapolated from films of the New Wave.

42. See for example John Hess, "La politique des auteurs," *Jump Cut*, nos. 1 and 2, 1974; John Caugie (ed), *Theories of Authorship* (London and New York: Routledge, 1988), pp. 35–38 and Thomas Elsaesser, "Two decades in another country: Hollywood and the cinephiles," in C.W.E. Bigsby, *Superculture: American Popular Culture and Europe* (London: Paul Elek, 1975).

43. Jim Hillier (ed), *Cahiers du cinéma*, vol. 2 (London: Routledge, 1986), p. 28.

44. Andre Bazin, Jacques Doniol-Valcroze, Pierre Kast, Roger Leenhardt, Jacques Rivette, Eric Rohmer: "Six characters in search of *auteurs*: a discussion about the French Cinema," in Jim Hillier (ed), *Cahiers du cinéma*, vol. 1 (London: Routledge, 1985), p. 32.

45. Ibid, p. 40.

46. See the interviews with Rohmer and Truffaut in Jim Hillier (1986), op. cit., pp. 84–94 and 106–9.

47. "Introduction: re-thinking and re-making French Cinema," ibid, pp. 27–34.

48. "Six characters in search . . .," op. cit., p. 42.

49. Jean-Louis Comolli, Jean Domarchi, Jean-Andre Fieschi, Pierre Kast, Andre S. Labarthe, Claude Ollier, Jacques Rivette, François Weyergans: "The misfortunes of *Muriel*," in Hillier (1986), op. cit., pp. 75–76.

50. François Truffaut, "A certain tendency of the French cinema," reprinted and translated in Bill Nichols (ed), *Movies and Methods*, vol. 1 (Berkeley and London: University of California Press, 1976) .

51. Ginette Vincendeau, "France 1945–65 and Hollywood: the *policier* as international text," *Screen*, vol. 33, no.1 (1992).

52. Ibid, p. 53; a point made clear by Godard in a 1962 *Cahiers* interview: "The dream of the *Nouvelle Vague*—which will never come about—is to make *Spartacus* in Hollywood on a ten million dollar budget . . . Everyone has always thought the *Nouvelle Vague* stood for small budgets against big ones, but it isn't so: simply for good films of any kind against bad ones." "From critic to film-maker: Godard in interview" in Jim Hillier (ed), op. cit., p. 63 .

53. Brian Jenkins and Nigel Copsey, "Nation, nationalism and national identity in France," in Brian Jenkins and Spyros A. Sofos (eds), *Nation and Identity in Contemporary Europe* (London and New York: Routledge, 1996), p. 109.

54. As Vincendeau notes, the project of the New Wave was unambiguous-
    ly endorsed ". . . by Andre Malraux [celebrated novelist and Minister
    of Culture under de Gaulle] who enshrined the ideological function of
    the New Wave in 1965 by declaring to the French Assembly: 'The
    French cinema that matters consists of a very small number of films,
    most of them made by young people,'" op. cit., p. 56. A few years ear-
    lier, in 1958, Truffaut was banned from the Cannes film festival for his
    critical views on French cinema.

3 IDENTITY, DIFFERENCE AND CULTURAL EXCHANGE

A S THE PREVIOUS chapter indicated, the concept of a national cinema is deeply problematic. Not only is the term riddled with conceptual and theoretical contradictions, but also the discourse of the "national" within European cinema is dominated by a rhetoric that privileges the "universal language" of film, the genius of the author that transcends nationality, and the humanist (and decisively European) belief in the ecumenical value and currency of great films. In addition, there is now in Europe such a significant shift towards co-productions that the very category of the national film is becoming increasingly problematic. These conceptual difficulties and pragmatic developments clearly influence the ways in which identities, and in particular national identities, are constructed in/by cinema.

Furthermore, in the last ten years questions of national identity have become particularly important in the European context. The very concept of national identity become the object of political and critical scrutiny, as nation-states and pan-European organizations are confronted with the urgent need to identify those unifying aspects of Europe that can possibly constitute a shared European identity, while, at the same time, allowing for the diversity of identities encountered within the geopolitical space of Europe and European nations. There are all the signs that this will become even more urgent in the coming decades as processes of unification and expansion of the European Union intensify and nationalist movements emerge in the political arena of Eastern and Western Europe. The crucial contradiction articulated on the level of both the nation-state and pan-European organizations is between the liberal demand to recognize and celebrate diversity and the essentialist need to hold on to an imaginary center, the shared experience of historical processes and the consensual acceptance of common moral, political and cultural values. This conflict is a cause of considerable anxiety in regional, national and international governing bodies and is omnipresent in the cultural policies pursued by both the European

Union and the Council of Europe, as discussed in the first chapter of this book.

At the same time national cinemas are experiencing a profound crisis that makes the role of pan-European funding and policy making bodies crucial for their survival into the new millennium. This crisis is evident on many levels, from the critical to the economic. Not only has the theoretical, pedagogic and practical usefulness of the term been repeatedly challenged in recent years,[1] but, perhaps more importantly, there is an emerging realization that the shrinking domestic markets have become in most cases inadequate for the financial survival of national films. As a result more and more filmmakers have to rely on state or European funding (and in many cases both) for their films. This in turn brings into play the contradictions in national and European policy discussed above and raises dilemmas of criteria and priorities: for example, is funding offered to films asserting difference or to these relying on the assumed shared repertory of "European" themes and values? The current policy of supporting both (albeit at varying degrees) might be revised in the future in the face of changing political priorities and market concerns.

Co-production is emerging as an important strategy for the survival of European cinema. Notwithstanding the negative criticism it attracts, co-production has, since the 1920s, facilitated the making of countless films belonging to both the commercial/popular and the art canons. The recent significant shift towards co-production represents, nevertheless, a qualitative leap, as the norm will almost certainly become (if it is not already) the transnational rather than the national production.[2] This is further reinforced by the prominent position that transnational co-operation plays in the funding criteria of the various initiatives of the MEDIA I and MEDIA II programmes of the European Union, and forms the basis of the European Council's influential fund EURIMAGES.

What is further emphasized by the funding criteria of such organizations is the ability of films to cross cultural and national borders across Europe. This is seen as essential not only because it provides a broader market for films but also because it is seen as accelerating the process of European cultural unification. Clearly there is a convergence between European film policy, the strategies of the industry and the reality of the market. In the new millennium the challenge that confronts directors, writers and producers, as well as national and transnational policy makers, is the financial survival of European cinema through the establishment and development of transnational partnerships and the production of films that can effectively cross cultural and national borders.

It is important, then, to evaluate some of the strategies employed by filmmakers in their attempts to make films that can "travel." In a sense, some of the dilemmas facing European cinema(s) are structurally similar to those clustering around national and European identity: how to discover "unity" (shared audiences and/or values) while respecting and encouraging diversity. Of particular interest is the increasing engagement of European films with precisely the issues of identity, similarity and difference, and cultural exchange. Questions of cultural difference and ways of overcoming it through/in cultural exchange have become crucially overdetermined in contemporary Europe and European cinema. While it is, in this context, logical and expected for films to explore themes of difference it might seem paradoxical that these concerns are also seen as a tactical weapon in attempts to attract transnational critical attention and, importantly, audiences. I shall examine textual strategies for representing difference in three recent European films: *Mediterraneo* (Gabriele Salvatores, Italy, 1991), *Bhaji on the Beach* (Gurinder Chadha, UK, 1993), and *Underground* (Emir Kusturica, France/Germany/Hungary, 1995). Each of these has successfully crossed national borders. I shall argue that these films offer two alternative ways of coping with difference, strategies that not only prescribe alternative futures for a transnational European cinema but also provide invaluable insights into conceptualizations of cultural difference and exchange within Europe.

I shall now address some key theoretical issues around identity, similarity and difference in the context of European cinema.

Similarity, Difference and European Cinema

HOMI K. BHABHA'S distinction between cultural diversity and cultural difference offers a politically and theoretically crucial insight, one that facilitates a productive and dynamic conceptualization of identity. In his article "The Commitment to Theory," Bhabha calls for a revision of the methodology and history of critical theory, which, he suggests, can only happen under the guidance of cultural difference, and not cultural diversity:

Cultural diversity is an epistemological object—culture as an object of empirical knowledge—whereas cultural difference is the process of the *enunciation* of culture as "knowledge*able*," authoritative, adequate to the construction of systems of cultural identification. If cultural diversity is a category of comparative ethics, aesthetics or ethnology, cultural difference is a process of signification through which statements *of* culture or *on* culture differentiate, discriminate and authorize the production of fields of force, reference, applicability and capacity. Cultural diversity is the recognition of pre-given cultural contents and customs; held in a time-frame of relativism it gives rise to liberal notions of multiculturalism, cultural exchange or the culture of humanity. Cultural diversity is also the representation of a radical rhetoric of the separation of totalized cultures that live unsullied by the intertextuality of their historical locations, safe in the Utopianism of a mythic memory of a unique collective identity.[3]

What is ironic about liberal celebrations of cultural diversity or even radical forms of cultural relativism is the fact that such recognitions of the value of the various cultures perceive them in isolation from each other; in the totalized existence that Bhabha describes cultures exist beyond politics and beyond interaction. From this perspective, many studies of national cinemas (especially European national cinemas) demonstrate the characteristics of the "cultural diversity" approach. National cinemas are usually studied in isolation,[4] with their individual "value" largely unquestioned (their study epistemologically justified precisely on the grounds of diversity), and often conceptualized in terms of a meta-discourse—their contribution to the international development of the film form.

Difference, on the other hand, must be understood as political, positional and essentially fluid:

The analytic of cultural difference intervenes to transform the scenario of articulation—not simply to disclose the rationale of political discrimination. It changes the position of enunciation and the relations of address within it; not only what is said but where it is said; not simply the logic of articulation but the *topos* of enunciation. The aim of cultural difference is to re-articulate the sum of knowledge from the perspective of the signifying position of the minority that resists totalization—the repetition that will not return as the same, the minus-in-origin that results in political and discursive strategies where adding *to* does not add up but serves to disturb the calculation of power and knowledge, producing other spaces of subaltern signification.[5]

The positional character of difference reintroduces the possibility of similarity, the possibility for a cultural product to reach out beyond the borders of its cultural (usually national) context to texts and constituencies placed in similarly marginal positions.

This is not just the way in which many filmmakers across Europe seem to increasingly approach difference (exploring at the same time its ability to transcend borders), but it is also crucial for film theory and criticism. Within Anglo-US film studies, the challenge to established critical hegemonies and historical paradigms has placed cinemas previously described as "other" firmly in the curriculum and in the center of critical and analytical activity. This, in turn, entails an engagement with culturally unfamiliar if not strange texts and practices. As a result, a key question raised by many sensitive critics is about the ways in which we approach such texts. In a sense, the critic is in a position similar to that of the director: s/he has to cross cultural and/or national borders in order to place texts and practices in their appropriate framework. The difficulty and dangers involved in undertaking such work have been repeatedly outlined, but this has not inhibited scholars from engaging with such paradigms.[6] These are issues that will be explored later in this book, but suffice it to say that on many levels the question of difference has become absolutely central not only for the study of European cinema but also for its material survival. Equally important is to conceptualize difference not as the assertion or creation of unbridgeable epistemological and cultural chasms, but as what initiates complex but knowable relations of exchange and interaction. As Bhabha notes:

> The very possibility of cultural contestation, the ability to shift the ground of knowledges, or to engage in the "war of position," marks the establishment of new forms of meaning, and strategies of identification. Designations of cultural difference interpellate forms of identity which, because of their continual implication in other symbolic systems, are *always "incomplete" or open to cultural translation.*[7] [emphasis mine]

Similarity and difference exist in a dialectic and dynamic relationship of mutual interdependence rather than of exclusion. The political nature of this relationship makes it flexible, adjustable and conditional. For example, it has been politically valuable to assert difference in order to challenge the imaginary (and oppressive) unity of national culture.[8] On the other hand, it has proved to be equally important for anti-racist politics to assert the essential similarity of all humans by mobilizing scientific discourses that challenge biological definitions of race.[9]

It is in this way that we must approach the question of difference in European cinema. Historically, the films that were considered to be able to cross barriers of cultural difference were of two kinds—either those of the great European *auteurs* which had and still have a guaranteed run in the art-house cinemas across the world, or blockbusters which explore "universal" themes and embrace the globally recognizable Hollywood production values and style. In both cases the relationship between similarity and difference is rather static and fixed. The *auteur* movie (of the realist, modernist or postmodernist kind) is perceived as encapsulating universal values (either moral or aesthetic) and in this sense, as subordinating the particular (and different) to the general (and similar). On the other hand, films such as *Four Weddings and a Funeral* (Mike Newell, UK, 1994), or *Notting Hill* (Roger Michell, UK, 1999), while exploring themes with worldwide currency (such as love and friendship), also introduce cultural difference as a marketing strategy. Both films rely heavily on stereotypical (and almost exotic) images of Englishness that negate any difference within the national culture that they represent. As I will demonstrate later, *Mediterraneo* also belongs to this category and will be analyzed as a representative example.

But a number of films engage with questions of difference and identity in a more dynamic way without necessarily aspiring to transcend national borders. This is the case with, for example, *cinéma beur* in France or with a film like *Bhaji on the Beach*, in which the motivation of their makers is not to transcend European borders at all, but instead to explore positions within national cultural formations. Interestingly, many of these films (*Bhaji on the Beach* and *Trainspotting* (Danny Boyle, UK, 1996) are obvious examples) do manage to cross cultural borders and often enjoy decent commercial success across Europe or even farther afield.

It is crucial to realize that there is similarity in difference. Because difference is positional and political, the fact that the sites of cultural production, circulation and consumption are specific and unique does not preclude structural similarities between positionalities and political contestations. Instead of imposing universal similarities or unbridgeable differences, filmmakers such as Gurinder Chadha and Emir Kusturica, who are involved in exploring the dialectics of similarity and difference, make this the basis for cultural border-crossing and exchange.

Mary Louise Pratt's work on transculturation is perhaps the most sophisticated approach to processes of cultural exchange. Chapter 5 will explore in detail her theorization and compare it to other critical perspectives, but a sketchy outline of Pratt's approach is necessary at this point. *Imperial Eyes: Travel Writing and Transculturation*[10] is a study of the work of metropolitan writers travelling in the colonies and her analysis focuses on how this encounter both shapes and is shaped by the values, beliefs, systems of knowledge and representation of the colonized. Transculturation, nevertheless, can be used to understand other forms of cultural exchange, as long as we understand that interaction takes place in a field of complex and unequal power relations, which transform to a degree both parties involved in the process. For the purposes of this chapter, transculturation operates on two interrelated levels in the three films considered here: on a textual level, as representation of cultural difference and exchange, and on a contextual level, as the relationship between the film and critical reception and/or audiences. The following analysis of the films explores the dynamics of cultural exchange/transculturation and also utilizes Homi Bhabha's diversity/difference binary in order to propose a conceptual framework for the mapping of representations of cultural difference in European cinema.

The Films

Mediterraneo

PERHAPS THE MOST successful of the three films examined here, *Mediterraneo* has the dubious credential of winning the Best Foreign Language Film Academy Award in 1992, and a solid box office return in Europe and the USA.[11] The film was produced by two small Italian companies (AMA Film and Penta Films) that specialize mainly in medium budget Italian productions, but with some involvement in international productions in Spain and New

Zealand. In the same year (1991) Penta Films was one of the many companies involved in the production of *Prospero's Books* (Peter Greenaway, France/Italy/Netherlands/UK, 1991). *Mediterraneo* was shot on location in the Greek Aegean island of Kastellorizo (presented in the film as "Meghisti") with the local community providing the background of the film and used largely as extras, but relying almost exclusively on Italian actors and crew. The notable exemptions are the actress Vanna Barba (who plays Vassilissa) and the production designer Thalia Istikopoulou who are both Greek.

Mediterraneo is the story of eight misfit Italian soldiers who in 1941 are sent to occupy the remote Greek island of Meghisti. As they become increasingly isolated from the rest of the world, they find pleasure in escaping the war and their national identity, eventually becoming "one" with the natives, as they dress, eat and dance like them, smoke Turkish hashish and sleep with the local women. The central theme of the film is precisely this erasure of national identity as the sea and the sun of the Aegean island wash out any traces of cultural or physical difference.

In the first twenty minutes of the film, Meghisti seems to be empty of people, with the soldiers involved in comic incidents that betray their apprehension of the (absent) natives and establish their manifest incompetence to act as an occupying force. Their fear and incompetence leads to a series of self-destructive actions (such as smashing their radio and shooting the mule) which effectively cut them off from the rest of the Italian army and the war. They eventually lose all traces of their military status, including uniforms and weapons.

Their first encounter with the locals occurs when the sentry, Farina (Giuseppe Cederna), is awakened by a group of Greek children who tease him. As panic takes over, the soldiers march in deadly silence, fully armed, through the paths and the squares of the village, looking for the enemy. They approach a washing line, with bright white sheets obscuring the view, and on parting them they discover the locals (children, women and old men) sitting in a café drinking ouzo and playing backgammon. When they inquire where the men are, they are directed to the local priest who not only speaks perfect Italian but also reassures them that "Greeks, Italians, one face, one race"! This assumed similarity between Italians and Greeks is something that the film exploits in various ways. The local priest asks them to re-decorate the frescoes of the church and the final result is a postmodernist, hybrid Greco-Roman iconography. The arrival of the British at the end of the war further emphasizes the similarity between the two Mediterranean "people" by playing the "whiteness" of the former against the "darkness" of the latter. At the same time the British soldiers are clearly marked as "other," looking completely out of place in the sun-soaked landscape, in their military uniforms and their formal and rigid body language and mannerisms. With the issue of difference/similarity settled in such a stereotypical fashion, the film sets out to explore such universal issues as friendship, love, destiny and the meaning of life. The opening ("in times like these escape is the only way to stay alive and to continue dreaming") and closing inter-titles ("dedicated to all those who are running away") are significant in these terms as they stress the global humanism of the film.

On the level of narrative the first encounter sequence functions as a reassurance for the invading but fearful soldiers that the invaded are not the hostile and dangerous "other" that a war enemy essentially is. On the level of the *mise-en-scène*, the disavowal of threatening difference takes the form of postcard type shots of the villagers engaged in their peaceful and stereotypically Greek activities. This is further reinforced by the vaguely Greek-sounding music that dominates the soundtrack. Reassurance here takes the form of a representation of the natives as a group of primitive, fun-loving, simple and friendly crowd who only come to life under the gaze of the Italian soldiers. The Greek villagers become an organic part of the wild but beautiful landscape that exists beyond history or conflict. The threatening but historically rooted difference of the enemy is replaced by a much more controlled difference, that of the objectified native abstracted from historical reality and re-packaged as local color. In this sense the historically specific becomes eternal and the encounter of the two cultures an existentialist issue.

The cultural encounter that the film dramatizes, inscribes positions for both the outsiders and the locals that are strikingly similar to those inscribed by "enlightened" forms of tourism. The invaders/tourists not only respect the customs of the invaded/locals but they appear to transform themselves in order to participate in the activities and the rituals of the community. The "experience" of this "other" environment becomes complete with the various sexual encounters of the soldiers. It is precisely these encounters, however, that give a clear indication of the real nature of the cultural exchange that unfolds in *Mediterraneo*. The use of deeply problematic clichés not only seriously questions the film's originality but also suggests that the terms of the cultural exchange between outsiders and locals are clearly informed by power structures operating most obviously in terms of gender. Farina falls in love with the local prostitute Vassilissa. The Munaron brothers (Memo Dini and Vasco Mirandola) enjoy a *ménage à trois* with the silent but aptly named in the credits Pastorella (Irene Grazioli). Strazzabosco (Gigio Alberti) impregnates and then abandons a local woman, who seems to be mysteriously delighted when she waves him goodbye. The fact that such sexual fantasies are not universal but clearly defined across gender divisions is a reminder that the cultural fantasy of the film operates along similar lines.

Bhaji on the Beach

A REASONABLY SUCCESSFUL film, *Bhaji on the Beach* was one of the first films released through mainstream distribution that directly addressed the black and/or Asian experience in the UK. The film was also shown abroad in film festivals (such as the Toronto film festival in September 1993) and in the cinemas in countries such as Germany and France. It was also shown in the USA where it made $735,192.[12] It was successful with critics both abroad and in the UK and it was nominated as Best British Film in the 1995 British Academy Awards.

The narrative of *Bhaji on the Beach* follows a group of nine Asian women who spend a day visiting the Blackpool illuminations. The film traces their complex relationships and has as its focal point Ginder (Kim Vithana) who, together with her son Amrik (Amer Chadha-Patel), is hiding from her violent husband Ranjit (Jimmi Harkishin) and his family. The film stresses multiplicities and interconnections and the narrative is episodic, structuring a network of interconnected sequences in which the characters are seen in relation to each other. The conflicts between the characters, as well as the possibility of resolving them, is the theme of the film.

In *Bhaji on the Beach* the sequence of the arrival of the women in Blackpool is structurally and thematically very similar to the one in *Mediterraneo*, but represents the encounter with the resort in a drastically different way. The women initially become a spectacle both for the residents of Blackpool and for the camera as they parade in front of both. Particularly interesting is the shot in which they enter the frame facing the camera and looking out of frame as Rekha (Souad Faress) exclaims "Bombay!" The shot that follows appears to be from their point of view as we see that what Rekha described as Bombay is in reality Blackpool and its illuminations: a crowded street, bustling with noise, with colorful ornaments dominating the view. As the camera tilts down, however, we redis-cover the group, part of the colorful and noisy crowd, distinct but not out of place. The next shot comes from Madhu's (Renu Kochar) and Ladhu's (Nisha K. Nayar) point of view, as they dis-cover the local lads Paul (Dean Gatiss) and Ray (Martin Greenwood) dressed as cowboys and serving burgers. Unlike the encounter between Greeks and Italians in *Mediterraneo* this sequence articulates the difference of the group as positional and relative, with the confusion of the point of view problematizing any division of the world into two fields. This not only involves the playful rejection of the shot/reverse shot pattern (which is essentially a division of narrative space in two worlds occupied by different characters and invested with different representational values), but also the systematic undermining of any position which unproblematically supports an us/them dichotomy. As Gurinder Chadha herself put it: "Britain isn't one thing or another. It isn't just *Howard's End* or *My Beautiful Laundrette*. There are endless possibilities about what it can—and is—already."[13]

This understanding of difference is further emphasized by plac-ing the story in Blackpool, a liminal space[14] par excellence, where individuals are abandoned to fantasies of flexible identities, escap-ing the routine of everyday life and exploring other possibilities. This is facilitated by the hybrid, profoundly orientalist iconography of the resort that the film playfully and systematically explores. Blackpool, which is in many ways quintessentially English, is also a place that imagines itself as transcending Englishness and offering an experience that escapes typicality and national boundaries. The women of the Saheli group are placed in a peculiar position in this set-up, as they are out of place within the orientalist *mise-en-scène* in two ways. They are excluded by the Englishness of the resort and they are subjected to the orientalist objectification that the resort mobilizes. In this sense the possibility of escape, of reimagining their identity is simultaneously enhanced and compromised by Blackpool.

Bhaji on the Beach does not negate difference and avoids placing the process of cultural exchange and interaction outside a field of complex power relations. This is brilliantly illustrated in the case of Asha's (Lalita Ahmed) holiday romance with Ambrose (Peter Cellier). In a fantasy staged in a Blackpool park and pastiching the musical numbers of Hindi melodramas, a romantic chase is choreographed with Asha and Ambrose dressed and made up as glamorous Indian stars. The point of view system is again peculiar. While this is clearly Asha's fantasy, the cinematic enunciation is that of a third person omniscient narrative with the camera revealing that the object of the fantasy, the glamorous Indian man, is really Ambrose. The narrative and cinematic points of view align at the very end as Asha looks at Ambrose's pale face marked by smudged brown make-up. This last shot functions as the ultimate sign of the impossibility of their romance. Ambrose has no place in the culturally specific *mise-en-scène* of Asha's fantasy. Particularly alarming is the fact that in this shot cultural difference is constructed in racial terms: Ambrose is the *wrong* color, the running make-up revealing his "Indianness" to be *false*. The fantasy is very ambivalent: it can be seen as Asha's resistance to Ambrose's orientalist attitude but it also places her within a racist discourse that disavows her romance and negates the possibility of cultural interaction. Furthermore, the point of view system undermines her desire and authority as her perception of Ambrose's "fakeness" is revealed to be based on a mistake: it is not Ambrose who is getting drenched but her. In a sense, the fantasy is not about Ambrose at all but it expresses Asha's inability to perceive *her* identity and *her* difference in ways that escape a fixed position in terms of race and gender. The film rigorously resists representations of difference as otherness while at the same time it engages in a thorough exploration of positions and power structures articulated around difference.

Asha's fantasies function as an important motif in the film and articulate the moral dilemmas that inform her actions and values. Her fantasies are "wild" (and this is most evident in terms of their *mise-en-scène*, with bright colors, spectacular camera angles and lens filters used excessively), but also very banal, motivated by ordinary events and referring to ordinary situations usually disrupted by improper behaviour. The fantasies are marked by an anxious questioning of the function of the extended family brought about by the transgressions of the younger members, as well as Asha's own position within this family and even her ability to construct a coherent and meaningful identity. As is the case with the one discussed above, Asha's fantasies are always exposed as based on or motivated by erroneous assumptions and leading to errors of judgement of the other women's character. This is clearly the case with Hashida (Sharita Khajuria) who in one of the fantasies is seen as smoking and coughing while in reality she coughs because she inhales the smoke from Rekha's cigarette. Furthermore, the narrative of the film seems to revolve around a moral universe that contradicts and rejects her views: it is Ranjit's violence that destroys his family and not Ginder's "modern ways." Asha's fantasies are not explorations of desire and/or exercises of freedom, but demonstrate an overwhelming anxiety about the moral order of the world and her position in the family; their function is undoubtedly oppressive, and they record her uncertainty and confusion.

The film remains ambiguous about the transformative potential that Blackpool, as a liminal space, offers to Asha. While she seems to suffer from the oppressive nature of her fantasies (and thus denies herself the pleasure of a holiday romance), she nevertheless manages to resist (albeit in problematic terms) Ambrose's orientalist objectification. She also dramatically and very effectively disclaims patriarchy in her intervention against Ranjit, which resolves this important narrative thread. Overall, there is a sense that the Blackpool trip has changed the members of the group, as they seem to change their attitude towards each other, but it also moves towards a criticism of patriarchal family structures and a spontaneous endorsement of the forbidden pleasures of the seaside resort.

Underground

THE FILM WON the *Palm d' Or* in the 1995 Cannes Film Festival and was released across Europe in 1995–96. As it appeared at the height of the Bosnian war it attracted extremely hostile criticism[15] for not offering a definitive position in relation to the history of the former Yugoslavia and the role of the nationalist movements. The film follows the lives of a group of Serbian people (at least this appears to be the general critical consensus, probably because the film is set in Belgrade, but the film does not define ethnic origins in any clear way) through fifty years of Yugoslavian history, beginning in 1941 and the World War II, moving to the Cold War and the 1960s and finally to 1991 and the bloody civil/independence wars.

History in the film consists of newsreel footage of recognizable events, *Forrest Gump*-like manipulations of this footage, a constructed propagandistic national history, and the story of the characters. In a tenuous and iconoclastic way, a link is created between "objective" history, constructed national mythology and the film's narrative. The film is not preoccupied with historical accuracy but is deeply historical: not just because the adventures of the heroes only make sense against a historical background, but also because history is in itself the subject matter of the film. There is a shrewd awareness of the political stakes and the power structures involved in producing and circulating a national history. The ground/underground divide is a clear representation of this power structure: the imposition of a national history from above has direct and tragic effects on the lives of those down below. But although the film seems to criticize this manipulation it does not suggest an unproblematic true/false dichotomy. The film is ambivalent in that respect: it foregrounds the constructed, manipulated and manipulative nature of history, but it also accepts an ultimate historical truth that exists outside the text. This truth is not sacred, nevertheless, as the narrative events are not organized with a strict adherence to the historical facts. For example, Blacky's (Lazar Ristovski) escape and the destruction of the cellar happen well before Tito's death and the eventual disintegration of the federation, while the inter-titles (which generally function in cinema as an authoritative enunciation of historical truth) are often openly satirical and historically inaccurate.

In true Foucauldian fashion *Underground* is concerned more with the effects that official national truth has on individuals and less on its historical accuracy.[16] Blacky is constructed by the nationalist propaganda as a hero of the nation and as an icon that "symbolizes anti-fascist struggle." The film not only challenges this through the explicit representation of Blacky's profiteering, opportunism and macho hedonism, but it also demonstrates how this icon is used in order to forge national unity. Significantly, Blacky's status as an icon is shown as clearly oppressive as he is confounded in the underground life of sensual and sexual deprivation. The alienating effects of nationalist myth-making are further explored in the hilarious sequence in which Blacky mistakes the propagandist film-within-the-film *Spring Comes on a White Horse* for reality and attacks the filming set with his son Jovan (Srdan Todorovic).[17] Life underground (cold war Yugoslavia if we follow the film's allegory) has rendered the occupants of the cellar incapable of distinguishing historical reality from fiction (Blacky) or even the moon from the sun (Jovan).

Underground very perceptively explores the power effects of the construction of national identity unified around the official version of national history. This is further emphasized by the weaker characters Jovan, Ivan (Slavko Stimac) and Bata (Davor Dujmovic). All three are related to the main characters (Blacky, Marco (Miki Manojlovic) and Natalija (Mirjana Jokovic)) and suffer from various physical disabilities as well as from the tragic historical events and their manipulations by the nationalist myth making.

The final sequence of the film, in which the characters emerge from the waters of the Danube to a utopian land beyond historical reality and power structures, is a celebration of communality with national unity and peace restored. While this is marked as fantasy, it contains aspects of the reality of the film: mannerisms, antagonisms, humour, references to narrative events, music. It is a utopia, a non-place which is both real and imagined, both culturally specific and transculturally recognizable. The symbolic "birth of a nation," with cattle emerging from the water to form a homeland, is also a death or rather a double death, the negation of a negation. This is expressed in terms of an overcoming of loss that works on several levels. The loss of the unity of the country, the loss of friendship and goodwill, the loss of physical and psychological capabilities, the loss involved in aging and death are all negated as the full cast of the film celebrate their reunion in an outdoor wedding party. The sequence not only exemplifies Benedict Anderson's notion of the imagined community as both sovereign and limited, real and imagined,[18] but it also demonstrates the fundamental dialectic between similarity and difference that informs national identity. The assertion of difference (the specificity of the nation, in this case the "fairy tale country Yugoslavia") is articulated in forms, processes and rituals that are transculturally similar. As Anderson observes, one of the fundamental paradoxes of nationalism is the conflict between

> the formal universality of nationality as a socio-cultural concept—in the modern world everyone can, should, will "have" a nationality, as he or she "has" a gender—vs. the irremediable particularity of its concrete manifestations, such that, by definition "Greek" nationality is sui generis.[19]

The longing for a lost unity and the imagining of a happy and peaceful community is what forms the basis of all nationalist sensibilities. Ivan's direct address to camera is emotionally charged, as he overcomes his speech impediment and articulates the simple and transcultural fantasy of individual and national harmony. The film's conclusion, with a piece of land separating from the mainland and drifting away to an uncertain destination and future, rearticulates the dynamic dialectic of similarity and difference. The imagined union (articulated verbally, visually and symbolically in Ivan's monologue and the wedding party, and celebrated by the music) is undermined by this splitting and drifting, which reintroduces the harsh reality of the painful and horrific dismemberment of the country. The film places the utopia of the recovery of the "lost country of the fairy tale" in the context of both the universal modality of nationalism and the specific historical reality of Yugoslavia. This is in remarkable contrast to the role of utopia and history in *Mediterraneo* where the cultural (and clearly utopian) unity of Greeks and Italians can only happen once the historical reality of the war is safely removed from the narrative of the film.

Diversity, Difference and Water

CONFLICTS AROUND NATIONAL and European identity, the representational regimes of the films under consideration, and the future strategies for a transcultural and transnational European cinema can be mapped around Bhabha's diversity/difference dichotomy. The demand for and celebration of cultural diversity can be seen as essentially European in terms of the assertion of values such as the democratic pluralism of culture and the freedom and autonomy of artistic expressions. In liberal cultural relativism and multiculturalism Europe discovers its enlightened uniqueness as well as a point of coherence in its fractured identity. *Mediterraneo* mobilizes these sensibilities by negating the specific historic context that defines the difference(s) between cultures in conflict. The erasure of difference enables the film to capitalize on the assumed universality of its themes. If *Mediterraneo* offers the comfortable perspective of the diversity of cultures, *Bhaji on the Beach* and *Underground* challenge the very possibility of such positions. As my analysis demonstrates, the point of view system in *Bhaji on the Beach* is emblematic of the complexity of positions and the impossibility of reducing difference into simple binaries. Similarly, *Underground* rejects any unproblematic view of Yugoslavian history and nationalism.

Crucially, in all three films water plays an important role. In the form of the sea that surrounds the island and gives the name to the film in *Mediterraneo*, in the form of Blackpool as a seaside resort in *Bhaji on the Beach*, as well as the water that initiates and dispels Asha's fantasies, and in the form of the water that splits the wedding party from the mainland in *Underground*, as well as the symbolism of death and re-birth that it provides. Water is a material and visual manifestation of fluidity, and in the case of all three films fluidity involves first and foremost the renegotiation of identity. This entails a restructuring of the relationship between similarity and difference that supports any identity.

In each of the three films, too, water has specific narrative and symbolic functions which represent distinctive ways in which cultural difference and exchange are conceived and constructed. Furthermore, in a geographical sense water seems to reproduce this dynamic relationship between similarity and difference, union and separation: seas and rivers are not only physical frontiers and markers of national borders, but also routes of communication linking and connecting ports, peoples and cultures. Thus, the Danube is the physical border between Bulgaria and Romania and between Romania and Yugoslavia but it also connects the Black Forrest with the Black Sea, linking in its flow Linz, Vienna, Bratislava, Budapest, Belgrade, Braila and Galati. Similarly the Mediterranean Sea separates Europe from Asia and Africa but throughout history it has also provided important links and exchange routes between the cultures and peoples of the three continents.

In *Mediterraneo* the cultural and historical difference between the Italian soldiers and the Greek natives is erased as the sea disconnects them from the flow of history and the fixity of national identity. But, as the first encounter sequence demonstrates, this assertion of similarity, of the essential sameness of the human condition, negates difference by placing it within a discourse and a regime of representation that can only divide the world into "us" and "them," the same and the other. The function of the sea, then, despite the rhetoric and tone of sameness, is to separate, to protect and insulate the island from history, reality and interaction, to turn it into a "desert" island where cultures exist in the totalizing loneliness of the "utopianism of a mythic memory of a unique collective identity" that Bhabha describes.

Bhaji on the Beach and *Underground* involve a far more dynamic approach: While cultural difference is acknowledged, it is placed in concrete historical and geographical contexts and with reference to a higher level of discourse that introduces similarity in difference. *Bhaji on the Beach* articulates difference as positional and political, stresses interconnectedness, and perceives cultural exchange as a complex relationship fully structured by both power relations and individual agency. *Underground* dramatizes the conflict between official versions of national history and identity on the one hand and individual experiences of history and the nation on the other. The film refers to contradictions in the formation of national identity that are not restricted to Yugoslavia. This seems to explain the critical controversy surrounding *Underground*: the film represents nationalism as a celebration of communality and unity *and* as politically oppressive and divisive. The complexity of this relationship not only underpins the formation of most national identities but also avoids representing Serbian nationalism as "other." The film does not divide the world in "us" and "them"—a division very much demanded by the new world order, and one that can offer a political position from which to make moral sense of history and administer the necessary punishment. *Mediterraneo* views the sea as disconnecting and dividing while *Bhaji on the Beach* and *Underground* preserve the fundamental dialectic of separation and unity, of similarity and difference.

The international/critical success of the films seems to negate critical assumptions about what kind of film "travels" well in Europe. In Angus Finney's comprehensive survey of European cinema in the 1990s it is suggested that

> [F]oreign-language films that perform well across borders don't necessarily depend on star pulling power. Rather, they are often films that are more emotionally resonant and universally accessible, including *Il Postino*, *Cinema Paradiso*, and *My Life as a Dog*.[20]

While *Mediterraneo* perfectly complies with Finney's assertion, *Bhaji on the Beach* and *Underground* stubbornly refuse to follow suit. Their success is proof that the exploration of difference rather than universality is not only a politically important cultural strategy but is also a viable commercial alternative.

It is also significant that all three films have strong comic elements and could plausibly be generically categorized as comedies, because comedy is used as "viewer friendly" way of dealing with such serious (if not depressingly grave) subjects as war (*Mediterraneo, Underground*), sexism/racism (*Bhaji on the Beach*), and national identity and nationalism (all three). But it is perhaps more important that comedy in all three films seems to operate in a way that invites a transgression of fixed individual and collective identities. This form of comedy centered around cultural difference and exchange is both nationally inspired and transnationally intelligible, and negates another of Finney's assumption that comedies are firmly rooted in a national context:

> The problem . . . is that comedies hardly ever succeed in travelling across borders. Germany's Otto series, starring Otto Waalkes; the Dutch Flodder series; the Italian comedy *Johnny Stecchino*, starring Roberto Benigni (which took more than $25 million domestically, and flopped abroad); and most recently, *Der Bewegete Mann*, which is now being remade by producer Bernd Eichinger into English, are all prime example's of comedy's failure to appeal across a domestic border.[21]

If cultural gaps are to be bridged and cultural frontiers to be effectively crossed in the production, circulation and consumption of European films, difference must be neither negated in the name of the universality of culture nor affirmed in the fortresses of national and cultural particularity. Like those travellers who for millenia have crossed the Mediterranean and sailed the Danube we need to discover what brings us together by exploring what constitutes our difference.

Notes

1. For example, Andrew Higson, "The concept of national cinema," *Screen*, vol. 30, no. 4, 1989; Stephen Crofts, "Reconceptualising national cinema/s," *Quarterly Review of Film and Video*, vol. 14, no. 3, 1993.
2. Angus Finney in *The State of European Cinema: A New Dose of Reality* (London: Cassell, 1996), notes that the percentage of European co-produced films rose from 12 percent in 1987 to 37 percent in 1993.
3. Homi K. Bhabha, *The Location of Culture* (London and New York: Routledge, 1994), p. 34.

4. See, for example, the excellent but strictly restricted in national contexts, Susan Hayward, *French National Cinema* (London and New York: Routledge, 1993) and Pierre Sorlin, *Italian National Cinema 1896–1996* (London and New York: Routledge, 1996).
5. Bhabha, op. cit., p. 162.
6. Important here is the debate around Fifth Generation cinema; see for example E. Ann Kaplan, "Problematizing cross-cultural analysis: the case of women in the recent Chinese cinema" in Chris Berry (ed), *Perspectives on Chinese Cinema* (London: BFI,1991) and a more thorough exploration of issues of cultural border crossing in her *Looking for the Other: Feminism, Film and the Imperial Gaze* (London and New York: Routledge, 1997); also Esther Yau, "*Yellow Earth*: Western analysis and a non-Western text," in Berry, op. cit.
7. Bhabha, op. cit., pp. 162–63.
8. For example see Stuart Hall's essay "New Ethnicities" in *Black Film, British Cinema*, ICA Documents 7 (London: Institute of Contemporary Arts, 1989), or Homi Bhabha's "DissemiNation: time, narrative and the margins of the modern nation," in Homi Bhabha (ed), *Nation and Naration* (London: Routledge, 1990).
9. See N. P. Dubinin, "Race and contemporary genetics," in Leo Kuper (ed), *Race, Science and Society* (Paris and London: The Unesco Press and George Allen and Unwin Ltd, 1975), pp. 68–94, and Albert Jacquard, "Science and racism," in *Racism, Science and Pseudo-Science* (Paris: The Unesco Press, 1983), pp. 15–49.
10. Mary Louise Pratt, *Imperial Eyes: Travel Writing and Transculturation* (London and New York: Routledge, 1992).
11. Grossing $4.532m in the USA and widely released throughout Europe (Internet Movie Database).
12. Internet Movie Database.
13. Interview with Gurinder Chadha, *Sight and Sound*, February 1994, p. 27.
14. See Rob Shields, *Places on the Margin: Alternative Geographies of Modernity* (London and New York: Routledge, 1992), especially Chapter 2, "Ritual pleasures of a seaside resort: liminality, carnivalesque, and dirty weekends," pp. 73–116, which, although specifically addressing Brighton, analyzes the liminal nature of British seaside resorts.
15. See for example, the film's review by Tony Ryans, *Sight and Sound*, March 1996, pp. 53–54; and Dina Iordanova's "Kusturica's *Underground* (1995): historical allegory or propaganda," *Historical Journal of Film, Radio and Television*, vol. 19, no. 1, 1999.
16. Michel Foucault's work, and in particular *The Order of Things* (London: Tavistock, 1970) and *The Archaeology of Knowledge* (London: Tavistock, 1972), is a detailed examination of the ways in which discourse establishes "regimes" of truth. Foucault examines the

power effects of these "truths." Significantly, in relation to *Underground*, Foucault's work is often placed in opposition to both Marxist epistemology and the regimes of "official truth" of the (ex) socialist countries. Foucault himself clarifies his position in a number of interviews, and the following quotation is characteristic of his line: ". . . this has always been my problem: the effects of power and the production of 'truth.' I have always felt uncomfortable with this ideological notion which has been used in recent years. It has been used to explain errors or illusions, or to analyze presentations—in short, everything that impedes the formation of true discourse. . . . In sum, the economics of untruth. My problem is the politics of truth." Michel Foucault "On Power," in Lawrence Kritzman (ed), *Michel Foucault: Politics, Philosophy, Culture* (New York and London: Routledge, 1988), p. 118.

17. This can also be read as comment on the Stalinist narrative that treats the "people" as the hero of history while at the same time alienates the "people" from the political process.

18. Benedict Anderson, *Imagined Communities: Reflections on the Origins and Spread of Nationalism* (London and New York: Verso, 1991), pp. 5–7.

19. Ibid, p. 5.

20. Finney, op. cit., p. 55.

21. Ibid, p. 55.

4 THE POPULAR AND THE EUROPEAN IN FILM STUDIES

IN THE DISCOURSE of Anglo-US film studies the terms "popular" and "European" seem to be mutually exclusive. On the level of signi-fication, "Europeanness" has clear connotations of high art; the "popular," on the other hand, usually refers to cultural products which are either non-European in essence because of their "base-ness" (even if they are produced in Europe), or come from outside Europe (in the case of cinema this usually means Hollywood). On the level of film theory, the conceptual categories of film studies do not take into consideration the popular European (and indeed any non-Hollywood) film. The exploration of these two levels of dis-course will facilitate an initial mapping of the methodological and conceptual difficulties involved in definitions and in the study of popular European cinema.

In the pioneering work in the field of popular European cinema,[1] Richard Dyer and Ginette Vincendeau have noted that the difficulty of pinning down the term should not be seen as an insurmountable obstacle inhibiting research, but as a "productive messiness," offer-ing privileged insights into the workings of theory and criticism and its relation to cultural production and consumption. Previous chap-ters of this book have explored to some degree the troublesome intersection between the "national" and the "popular," as well as the particular problems posed by recent developments in European cinema to the "national popular" compound. The increasing impor-tance of international markets, for instance, give to the basic, com-mon-sensical definition of popularity as commercial success a clear-ly transnational dimension and in this sense, force a *de facto* rethinking of both terms.

After exploring some of the contradictions of the term and the theoretical frameworks in which it has been used, I shall conclude this chapter with an analysis of a cycle of French comedies, the *Gendarme* series starring Luis de Funès, with specific reference to both national and transnational contexts.

The Popular

THE TERM "POPULAR" has a multiplicity of sometimes contradictory meanings that make it a notoriously difficult critical category. The aim of this section is not to discover and impose a strict and rigorous definition of the term (even if that was ever possible), but to explore what that the term has come to signify within a number of different discourses. After mapping out the broad field of signification I shall examine how the term is used in film studies.

Some of the confusion around the popular (especially "popular cinema") arises from the existence of a cluster of terms that are perceived and used as more or less interchangeable—crucially the terms "commercial," "entertainment," "mainstream" and "genre." I shall attempt to diminish the confusion by considering the similarities and differences between the terms and the connotations attached to them.

A useful point of departure is Raymond Williams's etymological and discursive history of the popular in *Keywords*.[2] Williams notes that the term was in its original use (in the fifteenth and sixteenth centuries) a legal and political term meaning "belonging to the people." In such context the term also carried connotations of "commonness" ("low" or "base") stemming from the binary opposition people/aristocracy. A variation of this binary can be found in a fundamental contradiction of modern nationhood discussed previously in passing. While popular mandate and approval offers political legitimacy to the nation-state, the cultural cohesion of the latter is maintained through the valorization of an elite culture,[3] which, nevertheless, also functions as a marker of distinction and exclusion.[4] This is the hypocrisy of the modern nation-state, in which the people are sovereign in terms of their political will but unreliable and in need of guidance in terms of their aesthetic orientation.

Williams also observes that within a legal/political discourse the popular became an adjective that involved a certain degree of manipulation; this is most obvious in description of policies as "deliberately popular." This indicates an uneven relationship of power in which the lines of force come from "above," seeking out the people "down there." As Meaghan Morris persuasively argues, an influential strand in cultural studies is informed by the political desire to challenge and debunk this power structure and, ultimately, to "understand and encourage cultural democracy."[5] It is within this political and critical context that a similar strand was developed in Anglo-US film studies in the 1960s and 70s, expressed most clearly in the successful establishment of Hollywood cinema as a legitimate object of academic study and critical practice.[6]

In the context of popular culture, Williams identifies two interconnected sets of meaning that persist in contemporary uses of "popular": connotations of inferiority (as in "popular literature" and "popular press" distinguished from "quality press") and intentionality (work deliberately seeking out to win favour, as in "popular journalism"). A particularly relevant discourse, in which these two overlapped meanings surface, is the area of European cultural policy-making, especially with reference to American popular culture. As witnessed in the GATT (General Agreement on Tariffs and Trade) negotiations, European decision-makers mobilize a rhetoric that describes American popular culture (and in particular Hollywood films) as aggressively expanding and overwhelming Europe with inferior products that threaten indigenous expression and tradition. Indeed, the exclusion of the audio-visual sector from the 1993 agreement signed at Marrakesh was seen as absolutely fundamental for the survival of European culture. This was a French initiative that was eventually adopted by and became the position of the European Union.[7] President François Mitterand most lucidly articulated the argument, using a distinctly "European" rhetoric:

> Creations of the spirit are not just commodities; the elements of culture are not pure business. Defending the pluralism of works of art and the freedom of the public to choose is a duty. What is at stake is the cultural identity of all our nations. It is the right of all peoples to their own culture. It is the freedom to create and choose our own images. A society which abandons to others the way of showing itself, that is the way of presenting itself to itself, is a society enslaved.[8]

While the French clearly spearheaded the attack on Hollywood, the British were more reserved. However, even the rather "Eurosceptic" Anthony Smith notes:

> The great fear of the 1990s, as a major political and economic unit begins to emerge in Europe, is that the outreach of Hollywood will become even more effective. The imagery of

America displaces national language and gesture, national fable
and landscape, and perhaps in time the sense of belonging to the
traditional national entity.[9]

While there is a long and well-documented history of
Hollywood's strategic and aggressive expansion in the European
market[10] that offers historical justification to the use of protectionist measures, the rhetoric used above reinforces connotations of inferiority and manipulation attributed to and associated with popular
forms. This, as we will see later, has important ramifications for the
future of European cinema, because the "defense" of European
identity and/or national European identities is seen as exclusively
depending on the promotion of "art" cinema.

A positive meaning of the popular, according to Williams, is
"well-liked by many people." It is in this sense that the term is
often used in film studies. Before exploring this further, it is worth
reminding ourselves that the semantic wealth of the term arises
from the presence of multiple, overlapping and often contradictory connotations that coexist in a variety of discourses. Thus, while
it is desirable for a politician to be well-liked by the people, it is
undesirable to have a "European audio-visual area"[11] flooded by
well-liked Hollywood movies. Here, as in the Mitterand quotation
used above, we see that the people are perceived as simultaneously sovereign and unreliable.

Richard Dyer and Ginette Vincendeau in their "Introduction" to
the *Popular European Cinema* collection, identify two paradigms
("one based on the market, the other drawn from anthropology")
which have been used in conceptualizations of the popular:

> The popular can refer to things that are commercially successful
> and/or to things that are produced by, or express the thoughts,
> values and feelings of, "the people."[12]

The market approach considers popular the films that are commercially successful. As Dyer and Vincendeau explain, there are
numerous problems in the various attempts to discover and evaluate
"success."[13] For instance are we referring to profit or ticket sales?
And what exactly do we take into consideration? The first release of
a film or the profit accumulated through subsequent screenings in
cinemas and television? Other important questions arise in relation
to the frame of reference of success: how can we compare the

relative success of a film made for domestic production targeting a strictly national (or even regional) market with that of a film with international scope? Is a film watched by 10 percent of the population of Finland or Portugal more successful than a film that attracted 0.001 percent of a global audience? It is very probable that while the latter made more money the former was vastly more efficient at reaching its target audience.

The anthropological approach works with a specific set of connotations of the popular, namely, work produced by or expressing the people. This, as Williams also notes, is a sense of the popular quite different from the ones discussed earlier, one that relates to the "culture of the people," a term that translates Johann von Herder's *Kulture des Volkes*.[14] Herder's obsession with folk songs indicates what cultural forms this "folk culture" privileges: artisan works involving traditional craft, locally produced and consumed and heavily depending on popular traditions and themes.

As Dyer and Vincendeau argue, the anthropological approach, exemplified by Harder's notion of "folk culture," has severe limitations when used in definitions of the popular in cinema. "Folk culture" refers to pre-industrial forms drastically different in their mode of production, circulation and production from cinema which is predominantly a modern industrial art. Additionally, a false opposition is created between, on the one hand, "authentic" and "pure" forms made by the people, and on the other hand, mass culture, which is seen as ultimately exploiting the people's need for entertainment. Nevertheless, the anthropological approach defines an interesting field of research around the use of traditional themes and forms in mass-produced and consumed films.

Through the above approaches (which also correspond to different connotations of the popular) we reach a polarity that maps the broad semantic field of the popular. At one extreme the popular is identified with the "commercial," which seems to place the process of production and consumption purely in the realm of an economic relationship. This leaves the researcher with a whole host of problems, most notably the lack of any attention to the textual workings of the popular/commercial films, but also the positioning of that type of film in opposition to the "art movie" or "high art" in general. I will explore the popular/art film binary later, but it is useful to note at this point that such a polarity leads to a misunderstanding of both types of film and of the processes of cultural production. Art movies do not exist in an idealistic, non-commercial sphere and popular films are not totally devoid of aesthetic sophistication or intentions of creativity.

At the other extreme the popular is identified with the "folk," with the people and their creative needs and expressions. While this stresses the involvement of the people in the production of art works, it is an understanding of the popular that is also consistent with postmodernist theorizations of audiences as powerful, free agents exercising control over the texts as they engage productively with them.[15] Apart from the theoretical problems involved in such positions, the shift of emphasis from production to the productiveness of consumption does not resolve any of the conceptual difficulties of the popular.

We can, however, conceptualize the polarity between the commercial and the folk in the popular as a relationship of mutual dependence rather than exclusion. If we overcome the semantic opposition, we can see that "popular cinema" refers both to socioeconomic structures of production, circulation and consumption of films and to ways in which audiences relate to the texts produced, circulated and consumed within these structures.

Victor Perkins's contribution to Dyer and Vincendeau's collection attempts such a synthesis by introducing a model of "accessibility":

> Popular cinema . . . is importantly a category of access identifying films whose comprehension and enjoyment require only such skills, knowledges and understandings as are developed in the ordinary process of living in society—not those that come with economic or cultural privilege. The terms of access unite the formal with the cultural since what is learned in the ordinary processes of life varies with place and time. Thus a film fully accessible to its French audience will no longer belong to the popular cinema when it arrives in England equipped with subtitles . . . Factors of those kinds contribute to the processes whereby movies popular in their countries of production enter the structures of art cinema abroad.[16]

While this might appear to be vague it raises a number of important issues:

Firstly, it suggests that the popularity of a film can be usefully examined in terms of the codes, values and systems of representation that it mobilizes and their relation with the codes, values and systems of representation available to a given culture at a certain time. We can also include under such examination the selective use of certain modes of production, distribution and exhibition, as well as financing and marketing strategies.

Secondly, Perkins asserts that popularity depends profoundly on the historical and cultural context in which films are produced, distributed and exhibited. This certainly places limitations on notions of the popular but the emphasis on locality and history is particularly useful for approaching European films which, unlike their Hollywood counterparts, have little or no claim at all to universal popularity. Perkins is certainly right in pointing out the "art cinema" connotations that subtitles have in the UK, but it must be stressed that this is to a great extent a peculiarity of Anglo-US film cultures. The popularity of Hollywood (or British films for that matter) does not suffer by the use of subtitles (or dubbing) in many other European countries.[17]

Finally, popularity is defined as operating within a social, cultural and aesthetic sphere marked by consensus. In this way, as Perkins notes, the popular is placed in opposition to experimental, avant-garde or art cinema that depends on the challenge and negation of established cultural and aesthetic paradigms.

After this initial exploration of the semantic richness of the term, I shall pay closer attention to the methodological and theoretical problems that revolve around two interrelated and overlapping binary oppositions involving the "popular" and the "European": art vs. popular cinema and European cinema vs. Hollywood.

Unravelling the Binaries: Art/Popular, Europe/Hollywood

THE RELATIONSHIP BETWEEN art and popular cinema has a peculiar history within Anglo-US film studies. While this history is informed by debates in cultural studies and philosophy it is also distinct in ways that I shall explore shortly. It is useful, however, to offer a brief and sketchy outline of positions taken within cultural studies (informed by philosophy) in relation to the art/popular binary. As the quotation from V. F. Perkins indicates, an influential way of thinking of the function of high art in society is one of exteriority and exclusion: the production and consumption of high art is the privilege of the few.

But this explicit elitism of high art is not necessarily perceived as politically undesirable and undemocratic. On the contrary, Jürgen

Habermas suggests that the ever increasing autonomy of art in modern European societies is fundamental for the (yet incomplete) project of modernity, which is ". . . the enrichment of everyday life, . . . the rational organization of everyday social life."[18] This project involves the inevitable marginalization of the artist and of high art from the mainstream of social life and activity:

> The autonomy of the aesthetic sphere could then [around the middle of the 19th century] become a deliberate project: the talented artist could lend authentic expression to those experiences he had in encountering his own de-centered subjectivity, detached from the constraints of routinized cognition and everyday action.[19]

This understanding of high art as operating in an autonomous sphere (and thus maintaining a distance from shared or mass culture) is echoed by Jean François Lyotard's definition of the avant garde as operating outside and against social and cultural consensus,[20] as well as by Peter Bürger's analysis of the "detachment of art from the praxis of life."[21] This autonomy of art (and its liberating, enriching, even oppositional potential) is threatened by the culture industry (Adorno and Horkheimer[22]) and what is seen as the erasure of the high art/popular culture distinction comes to define (in what is clearly a negative manner) our contemporary, postmodern life (Fredric Jameson[23]).

In relation to this tradition, film studies has a position that oscillates and shifts in its history. As film was initially perceived to be an industrial cultural form it was seen as not falling on the art side of the high art/popular culture binary. Part of the project of Cahiers du cinéma's politique des auteurs was positing the director as the creative force who manages to stand outside the production pressures of the big studios, generic constraints and commercial calculations. An early project of film critics and historians was to establish cinema as an acceptable form of art, indeed the "seventh art."

This, nevertheless, was replaced by a polemical attempt to establish "popular culture" (and consequently cinema) as a legitimate object of academic study and worthy of critical attention. As Steve Neale notes:

> During the 1960s and early 1970s in particular, at a time when the polemics surrounding "popular culture" and Holywood

were at their height, Art Cinema was often defined as the "enemy": as a bastion of "high art" ideologies, as the kind of cinema supported by *Sight and Sound* and the critical establishment, therefore as the kind of cinema to be fought. To parody the debate somewhat, it was a question of Siegel, Fuller, Hitchcock, Hawks and Corman versus Antonioni, Bergman and Fellini, of genre versus taste, hysteria versus restraint, energy versus decorum and quality, *Underworld USA* (1960) and *Bringing up Baby* (1938) versus *Persona* (1966), *La Dolce Vita* (1960) and *The Red Desert* (1964).[24]

The concept of art cinema, however, did not properly surface in Anglo-US film studies until the 1970s, and it was David Bordwell[25] and Steve Neale who attempted early definitions of the term. Both critics conceptualized "art cinema" as both a critical category (a way of classifying and judging films) and an institution (a mode of production/consumption and a set of formal characteristics).

In terms of the latter, it is important to note the centrality of the "art house" venue as the outlet of the products of art cinema. However, the definition of "art films" as those shown in art house cinemas is deeply problematic in Britain and the USA. As V. F. Perkins indicates, the mere presence of subtitles classifies a film as an art film suitable only for art houses. Tino Balio defines the art film in the American context as ". . . foreign-language films and English-language films produced abroad without American financing."[26] What is obvious here is that the distinction between art and popular film ceases to exist when a foreign film is involved. The situation is not very much different in the UK. European films are usually distributed and exhibited as art films without paying particular attention to formal characteristics or the mode of production. It is also important to note that the UK proved to be the most resistant market in terms of importing popular European films. Christopher Wagstaff's comparative study of Italian films in the French and the British markets in the 1950s and 60s indicates that even when popular Italian films were imported in Britain they would almost exclusively end up as B-movies in double bills after having been cut considerably.[27]

While the articles by Bordwell and Neale were valuable in terms of offering a specific definition to a category that was previously unproblematically demonized or idolized, they also introduced some broad generalizations that become particularly evident in the context of popular European cinema. The main difficulty is that art cinema as an institution and as a critical category is defined in purely negative terms and in clear opposition to Hollywood. There is in this sense a transformation of the initial binary art cinema/popular cinema into (what both critics assume to be) an identical binary, art cinema/Hollywood. Furthermore, the examples offered by Neale in the quotation cited above seem to suggest yet another shift: all the art films and directors are European while the popular ones are American. This establishes an equivalence between art cinema and Europe and popular cinema and Hollywood. Obviously this poses serious problems for the study of popular European cinema, as Dyer and Vincendeau have noted.[28]

The art cinema/popular cinema binary is also problematic in terms of the way it defines the formal characteristics of these two types of cinema as existing in clear opposition and even as being mutually exclusive. While useful (if a bit unimaginative) when it comes to distinguishing between *Wavelength* (Michael Snow, Canada, 1967) and *Batman* (Tim Burton, USA, 1989), the binary is counter-productive when films such as *La dolce vita* or *Jour de fête* (Jacques Tati, France, 1948) and directors such as Tati and Lina Wertmüller are examined. Furthermore, theorists suggest that in postmodernity the art/popular distinction has lost its critical currency and, more importantly, the reality of contemporary European film production renders such classification meaningless. As the previous chapter has suggested, the material survival of European cinema depends on the ability to cross boundaries, not just in terms of national borders but also in terms of transcending the art/popular distinction. *Until the End of the World*, *Bhaji on the Beach*, *Mediterraneo* and *Underground* are all examples of a European cinema that negotiates (albeit with varying degrees of success) the marriage of traditional high art themes and aesthetics with popular forms. In this sense the art/popular binary is not only inaccurate but also obsolete.

Equally problematic is the way in which the terms "mainstream," "commercial," "popular" and "Hollywood" are used interchangeably. This not only produces Hollywood cinema as a normative category in Anglo-US film studies, but it also places other types of cinema in a position of epistemological and ontological otherness. When Hollywood production values are accepted as the norm, as setting the international standards as it were, the products of other popular cinemas are inevitably seen as inferior. The difference of such cinemas, then, is not perceived as neutral, not even in the sense of liberal "cultural diversity" discussed in the previous chapter, but as carrying with it implicit value judgements of aesthetic inferiority.

Allowing Hollywood to monopolize the popular leads into a series of methodological difficulties and critical (mis)judgements. While Hollywood can be usefully described as a mode of production, as a specific practice against which the texts can be placed and examined, this is not the case with popular European cinema. Not only because different practices prevail in different countries and at different times, but also because there are very few established studios organized in ways even remotely approximating the consistency and tradition of Hollywood studios. The following two chapters will explore how such methodological difficulties surface in two key areas of study of popular European cinema: the study and evaluation of genres (European genres are generally perceived as inferior, failed imitations of the Hollywood prototypes) and authors (directors of popular European films are very rarely acknowledged as *auteurs*).

Indicative of the critical prejudice against popular European (but also international) films is the assertion expressed by David Bordwell and Janet Steiger, in the influential *The Classical Hollywood Cinema: Film Style and Mode of Production to 1960*:

> It is evident that the "ordinary film" of France, Germany, and even Japan and Russia constructed causality, time and space in ways characteristic of the normal Hollywood film. The accessibility of Hollywood cinema to audiences of different cultures made it a transnational standard. This trend has, of course, continued to the present.[29]

This not only seems to contradict the theoretical premise of their argument (if their claim is true, how can the European style be identical to Hollywood while the mode of production is drastically different?), but also demonstrates a rather offensive disregard for the difference in aesthetic values and textual practices of other cinemas. Clearly Bordwell and Steiger acknowledge the existence of international styles of cinema which are different from Hollywood, but they are located in the works of the great *auteurs* (such as Ozu, Jancso, Mizoguchi and Dreyer).

It is important, however, to recognize the role of Hollywood within the film culture of other nations. The need to address popular European films in their own terms (rather than as poor imitations of Hollywood) must be carefully balanced with an acknowledgement and a detailed investigation of Hollywood's influence on modes and patterns of indigenous film production and consumption. As Andrew Higson suggests in the context of British cinema:

> American cinema has for many years been an integral and naturalized part of the popular imagination of most countries in which cinema is an established entertainment form; in other words, Hollywood has become one of those cultural traditions which feed into so-called national cinemas: "America is now within." Hollywood thus functions as a doubled mode of popular fantasy, being both a naturalized part of national culture, and, at the same time, "other," visibly different, even exotic.[30]

The next chapter of this book will investigate how Italian cinema negotiates its relationship with Hollywood with specific reference to the spaghetti western, but at this point it is important to identify some of the problems that the hegemonic position of Hollywood poses.

Based on the ill-informed assumption that national popular films are inferior imitations of Hollywood products, critical discourses on national cinema tend to seek the "national" not in the popular, but in art cinema. There are countless examples of otherwise meticulous studies of national European cinemas that totally dismiss popular films. This is deeply problematic, as films extremely popular with national audiences seem to have no place within the formation of a national cinema. This not only mobilizes the elitism inherent in the high art/popular culture binary and the suspicion of popular taste that it entails, but also places the "national" in a sphere which is predominantly international: that of a modernist art cinema which aspires to universal aesthetic and moral values.

Both art and popular cinema must be located within complex and dynamic relationships between the national and the transnational. Both types of cinema articulate and express key ideological themes and visions of nationhood (which might or might not be in opposition to each other), while at the same time they both operate within transnational critical, historical and cultural contexts. While film scholarship has paid particular attention to this complex framework, it has done so almost exclusively with reference to art cinema.

A detailed study of popular films is required in order to understand how such texts selectively negotiate national and international filmmaking practices and traditions. The assumption that it is all down to Hollywood when it comes to popular entertainment films is not only blatantly biased but also incorrect. As Higson, again, notes in the British context:

> One implication of this scenario is that, for a cinema to be nationally popular, it must paradoxically also be international in scope; that is to say, it must work with Hollywood's international standards. To some extent, this has indeed been the case. But there is also the possibility of working with different standards, whether economic, or cultural, or both.[31]

In the following section, I shall examine in detail the cycle of the six *Le Gendarme* films, which from 1964 to 1982 proved to be extremely popular both in France and abroad. My study will demonstrate that these films operate with close reference to national and international cinematic traditions and engage with fundamental issues of French national identity. Furthermore, the films express the latter as being in a fluid process of change by dramatizing a conflict between the "old" and the "new" and by placing this conflict within an international process of modernization.

The National, the Popular and *Le Gendarme*

The Films

THE CYCLE OF *Le Gendarme* films consists of the following six films:

> *Le Gendarme de St. Tropez* (1964)
> *Le Gendarme à New York* (1966)
> *Le Gendarme se marie* (1968)
> *Le Gendarme en balade* (1970)
> *Le Gendarme et les extra-terrestres* (1979)
> *Le Gendarme et les gendarmettes* (1982)

The films follow the life and adventures of a group of gendarmes stationed in cosmopolitan St. Tropez. The group is led by Adjudant Gerber (Michel Galabru) and Inspecteur Cruchot (Louis de Funès), with the antagonistic relationship of these two being a constant source of comic events. What is remarkable about this cycle of films that spreads over eighteen years is that they rely heavily on the same core group of actors and crew. This gives the series a very consistent and distinct look and feel. The original story idea and characters were the invention of Richard Balducci, who had an otherwise undistinguished career as a writer, director and actor. Indeed his only other possible claim to fame is his appearance as Tolmatchoff in *A bout de souffle* (Jean-Luc Godard, France, 1959). All six films were directed by Jean Girault, who died during the shooting of *Le Gendarme et les gendarmettes* and the film was finished by his assistant Tony Aboyantz— interestingly, this film was also the last in de Funès' career. The films were co-scripted by Girault and Jacques Vilfrid, with Balducci collaborating in the first of the series. In all of the films the original music score is by Raymond Lefebvre and the art direction by Sydnay Bettex.

The main characters, Inspecteur Cruchot, Adjudant Gerber and the gendarmes Tricard (Guy Grosso) and Berlicot (Michel Modo), appear in all six films, with the gendarmes Fougasse (Jean Lefebvre) and Merlot (Christian Marin) featuring in the first four of the series. Cruchot's daughter Nicole (Genevieve Grad), who appears in the first three films, left the series after Cruchot's marriage in *Le Gendarme se marie*. Madame Cruchot is a central character in the remaining films, played by Claude Gensac in three of them and by Maria Mauban in *Le Gendarme et les extra-terrestres*.

The undisputed protagonist of the series is Louis de Funès (1914–1983), one of the most popular French actors ever. His career took off in the 1960s, and the success of the *Gendarme* series was fundamental to his popularity. Unchallenged king of French comedy,[32] de Funès was voted France's favorite actor in 1968 and enjoyed incredible success internationally. While the *Gendarme* series was his most successful set of films, he appeared in well over a hundred films with *La Grande vadrouille* (Gerard Oury, France, 1966, costarring Bourvil) one of the highlights of his career and one of the biggest box office successes in French film history. In France *La Grande vadrouille* attracted 17.7 million viewers, while the 777,000 tickets that the film sold in Sweden provided an indication of its international success.[33] The *Gendarme* films were also widely exported and, although virtually unknown in the UK, they were very popular around Europe in Scandinavian and Mediterranean countries and in Germany, the USSR, Poland and Hungary.

The Context

A CLEAR INSPIRATION for the *Gendarme* films was the *Pink Panther* series, the Hollywood production of the adventures of Inspector Clouseau, starring Peter Sellers. Like Cruchot, Clouseu is an incompetent French policeman caught in the middle of international intrigue. The two *Pink Panther* films (*The Pink Panther*, 1963, and *A Shot in the Dark*, 1964, both directed by Blake Edwards) that preceded *Le Gendarme de St. Tropez*, were huge successes internationally, and they set the tone for the series: cosmopolitan settings, police infighting and ineptitude, ingenious criminals. The cast was usually a galaxy of international stars: Peter Sellers, David Niven, Claudia Cardinale, Robert Wagner and Capucine in *The Pink Panther*; Sellers, Elke Sommer, Herbert Lom and George Sanders, in *A Shot in the Dark*. The nine films of the series (and the cartoon spin off) were fundamental for United Artists' financial success in the 1960s and 70s.

While there is no doubt that *The Pink Panther* inspired the *Gendarme* series and that there are startling similarities between the two, there are also important differences. A brief consideration of some of these differences will help to clarify crucial aspects of the complex relationship between Hollywood and other popular films.

Particularly useful for such comparison is the second film of the series, *Le Gendarme à New York*. While the other films are located exclusively in France, *Le Gendarme à New York* takes the French policemen to the USA to represent France in an international police conference. Important here is the sharp awareness of national particularity that the film demonstrates. The move from France to New York is dramatized as a difficult and problematic narrative event. The film pays particular attention to the actual process of getting there, with the first quarter of the film narrating this transition, as we follow the gendarmes in their (slow) journey on the boat to America.

Particularly interesting are the scenes in which Cruchot teaches the other gendarmes English. In these scenes, as in many other scenes in New York, we witness the difficulty that the policemen have with English, and their linguistic incompetence is fully exploited for its comedic potential. This offers a clear indication of position: this is a French film, telling the story of a group of French people (played by French actors), who move to a strange, foreign location, where they face all sorts of problems precisely because they are foreign. *The Pink Panther*, on the contrary, is oblivious to such difficulties and to national limitations, positions and borders. The film moves freely around the globe, changing locations constantly and placing the international characters (played by international stars) in various settings. The freedom of movement and smoothness of transition do not seem to indicate that foreign locations pose any kind of challenge for this film (but what can be foreign in such an international film?). There is not even the slightest sense of awareness that this film is a national product.

A fundamental difference between the films is the treatment of language. In typical Hollywood fashion, it is an Anglophone actor who plays the French policeman in *The Pink Panther*. Indeed, for many people the enduring comic memory of the series is Peter Sellers' English accentuated with a phoney French accent.[34] This has a powerful effect: it constructs English as the universal (and essentially neutral) language of film and disguises the reality of linguistic difference. What *The Pink Panther* renders comic in language is the French version of English, interpreted in this sense as a French failing, while it disguises completely the fact that Peters Sellers is a British actor who cannot (or will not) speak French. *Le Gendarme à New York*, on the other hand, foregrounds the difficulties that the French characters/actors encounter in a foreign linguistic environment. In this case the comic element does not come from the linguistic environment itself but by the incompetence in English that the characters/actors demonstrate.

What distinguishes *Le Gendarme* from *The Pink Panther* is the former's awareness of the limits and limitations of the diegetic world, which are determined by the national particularity of the film. As is the case with the popular films of nations other than the USA, French films demonstrate an awareness of their existence in relation to other cultures and other cinemas.[35] This can also be seen in terms of the numerous references to Hollywood films typical of the films of *Le Gendarme* series. In *Le Gendarme à New York*, for example, the scenes in the playground are clear references to the *West Side Story* (Jerome Robbins and Robert Wise, USA, 1961). And the fifth film of the series, *Le Gendarme et les extra-terrestres*, is clearly influenced by *Close Encounters of the Third Kind* (Steven Spielberg, USA, 1977), as the scenes of the spaceship landing and the gendarmes approaching demonstrate.

More broadly, St. Tropez as the setting of *Le Gendarme* must be placed in the context of the increasing trend towards mass tourism in

Mediterranean countries since the late 1950s. In the 1960s St. Tropez (as well as places such as Capri, Monte Carlo or Mykonos) emerged as a center of attraction for an upper class, cosmopolitan type of tourism. In this sense, the very setting of the series places the films in a concrete historical and cultural context, within which French values and issues are given an international perspective.

But the *Gendarme* films must also be seen in the context of the shorter-lived (1964–66) *Fantômas* series, which comprised three films: *Fantômas*, 1964, *Fantômas se déchaîne*, 1965 and *Fantômas contre Scotland Yard*, 1966, which were all directed by Andre Hunebelle and starred Louis de Funès, Jean Marais and Mylène Demongeot. While the series is clearly indebted to both *The Pink Panther* and the James Bond films (the stories revolve around Fantômas, a super-criminal and master of disguises, who is running circles around Louis de Funès' Inspecteur Juve), it also relies heavily on a specifically French film heritage. Indeed, the settings and the main characters (Fantômas, Juve and Fandor) are borrowed from the earlier *Fantômas* series directed by Louis Feuillade (the first film of that series was released in 1913). There is a marked difference, nevertheless, in the moral tone of the two series: the original was in many ways a celebration of imaginative criminality, whereas the 1960s series (clearly targeting family audiences) seems to reject any notion that "crime pays in the end."[36]

What this exploration of the context of the *Gendarme* series seems to suggest is that popular films work with and exploit the popularity of both national and international forms and traditions. To reduce this complexity into a simple hegemonic model of Hollywood superiority is to grossly misunderstand and misrepresent the dynamics of popular films. Equally reductive is the unwieldy opposition posed by critics between popular and art films. Again, the *Gendarme* series offers some valuable insights into the difficulties involved in sustaining such neat binarism.

All the films were produced or coproduced by SNC (Societe Nouvelle de Cinematographie). SNC's partnerships involved other French companies (such as Franca Films in *Le Gendarme de St. Tropez*) and Italian companies (such as Medusa Distribuzione in *Le Gendarme se marie* and Mega Films in *Le Gendarme en balade*). It is difficult to categorize SNC as producers. A French company, they were (and still are) very much interested in both national and international co-productions. Furthermore, their production activities (as

is actually the case with many small to medium scale European producers) seem to transcend the art/popular cinema binaries, as SNC
have financed and produced films that fall on both sides of the
dichotomy. They were involved in the production of a number of
Godard films: *A bout de souffle*, 1960, *Pierrot le fou*, 1965, and
arguably the most avant-garde of his films, *Numero deux*, 1975.
They also participated in productions exploring popular genres. Best
examples of the latter are the French/Italian co-production, *L' invin-
cibile cavaliere mascherato* (AKA, *Terror of the Black Mask*,
Umberto Lenzi, 1962, one of the hybrid by-products of the peplum
genre), *Winnetou II* (Harald Reinl, 1964, a genuine European western involving Germany, France, Italy and Yugoslavia), and the
French/Italian/Spanish/British western, *Les Petroleuses* (Christian-
Jaque, 1971, a Brigitte Bardot and Claudia Cardinale vehicle).

While the production background of *Le Gendarme le St. Tropez*
challenges the art/popular opposition in pragmatic terms, certain
formal aspects of the films challenge the textual definition of the
binary. This is partly a generic characteristic, as comedies seem to
challenge many of the conventions of verisimilitude, causal and
plausible narrative and performance styles.[37] But the *Gendarme*
films demonstrate elements of self-reflexivity that go beyond genre
boundaries and even beyond the limited intertextuality of certain
types of Hollywood film cycles.[38]

The fourth film of the series, *Le Gendarme en balade*, narrates
the events following the retirement of the whole of the St.
Tropez/Cruchot police group. The opening sequences of the film
show Cruchot living an affluent but extremely boring life with his
wife in her family castle. An unexpected visit from the Gerbers gives
Cruchot the opportunity to spend some time with his ex-Adjudant
reminiscing about their past adventures. In the castle Cruchot has
set up a museum dedicated to the previous *Gendarme* adventures.
Inside, Cruchot and Gerber examine many of the sets and props
used in the series and watch the projection of scenes from the films.

Le Gendarme en balade uses a number of devices to explore the
fact that it is the fourth film of a series and this reference to the past
is happening on many interrelated levels. Cruchot's diegetically
motivated nostalgia for the good old days is used as a pretext for the
presentation of material that is clearly extra-diegetic. This strategy
only partially masks what is a self-reflexive moment in which the
present film celebrates the success of the whole of the series,

exposing in the process the various elements that contributed in the construction of the filmic reality (sets, props, music).

When Merlot bursts into the castle to announce that their old colleague Fougasse was involved in an accident that led to amnesia, Cruchot decides to re-form the group. He hopes that reliving the past (or, rather, live like in the past) will help Fougasse to recover his memory. Once again, a diegetic excuse is offered for the unfolding of events that inevitably draw attention to the constructed nature of the film and the series in general. The gendarmes have to re-create the "typical" experience of the past, a process that involves retrieving their old uniforms, returning to St. Tropez, but more significantly, going through adventures like the ones that they had in the past (raiding a nudist camp, causing chaotic traffic jams). While the narrative of the film is perfectly plausible, coherent and entertaining, it also foregrounds the underlying structural components of the story(ies). If Cruchot's museum exhibits the audio-visual aspects of the series, the overcoming of Fougasse's amnesia offers the narrative "recipe" for the series.

It is evident, then, that the film demonstrates a sharp and very entertaining awareness of cinematic conventions and explores the relationship between diegetic and extra-diegetic components in interesting ways that challenge the assumptions of textual constraints and limitations that inform the art/popular binary. Furthermore, the diverse production activities of SNC and the complex relationship of the series with national and international film traditions render the binary almost meaningless.

Le Gendarme and National Identity

THE FIRST FILMS of the series were produced at the height of de Gaulles's Fifth Republic, a period marked by the reinvention of France as a modern state with a unique role in Europe and the world.[39] The themes, characters and story lines of the series revolve around the crisis that traditional French institutions experience due to the process of modernization. The heroes of the films, the *gendarmerie*, represent one of the most profoundly traditional institutions, symbolizing conservativism, backwardness and the rural past, as they are a police force by definition excluded from urban modernity. In many ways the films are about the ambiguous, awkward (almost comic) function of such an instantly recognizable national (and furthermore, *so* French) institution in a period of restructuring, internationalization and change.

Cruchot, as the gendarme in the center of the narrative, is the embodiment of a Frenchman in social, cultural and moral conflict. The first film of the series articulates the contradictions in Cruchot's personality by offering a personal history, a past that introduces the series and places St. Tropez in perspective. *Le Gendarme de St. Tropez* opens with a short (2'30") black and white pre-credits sequence that very economically defines Cruchot's life *before* St. Tropez. The opening slow pan of mountainous landscape, accompanied by soft, instrumental music, reveals Cruchot leading a "criminal" to the police station of a small isolated village whose streets are jammed with flocks of sheep. In what follows, Cruchot is exposed as a narrow-minded, authoritarian bureaucrat who takes pleasure in punishing petit criminals. Very protective of his young daughter, he is shown as religious, with a deep-rooted respect for authority and hierarchy. At the same time he is very sly, using childish tricks to trap his opponents, and has ambitions of personal success and social mobility and recognition. The sequence ends with news of his promotion and transfer to St. Tropez.

The credits sequence that follows offers an audio-visual counterpoint to the opening shots: in brilliant color a helicopter shot approaches from the sea the harbour of St. Tropez, bustling with yachts, cafés and glamorous tourists. The pop song "Yeah, Yeah, Yeah, St. Tropez" dominates the soundtrack while Cruchot arrives by bus.

Even before the film "properly" begins, Cruchot is introduced as a character in transition and conflict. The two sequences set up the terms of the opposition and the values attached to them: past/future, mountain/sea, village/resort, church/café, isolation/cosmopolitanism, black and white/color, sheep/yachts, pastoral/pop music, country road/promenade. In St. Tropez, Cruchot's inward and backward mentality is severely tested by the international, modern orientation of the resort, with the comedic elements of the series arising from the striking difference between the place and the man. In a brilliant way the series dramatizes some of the key ideological contradictions of French national identity in the Fifth Republic by simply placing Cruchot in St. Tropez.

Cruchot's Frenchness is beyond doubt, not necessarily in terms of typicality, but mainly because of his self-definition. In an early scene of *Le Gendarme de St. Tropez*, the *gendarmes* take a nap in a field, and in a montage sequence we witness their dreams. While the other gendarmes have sexual fantasies that pastiche film genres (westerns, historical epics and "exotic island" films), and involve themselves in positions of control over young women, Cruchot's dream is of the war film genre, where as a French partisan he defeats and captures German soldiers. The sequence emphasizes Cruchot's narrow and naïve nationalism, as well as his conservative family values that reject any acknowledgement of sexual desire. Throughout the series, Cruchot is particularly keen in combating international crime or fighting against corrupting foreign influences: his epic battles are against hippies, nudists and art smugglers.

Clearly, around the figure of Cruchot, the *Gendarme* series constructs representations of French national identity in conflict, marked not by homogeneity but by diversity and placed in specific national and international socio-cultural contexts. There is a definite ambiguity about the political position that the films take in relation to social change, modernization and nationalism. This is often the case with comedies, as the critical disagreement around the subversive potential of the genre indicates.[40] In the *Gendarme* series there are definite moments of open racism and sexism (most obviously evident in *Le Gendarme et les gendarmettes*), as well as narrative themes that can be interpreted as traditional and conservative.

Right at the outset and in the form of intertitles the films pay homage to the noble and heroic national police force. The ending of all the films, with a parade of the triumphant *gendarmerie* in the streets of St. Tropez, is arguably a celebration of national unity constructed around the maintenance of law and order. But on closer inspection the *gendarmes*, in their pompous uniforms, posture and music, are genuinely comic, grotesquely out of place as they are accompanied by majorettes and are surrounded by informally dressed tourists. The tensions between change and stasis, tradition and modernization, insularity and internationalism, that were introduced by the two sequences that initiate the series, are not to be resolved by the films but simply exploited for their comedic potential. This perhaps explains the popularity of the series: French social anxieties and frictions are represented in a form that simultaneously registers them and makes fun of them.

The *Gendarme* series seriously challenges the critical adequacy or even relevance of the binaries popular/art, Hollywood/Europe as well as a limited, narrow definition of the "national." This case study has explored some aspects of the dynamic relationship between national European and Hollywood cinema that I shall explore further in the next chapter and in the specific context of genre.

Notes

1. Richard Dyer and Ginette Vincendeau (eds), *Popular European Cinema* (London and New York: Routledge, 1992).
2. Raymond Williams, *Keywords: A Vocabulary of Culture and Society* (London: Fontana Press, 1988), pp. 236–38.
3. See Ernest Gellner, *Nations and Nationalism* (Oxford: Blaxkwell, 1983).
4. See Pierre Bourdieu, *Distinction: A Social Critique of the Judgement of Taste* (Cambridge: Cambridge University Press, 1986).
5. Meaghan Morris, "Banality in cultural studies," in Patricia Mellenchamp (ed), *The Logics of Television: Essays in Cultural Criticism* (Urbana: Indiana University Press, 1990), pp. 14–43.
6. Thomas Elsaesser traces the origins of this tendency in the polemics of *Cahiers du Cinéma* in the 1950s and explores many of its contradictions in his article "Two decades in another country: Hollywood and the cinephiles," in C. W. E. Bigsby (ed), *Superculture: American Popular Culture and Europe* (London: Paul Elek, 1975).
7. For discussions of the 1993 GATT accord and the French position see: Jean-Pierre Jeancolas, "From the Blum-Byrnes agreement to the GATT affair," in Geoffrey Nowell-Smith and Steven Ricci (eds), *Hollywood and Europe: Economics, Culture, National Identity 1945–95* (London: BFI, 1998); Toby Miller, "The crime of Monsieur Lang: GATT, the screen and the new international division of labour," in Albert Moran (ed), *Film Policy: International, National and Regional Perspectives* (London and New York: Routledge, 1996); on Jack Lang's film policy see Susan Hayward, "State, culture and the cinema: Jack Lang's strategies for the French film industry 1981–93," *Screen*, vol. 34, no. 4, 1993.
8. As quoted in Jeancolas, op. cit., pp. 57–59.
9. Anthony Smith, "Speaking in tongues: words and images as vehicles for the cultures of Europe," in Rod Fisher, 1993: *The Challenge for the Arts: Reflections on British Culture in Europe in the Context of the Single Market and Maastricht* (London: The Arts Council of Great Britain, 1994), p. 81.
10. See for example Gian Piero Brunetta, "The long march of American cinema in Italy from fascism to the cold war," in David Ellwood and Rob Kroes (eds), *Hollywood in Europe: Experiences of a Cultural Hegemony* (Amsterdam: University of Amsterdam Press, 1994), pp. 139–54; Thomas H. Ghuback, "Hollywood's international market," in Tino Balio (ed), *The American Film Industry* (Madison: University of

Wisconsin Press, 1985), pp. 463–86; Ian Jarvie, "The postwar economic foreign policy of the American film industry: Europe 1945–1950," in *Film History*, vol. 4, 1990, pp. 277–88.

11. As envisaged by the Single European Act.
12. Dyer and Vincendeau, op. cit., p. 2.
13. For a discussion of some of the problems see Christopher Wagstaff, "A forkful of westerns: industry, audiences and the Italian western," in Dyer and Vincendeau, ibid, pp. 245–61.
14. Johann Gotfried von Herder, *Ideen zur Philosophie der Geschichte der Menschheit* (Darmstadt: Melzer, 1966).
15. The argument of "viewer power" is most clearly expressed in John Fiske, *Television Culture* (London and New York: Routledge, 1989).
16. V. F. Perkins, "The Atlantic divide" in Dyer and Vincendeau, op. cit., pp. 195–96.
17. In countries where the "norm" is dubbing (Spain for example) the use of subtitles in selected cinemas has the function of distinguishing between different types of audience (the choice of the original version over the dubbed version demonstrates familiarity with the culture and language of the foreign film) and not between different types of film.
18. Jürgen Habermas, "Modernity—an incomplete project," in Hal Foster (ed), *Postmodern Culture* (London: Pluto, 1985), p. 9.
19. Ibid, p. 10.
20. See Jean Francois Lyotard, "Philosophy and painting in the age of their experimentation: contribution to an idea of postmodernity," *Camera Obscura*, no. 12, 1985; "Presenting the unpresentable, the sublime," *Artforum*, April 1982; "The sublime and the avant-garde," *Artforum*, April 1984.
21. Peter Bürger, *Theory of the Avant-Garde* (Manchester: Manchester University Press, 1984).
22. Theodor Adorno and Max Horkheimer, *Dialectic of Enlightenment* (London: Allen Lane, 1973); for a different reading of Adorno and Horkheimer on the culture industries see John Caughie, "Adorno's reproach: repetition, difference and television genre," *Screen*, vol. 32, no. 2, 1991.
23. Fredric Jameson, *Postmodernism or the Cultural Logic of Late Capitalism* (Durham, NC: Duke University Press, 1990).
24. Steve Neale, "Art cinema as institution," *Screen*, vol. 22, no. 1, 1981.
25. David Bordwell, "The art cinema as a mode of film practice," *Film Criticism*, vol. 4, no. 1, 1979.
26. Tino Balio, "The art film market in the new Hollywood," in Nowell-Smith and Ricci, op. cit., p. 63.
27. Christopher Wagstaff, "Italian genre films in the world market," in Nowell-Smith and Ricci, op. cit.
28. Dyer and Vincendeau, op. cit., p. 1.

29. David Bordwell and Janet Staiger, "Alternative modes of film production," in David Bordwell, Janet Staiger and Kristin Thompson, *The Classical Hollywood Cinema: Film Style and Mode of Production to 1960* (London: Routledge, 1994), p. 379.
30. Andrew Higson, *Waving the Flag: Constructing a National Cinema in Britain* (Oxford: Oxford University Press, 1997), p. 8.
31. Ibid, p. 9.
32. Ginette Vincendeau (ed), *Encyclopedia of European Cinema* (London: Cassell and BFI, 1995), p. 164.
33. Data taken from the Internet Movie Database.
34. Encyclopedia of European Cinema, op. cit., p. 382.
35. See also the discussion of popular Greek cinema in the final chapter of this book.
36. For a discussion and comparison of the two *Fantômas* series see: Raymond Durgnat's Review in *Films and Filming*, vol. 15, no. 4, 1964, and George Lellis, "Fantômas," *Cinema Texas Program Notes*, vol. 5, no. 10, 1973.
37. For discussions of comedy as a genre and in particular its distinctiveness from other Hollywood genres see Donald Crafton, "Pie and chase: gags, spectacle and narrative in slapstick comedy," and Tom Gunning, "Crazy machines in the garden of forking paths: mischief gags and the origins of film comedy," both in Kristina Brunovska Karnick and Henry Jenkins III (eds), *Classical Hollywood Comedy* (London: Routledge, 1995), and Steve Seidman, *Comedian Comedy: A Tradition in the Hollywood Film* (Ann Arbor: UMI Research Press, 1981).
38. For a discussion of film cycles and their relationship to film genres see Rick Altman, Chapter 4 "Are genres stable?" in *Film/Genre* (London: BFI, 1999).
39. See the case study on the *Nouvelle Vague* discussed in the previous chapter.
40. See for example, Kathleen Rowe, *The Unruly Woman: Gender and the Genres of Laughter* (Austin, University of Texas Press, 1995) in opposition to Steve Neale and Frank Krutnik, *Popular Film and Television Comedy* (London: Routledge, 1990).

5 GENRE CRITICISM AND THE SPAGHETTI WESTERN

THIS CHAPTER USES a historically and nationally specific popular European genre, the spaghetti western, in order to point out the limitations of conventional genre criticism. I shall initially explore the numerous ways in which the spaghetti foregrounds the inconsistencies, hidden assumptions and open bias of many forms of genre criticism. Particular attention will be paid to the challenges posed by the spaghetti to concepts of national identity and national cinema. Theories of hybridity and transculturation will be examined in order to offer methodological frameworks for addressing these challenges in a way that takes into account the dynamic relationship between Italian production practices and American film forms. In order to further understand this relationship I shall examine in detail the international context within which the spaghetti surfaces, as well as the textual peculiarities of the genre. I shall return to questions of national identity and national cinema and suggest a rethinking of these categories that accounts for and explains the spaghetti phenomenon. I use the term "spaghetti western" throughout this chapter, despite its negative connotations: indeed I consider the term crucial for understanding the "violence" involved in generic classifications, the normative position that Hollywood cinema occupies in critical discourses and the "impure," hybrid nature of the genre.

Genre Criticism and Spaghetti Westerns

IT IS INTERESTING to consider briefly the generic classification "spaghetti western." The term, coined by American critics,[1] can be seen as a hybrid *par excellence*, an impossible mixture of cooking and filmmaking. "Spaghetti" here not only connotes inferiority and foreignness but also contamination as a dangerous and degenerate impurity. In this way, merely as a generic classification, the Italian engagement with an American genre is precluded to be an inferior, impure and contaminating exercise.

We need to pay some attention to the ambiguity of the term "hybrid" in discussions of film genres. A Ford western, a Sirk melodrama, a Hitchcock thriller and a Minnelli musical are all hybrids in the sense that they involve a transformation, a reworking of the formula, an intersection between creative impulse and long established tradition. The hybrid nature of these texts is celebrated, as the creative genius' intervention is not perceived as a contaminating destructive influence, but as an invigorating force that takes care of the renewal of the genre, of the successful balance between the new and the established. On the other hand, a Hong-Kong gangster movie, an Indian melodrama, a French comedy and a German spy film are all hybrids of a different order. They exist as specific local or national transformations of Hollywood generic conventions, the latter perceived as simultaneously national and global/universal. The normative position that these conventions occupy in Anglo-American film theory effaces the cultural and historical specificity of their production.

But the spaghetti western is a troublesome category, and its hybrid nature calls into question the purity (and the accuracy) of the fundamental classificatory activity of genre criticism. The hybrid nature of cultural products in general also becomes obvious when discussed in the context of genre criticism. Very few (and carefully selected) texts fit unproblematically into the almost Platonic ideal form of a genre. Indeed critics have identified the empiricism and arbitrariness involved in the process of classification and of establishing a genre as one of the fundamental difficulties of genre criticism.[2] One of the important consequences of this is the *de facto* empowerment of the film critic, who is in a position not only to decide the essential characteristics of a genre, but also to establish the essential corpus of films that belong to it. This in turn leads to a series of implicit value judgments concerning individual films or even whole groups of films: the spaghetti western is an obvious example.

There are, however, important advantages in the ways in which film genre criticism has historically attempted to define an object of study and undertake its analysis. Perhaps the most significant accomplishment of genre criticism is the fact that the study of specific formal characteristics of films (for example, narrative structures, themes and patterns, editing, soundtrack, *mise-en-scène*) is usually accompanied with detailed references to history/ideology (through the examination of iconography, the

cultural/historical referent or the myth-making processes in genres) and a consideration of the conditions, methods and strategies
of the film industry. It is precisely this ability of genre as a critical category in film studies to cover and link multiple concerns
that is assumed to be an advantage that film genre theory has over
literary genre theories.[3]

It is not my intention to revisit the theoretical controversy
around genre criticism, but to raise some specific questions relating
to the adequacy and appropriateness of the discourse for the better
comprehension and analysis of popular European films. With a
handful of notable exceptions,[4] the theoretical work produced
addresses either specific Hollywood genres or genre in general, but
in the context of Hollywood narrative cinema. Where does this leave
non-American film industries and genres? Research undertaken in
the area of Hindi popular cinema, for example, suggests that existing generic classifications are largely irrelevant in that context.[5]
Furthermore, is the argument (often and controversially put for-
ward) that genre categories were introduced and extensively used by
the industry referring only to Hollywood? If this is the case, through
what process did the rest of the world accept such classifications?
And if this is not the case where are the studies of the role of other
(non-American) film industries in genre formation?

The spaghetti western has been identified by theorists as a crucial category in terms of the problems that it poses for genre criticism. For example *The Cinema Book* suggests that:

> The films [spaghettis] clearly mark a challenge to the dominance
> of Hollywood over genre production, complicating the question
> of the relation of genre motifs to the culture which produced
> them, and demonstrating the work of translation and transfor-
> mation that goes on between cultures, especially in the cinema.[6]

But here—as in other in passing references to the "problem" of
the spaghetti—we encounter a remarkable hesitation to elaborate
further by avoiding even naming the problems, let alone addressing
them. I shall first attempt to identify the specific challenges that
spaghetti westerns pose to current critical paradigms and, throughout this chapter, suggest ways in which they necessitate a rethinking
of the terms and frame of reference of genre criticism.

Firstly, the derogatory title "spaghetti" in the hybrid
"spaghetti western" foregrounds critical agency in the process of

generic classification, evaluation and theorization. Genre criticism rarely discusses and problematizes the function of the critic in establishing the object of study. The usual argument in such cases is that the critic only responds to and utilizes generic labeling established through production processes and marketing strategies. If this is indeed the case with many Hollywood genres (although even this assertion has been challenged recently) it is definitely not the case with the spaghetti, a term that was never accepted by the Italian film industry. Furthermore, the generic status of the spaghetti western is ambiguous. Is it a genre in itself or really something less of a genre, possibly a sub-genre of the western? And if the latter is the case (as the critical consensus suggests) in what way is it a sub-genre? The assumption here can be that the short life span of the spaghetti (ten to fifteen years) makes it only a minor incident in the longer life of the western. Or, alternatively, that the formal characteristics of the spaghetti form a coherent group clearly contained within a broader group, that of the western. Both assumptions contribute to an understanding of the spaghetti western as a minor, inferior genre. But more, importantly they define and judge the spaghetti in comparison to a more general category, that of the western. By equating "western" with "American western," a hegemonic position within historical, critical and theoretical discourses is produced for Hollywood cinema. It is worth noting at this point a theoretical inconsistency that I shall explore in more detail later. The study of individual genres entails the examination of the complex but historically and culturally specific relationships between institutions, formal characteristics and audiences, and in this sense makes the American paradigm problematic and limited when a different set of relations is involved.

Secondly, the term "spaghetti western," as discussed above, evokes notions of impurity and is suggestive of change. Both impurity and change are notoriously difficult for genre criticism. While critics acknowledge that genre-mixing is as pervasive and common as the adherence to generic formulas, the overwhelming majority of scholarly work concerns the study of "pure" genres, or the analysis of films as example of identifiable, singular genres. On the other hand, notions of transformation surface in the context of accounts of the diachronic aspects of genres. An evolutionary paradigm emerges, with genre histories consisting of early, classic and late or post-classic periods. The difficulty of such approaches revolves around the obligation to maintain a sense of change and history, and at the same time to establish a core of generic characteristics. The spaghetti further aggravates these general difficulties. If it is impure, it is not so in terms of genre-mixing (in such case what would the "ingredient" genres of the mixture be?)—instead the contaminating agent is its Italianness. If it represents a change, a transformation of and a departure from the formula, it cannot be placed within an organic, evolutionary model, as it is essentially a "foreign body," a development outside the historic production basis of the western.

Thirdly, in many instances genre theories, as well as analyses of individual genres and genre films, conceptualize generic structures as operating against the more general framework of narrative/mainstream/Hollywood cinema. Steve Neale is explicit about this: "Genres constitute specific variations of the interplay of codes, discursive structures and drives involved in mainstream cinema."[7]

While the previous chapter of this book has already discussed the problems involved in identifications of mainstream cinema with Hollywood, it is important to note at this point that this is yet another way in which Hollywood cinema is elevated to a hegemonic and normative position. The assumption underlying such approaches is that the conventions of Hollywood cinema have become the international language of film, and have been wholeheartedly adopted by film industries around the world. The effect of this is that the spaghetti western is defined, analyzed and judged only in relation to Hollywood cinema, while frames of reference other than a simplified, essentialized notion of Italianness, are overlooked.

It becomes then increasingly evident that the spaghetti western as a generic category and in a variety of other ways brings into critical attention the national and cultural specificity of genres as well as the blindness of the theorists to issues related to nationhood and national identity. While the most influential examples of genre criticism locate clearly their frame of reference in American cinema, the status of the knowledge that these works produce is ambiguous. What is included under the general rubric of genre theory or genre studies is the extensive, detailed analysis of the phenomenon of genre in the context of one national cinema, Hollywood. The theoretical discourse, the generic classifications and the analysis of genres that such critical/theoretical activity produces, despite the limited frame of reference, are endowed with "universal" theoretical and practical applicability. The theoretical/critical work on genre mirrors the remarkable (but also normative) ability of national American cinema to disguise itself as universal. The problem is further aggravated by the absence of work on popular European genres that challenge the historical, critical and theoretical hegemony of the Hollywood paradigm. The precious few instances of such work remind us of the necessity to define and examine appropriate contexts and frames of reference.[8] Of course, it would be a mistake to completely reject the relevance of Hollywood genres. It is clear that in most cases popular European genres enter into some form of relationship with Hollywood forms and standards, but the latter are only one (often minor) part of a richer and more complex framework that informs the production and circulation, as well as the formal characteristics, of European films and genres.

The final problem that the spaghetti western poses is closely connected to the Hollywood/European cinema relationship. The spaghetti western foregrounds the national aspect of genre in two ways: by defining a national (American) context for Hollywood genres, but more importantly for the theoretical perspective of this book, by raising questions around national European cinemas. By condemning the spaghetti as an inferior genre, as a deviation from the classical paradigm that is unworthy of their attention, critics either completely overlook or oversimplify the complications that the spaghetti inflicts on models of national cinema. Crucial questions arise concerning the place of such a genre in the discourse of national cinema in general, and more specifically around the contribution (or lack of contribution) of the genre to formations of Italian nationhood and national identity. To simplify to the extreme, what does the phenomenon of the spaghetti western, of the Italian version of the "American film *par excellence*" (Bazin), say about Italy and Italian national identity? If the spaghetti western "demonstrates the work of cultural translation and transformation," as *The Cinema Book* proposes, how are we to approach and analyze this work? What theoretical paradigm and what methodology can accomplish such a task?

Hybridity and Transculturation

IT IS USEFUL to understand the spaghetti western (at least initially) as a phenomenon closely linked to the process of globalization. This not only follows accounts of Hollywood as global cinema but also highlights the accelerated mobility of cultural products around the world and their increasing detachment from national contexts. Such a model implies the weakening of national identities and perceives cultural production as operating not on a national but on a transnational, even global level. The spaghetti western offers an example of this process both as a response to Hollywood's global reach and as an economically and culturally transnational product.

Causally and historically linked to globalization is the process of cultural hybridization,[9] which is perhaps the most promising line of enquiry into the phenomenon of the spaghetti western. The advantage of such an approach lies in the possible conceptualization of the genre as a hybrid form, as well as in the semantic multiplicity and methodological flexibility that it offers. It is important, however, before adopting such an approach, to pay some attention to the different definitions and uses of the term "hybridity" and to evaluate their theoretical and practical usefulness.

The term "hybrid" originates in nineteenth-century biology and it is, in this sense, burdened with the dubious history of that discipline. Initially a term with unambiguously negative connotations of impurity, the hybrid was later linked to positive processes of genetic enrichment. In more recent applications it retains both positive and negative connotations. In economic discourses, the increasing internationalization of capitalism renders national economies interdependent, as foreign capital penetrates nation-states and produces hybrid economic spaces. While this can be seen as a severe blow against ideologies and practices of nationalism, it also raises questions around the politics of and power relations involved in local/global interactions.[10] Technological discourses are linked to such notions of globalization/hybridization. This is evident not only in fantasies of a media-rich world constituting a global village,[11] but also in the concept of the cyborg, which, for critics like Donna Haraway, offers a politically desirable model for contemporary identity.[12]

In literary theory, the work of Mikhail Bakhtin directly addresses issues of linguistic hybridization in ways that offer particularly useful insights into the workings of generic forms. In *The Dialogic Imagination*, Bakhtin draws a distinction between unconscious, organic hybridity and conscious, intentional hybridity.[13] The former describes cultures as evolving historically through unconscious borrowing, mimetic appropriations, exchanges and inventions. This constitutes the ground on which a second type of hybridity is based. Intentional hybridity involves the deliberate production of hybrids that challenge the unity and authority of monological forms. Despite Bakhtin's recognition of the impure nature of culture, most literary theories of hybridity remain locked within evolutionary accounts of shifts in genre hierarchy.[14]

While notions of the "dialogical" and "heteroglossia" have had considerable impact on research in film studies, even more important were developments in cultural studies and postcolonial criticism. Stuart Hall's work has been particularly influential in Britain. In the seminal essay "New Ethnicities," Hall suggests that identities are essentially hybrid and attaches a political imperative to his assertion: the purity and unity of a British identity is not only a fantasy but also a politically suspect concept.[15] This is very much in agreement with the way hybridity (in terms of identities and/or cultural products) is theorized in postcolonial criticism, in particular the part of the discourse that is heavily influenced by postmodernism and poststructuralism.

Particularly relevant is Homi K. Bhabha's work, which has very effectively challenged essentialist understandings of culture and identity as static and pure and problematized notions of authenticity and origins/roots.[16] The shift in emphasis from position to process, from the enunciated to enunciation is extremely important both in terms of conceptualizing culture and in terms of articulating flexible and efficient politics of national identity and cultural production in the complexity of the post-colonial condition. It is the emphasis on the interstices, the spaces "in-between," that makes Bhabha's approach to hybridity a valuable theoretical tool in dispelling the critical prejudices against cultural products such as spaghetti westerns.

There are, nevertheless, certain practical and pragmatic difficulties in using hybridity as a method of analysis of specific cultural forms such as spaghetti westerns. The tactical emphasis on the hybrid nature of all cultural production that Bhabha and others justifiably and convincingly posit opens up a very important space for politics of identity, but it limits the scope of our understanding of the conditions of production and consumption of specific cultural forms. In other words, the assertion that all films and all genres are hybrids defends spaghetti westerns against dismissive comparisons with Hollywood products, but it does not say very much about spaghetti westerns. It is Bhabha's clearly stated intention to challenge essentialist notions of purity, authenticity and origins; his theory of hybridity achieves this, but its use for the study of spaghetti westerns is limited. Ironically, and despite Bhabha's intention and theoretical elaboration, hybridity is usually employed in an oversimplified, rather crude manner in which the hybrid form is reduced to a composite secondary form "informed" by two essential and primary forms, in between which it exists.

Christopher Frayling's valuable work on spaghetti westerns (although it predates the recent debates on hybridity) is typical of the attitude described above.[17] Spaghetti westerns are analyzed in terms of an essential Italianness that he identifies in the themes of the films and which accounts for the transformation of the "original" Hollywood forms and conventions. It is rather surprising that Frayling's detailed study of the genre relies very heavily on Luigi Barzini's *The Italians* (1964) for the analysis of the Italian part of the hybrid. While Frayling acknowledges that the stereotypes that Barzini offers "cannot, of course, be treated as serious sociology" he is also quite happy to suggest that

> if one acccepts Barzini's account of these stereotypical themes at face value, one gets the unnerving (although not necessarily surprising) impression that contemporary Southern Italian society bears more than a superficial resemblance to the world of the Spaghetti Western. . . . This is clearly an impressionistic, cavalier view of Italian life—which might explain why its emphases mirror so closely those of the Spaghetti Western.[18]

Equipped with this implicit endorsement of Barzini's essentialism, Frayling criticizes Will Wright's reading of Sergio Leone westerns[19] for failing to consider "Italian values." Frayling then proposes the "Italian plot" as a separate category (with three "narrative variants") that accounts not only for the narrative structure of spaghetti westerns but also reflects the historical development of the genre.[20]

It is important to be aware of and challenge such reductive (mis)interpretations and uses of hybridity. There is a tendency to treat the process of hybridization as a "natural" process, part of the evolution of culture, or as the inevitable and unstoppable effect of colonization and globalization. In either case, the fact that "everything is a hybrid" should not be a point of arrival but a point of departure in the investigation of the different conditions and forms of hybridization. Furthermore, a rather biological understanding of the hybrid (as the impure product of two pure primary entities) persists in many critical approaches to postcolonial cultures and identities.

While it is beyond doubt that hybrid forms such as spaghetti westerns are the product of cultural interaction and exchange, there is a need for a theoretical approach that accounts for the textual specificities of the films and offers an understanding of how these forms relate to a broader field of power relations and to national and international historical contexts.

Mary Louise Pratt's work on transculturation proposes a much more useful articulation of the dynamics of cultural interaction. In the context of travel writing Pratt borrows the term transculturation from ethnographers, who

> have used this term to describe how subordinated or marginal groups select and invent from materials transmitted to them by a dominant or metropolitan culture. While subjugated peoples cannot readily control what emanates from the dominant culture, they do determine to varying extents what they absorb into their own, and what they use it for.[21]

Pratt's formulation addresses the works of metropolitan writers travelling in the colonies, and her analysis focuses on how this encounter both shapes and is shaped by the values, beliefs, systems of knowledge and representations of the colonized. Such encounters take place in what she calls

> "contact zones," social spaces where disparate cultures meet, clash, and grapple with each other, often in highly asymmetrical relations of domination and subordination—like colonialism, slavery, or their aftermaths as they are lived out across the globe today.[22]

Pratt indicates ways in which transculturation can be used to understand forms of cultural interaction that are not as clearly defined in terms of power structures as the colonial encounter. She discusses, for instance, how *arpilleras*, fabric pictures which emerged as an exportable art form in Peru in the 1980s, combine folkloric forms of representation with nineteenth-century colonial systems of knowledge and representations of nature in a complex historical process of transculturation:

> A product of the contact zone, the *arpillera* perhaps makes . . .
> an autoethnographic gesture, transculturating elements of met-
> ropolitan discourses to create self-affirmations designed for
> reception in the metropolis. In such autoethnographic represen-
> tations, subjugated subjects engage, and seek to engage, the
> metropolis's constructions of those it subjugates.[23]

It is possible to conceptualize the spaghetti western as functioning in a similar but also drastically different way from the *arpillera*.
Unlike the *arpillera* the spaghettis are particularly difficult to interpret as moments of autoethnography. And like the *arpillera* the
spaghetti western can be seen as the product of an encounter
between local culture and Hollywood's global cinema, as the latter
creates infinite "contact zones" around the world.

As I shall argue later, the spaghettis can be seen as a form of
"fantasy tourism" that transforms the myth of the Wild West in the
process. Given that Pratt's work is located within the context of
travelling and travel writing the usefulness of her work for the study
of the spaghetti western becomes clearer. Let us consider for a
minute the dynamics involved in the production and consumption of
tourist souvenirs. Like spaghetti westerns, souvenirs are hybrid
products, neither authentic nor inauthentic, existing within a complex system of transculturation. A tourist artifact, sold in a shop in
Spain, Greece or Turkey is informed by the local producers' understanding of what the tourists might consider as representative of the
local culture. As the manufacturer of tourist artifacts tries to imag-
ine and anticipate the expectations of the foreign buyer and the latter seeks to obtain an object representative of the local culture, they
are both involved in an act of transculturation.

Clearly this exchange takes place in a complex field of power
relations that brings into play a number of factors. Some of these are
the financial power of the tourists and their purchasing potential, but
also the profit that the seller makes; the stereotyping of the local culture that is, nevertheless, an act of deception in which the local mas-
querades as authentic, the specially-designed-for-the-tourist product;
the fact that many tourists are sophisticated enough to know that
what they buy is not really authentic, and so on and so forth.

Transculturation, as theorized and used by Pratt, involves an
understanding of cultural products as informed by a complex and
reciprocal relationship between producers and consumers that exists
in a broader field of national and international, historically specific

power relations. In this light and very simplistic way the Italian production of (spaghetti) westerns can be conceptualized as being
involved in a process of "buying" and "selling." The American
genre functions as raw material, which after its transformation in
the process of production, is delivered to national and international
markets, usually (but not always) disguised as American. It is worth
noting that while this may be upsetting for American film critics it
is not very much different as a process from Hollywood's use of
international locations and cultural traditions in the production of
its global cinema.

We have thus identified three interrelated areas that require further exploration. On the level of production, distribution and exhibition there is a need to understand the mode of production of the
spaghetti, the position of Italy in the world film market and the
dynamics of the relationship between Hollywood and Europe. On
the level of aesthetics it is important to examine the textual practices
of the spaghetti and their difference from the American version. And
on the level of national cinema we need to understand fully what is
involved in the production of representations and identities
expressed through/in the re-working of an American genre.

The Italian Film Industry and the International Market in the 1960s

IT IS NOT my intention to extensively discuss the complex postwar
history of the Italian film industry or to offer a convincing, insular
narrative about the emergence and decline of the spaghetti western.
Instead, I want to identify four areas that are crucial for an understanding of the place of the spaghetti western in the volatile international market of the 1960s: the close (sometimes friendly, sometimes bitterly antagonistic) relationship between the Italian and the
American film industries; the remarkable strength of the Italian
industry from the mid-1950s to the mid-1970s; production/distribu-
tion/exhibition conditions of the spaghetti western; and the international marketing strategies of the spaghetti western.

The strong American presence in all sectors of the Italian film
industry in the post-war period is well documented, as is the Italian
response to it.[24] Immediately after the end of the war American films
flooded the Italian market, which in the late 1940s was completely
dominated by distributors and exhibitors very keen to satisfy
American interests. This was eventually countered by protectionist

measures that blocked American film earnings in Italy and encouraged domestic production and the distribution of Italian films. One of the ways in which the American companies responded to that was by getting involved in the production and distribution of Italian films. As Thomas Guback notes, ". . . in the decade up to 1967 American companies spent a yearly average of about $35 million to acquire and finance Italian features, and to make their own films in Italy."[25]

Flexible strategies were developed to this end: American companies established foreign branches, co-productions with Italian and other partners were used, films with major American financial interests were disguised as Italian. Characteristic here is the case of the peplum, which from the mid-1950s to the early 1960s involved considerable numbers of American producers, actors, directors and other crew, in close collaboration with Italian crews and shooting in Italian studios. Many directors who made spaghetti westerns (for example Sergio Leone, Sergio Corbucci and Mario Bava) started their careers as assistants to Americans.

In distribution, despite the absence of big monopolistic chains in Italy, American companies (and their domestic branches) exercised a strong influence on and had major interests in the Italian market (second to the UK in the 1950s and the largest in Western Europe in the 1960s and 70s). A side effect of the strong American involvement in film production in Italy, nevertheless, was that Italian producers and distributors gained access to the world wide distribution networks of the Americans and to international markets. The accessibility of the international markets was also facilitated by the success of the neorealist films of the late 1940s and 50s, which opened a number of foreign markets to Italian distributors.

In terms of exhibition it is important to note that while domestic films came to dominate the Italian market in the period between 1955 and 1975, American films maintained a strong presence. Starting with an average of well over 50 percent of box office receipts in the 1950s, they fell to around 30 percent in the 60s, with a further drop in the early 70s before they went up again later on in that decade. The fall of the 1960s and early 70s, however, must be qualified in terms of the size of the Italian market in comparison with the other important European markets. In terms of attendance the Italian market was almost equal to the combined French, British and German markets. In 1969, for example, the Italian attendance was 557 million, in Germany 181 million, in the UK 215 million and in France around 200 million.[26] Furthermore, as Christopher Wagstaff argues:

> It thus appears that the commercial success of Italian films was being achieved at the expense of American films. However, if the percentage of box-office receipts going to American films dropped, it did not necessarily mean that Hollywood's receipts from Italian box-offices dropped to the same extent, because money earned by some Italian, French and British films actually went to American investors in those films. Moreover, American distributors distributed Italian films; Warner Brothers' biggest earner in Italy in the 1958—59 season was an Italian film *Europa di notte*, directed by the grand old man of Italian cinema, Alessandro Blasetti.[27]

The remarkable strength of the Italian film industry in the 1950s, 60s and 70s is also well documented. In that period Italy produced more films, attracted more spectators in more cinemas than any other European country. In terms of number of films produced, in the 1960s and early 70s Italy consistently outnumbered the USA: 242 to 174 in 1962, 241 to 155 in 1963, 270 to 181 in 1964, 245 to 168 in 1966, 258 to 215 in 1967, 237 to 156 in 1974.[28] In Cinecittá, Italy possessed the most Hollywood-like complex of studios in Europe, with advanced technology and facilities used in the production of a vast number of different kinds of films from peplums and spaghettis to Fellini films.

Crucial for understanding the spaghetti is the international orientation of Italian cinema since the mid-1950s. The most obvious ways in which this "outward look" is expressed are co-productions and the massive increase in Italian films exported around the world. Wagstaff relates both of them to the needs of the Italian industry at the time:

> The basic problem afflicting the Italian production sector was that its home market was not large enough to provide box-office receipts to an Italian film that could cover the costs of production. The obvious solution was to follow the American lead and enlarge the market. Two devices were available, co-production and export.[29]

Co-production became the main mode of production, accounting for more than half of the overall Italian production in the years that the spaghetti western was launched and consolidated. In 1963 there were 134 co-productions out of 241 films made, in 1964 153 out of 270, in 1965 126 out of 188, in 1966 145 out of 245, in 1967 125 out of 258, in 1968 123 out of 254.[30] Co-productions are usually despised by critics as opportunistic ways of raising finances that have nothing to do with "genuine" transnational cooperation. While there is certainly an element of opportunism involved in many partnerships, it is worth listing the advantages that co-productions offer to producers, as compiled by Colin Haskins, Stuart McFadyen and Adam Finn in their study *Global Television and Film: An Introduction to the Economics of the Business*:[31] pooling of financial resources, access to foreign government's incentives and subsidies, access to partner's market, access to third country market, access to a project initiated by partner, cultural goals (in recognition of the "good" intentions of some producers), desired foreign locations, cheaper inputs in partner's country and learning from partner. What the list demonstrates is the fact that co-productions operate on many levels and necessarily implicate the producers in rather complex processes of exchange with and exploration of international markets and partners.

Additionally, since the mid-1950s the Italian film industry has expanded in world markets and captured significant fractions of audiences in Europe, North Africa, the Middle East, the Far East and Latin America. The number of total export permits granted to Italian films rose from 848 in 1950 to 3947 in 1964,[32] while at the same time Italian films outnumbered European films and in some international markets (for example, in Iraq, Algeria, Spain, Turkey, Greece and Portugal) Hollywood films. While this expansion took place, Italy continued to massively import Hollywood films: in 1970 51.7 percent of the imported films (271 in all) were American.

Frayling is only partially correct when he suggests that the spaghetti western was targeting Southern Italian audiences. This seems to be the case in terms of domestic audiences but, as it has been persuasively argued,[33] the spaghetti also spearheaded the expansionist orientation of Italian producers in the 1960s and 70s, and it was the most successful example of the "new genres for new markets" strategy. From the early 1960s to the late 1970s over 400 spaghettis were produced, often in co-production with Spanish, French or German companies. The emergence of the spaghetti coincides with the decline in terms of production numbers of the

American western: while in 1958 Hollywood produced 54 westerns, in 1963 the number fell to 11.[34]

The timing of the appearance of the spaghetti western is interpreted by many as strong evidence of the opportunism of the Italian film producers and directors who identified and exploited the lack of supply of westerns in the international markets. What seems to further support the accusation of opportunism is the way in which the producers of spaghetti westerns promoted and marketed their films nationally and internationally. Following this reasoning, *The Companion to Italian Cinema* suggests

> [t]he Italian Western is both the most original and the most parasitic genre to emerge in Italy in the 1960s. It began as a counterfeit, not only an imitation of the foremost American genre, but under the pretence of being American, with directors, actors and technicians credited with English pseudonyms.[35]

Leaving aside the labels "parasitic," "counterfeit" and "original," it is important to contextualize the opportunism of the Italian producers and bring to the attention certain ambivalent aspects of the spaghetti's "pretense of being American."

The Italians were by no means the first Europeans to make westerns. Indeed, there is a long history of international engagement with and production of such films. Over thirty westerns were made in Britain before 1920[36] and then again in the 1940s, 50s and 60s. A partial list includes the "straight" western *The Singer not the Song* (Roy Ward Baker, UK, 1961) starring Dirk Bogarde; *Diamond City* (David MacDondald, UK, 1949) and *The Hellions* (Ken Annakin, UK, 1961), both set in the "Wild South" of South Africa; the Australian-set *Eureka Stockade* (Harry Watt, UK, 1949). The Germans produced westerns in the 1920s (*Der Todescowboy/ Cowboy of Death*, 1920), the 30s (*Der Kaiser von Kalifornien* [Luis Trenker, Germany, 1936]) and just before the Italians in the early 60s (*Der Schatz in Silberbese/The Treasure of the Silver Lake* [Harald Reinl, Germany, 1962]) and the Winnetou series which started with *Winnetou the Warrior* (Harald Reinl, 1963, Germany).

Furthermore, the Italians were not the first to disguise their films as those of a different nation. There was, as we have already seen, an established tradition of American producers and investors who developed very sophisticated ways of presenting their films as European in order to beat the protectionism of national governments—nowhere was that more evident than in Italy in the 1950s.

There is an essential ambivalence around the Italian expansion, and more specifically the spaghetti western. Italian producers, directors and actors were able to shake off Hollywood's domination and very successfully produce and export their own work, but on the other hand, one of their strategies (for the early period of the genre at least) was to do so by pretending to be Americans. This is demonstrated by the massive operation of re-naming directors, actors and films, and by the importance given to an extremely complex and sophisticated system of dubbing. There is nothing of the confidence of Hollywood in the international expansion of Italian cinema. There are no battles against protectionist laws of national governments, not instantly recognized (or systematically introduced) system of genres or galaxy of stars and no acclaimed production values and standards. Instead there is marketing improvization, low risk investment strategies and unexpected success.

But the ambivalence goes deeper than that. In the process of re-naming the creative personnel of the spaghettis the Italians were clearly playful, ironic and even sarcastic. How else are we going to interpret the fact that the director Mario Costa, after a successful career in the industry from the 1930s, called himself John W. Fordson for the only western that he directed (*Buffalo Bill, L'eroe del Far West*, Italy/France/Germany, 1964)? Or that the well-known actor Giuliano Gemma changed his name to Montgomery Wood and the less known actress Anna Miserocchi was re-named Helen Wart? When critics ridicule the spaghettis for their perceived ineptitude in imitating the American westerns (so incontrovertibly demonstrated by the "silly" names of the films, the actors and the directors) they overlook the playfulness and the self-consciousness of those involved.

There are several layers superimposed in the spaghetti western that describe a process of transculturation: the growing confidence of the Italian film industry, the strategic decision of the industry to export films masquerading as American, the fact that this strategy goes hand-in-hand with an elaborate system of re-inventing and re-launching the careers of numerous Italian actors and directors, that this necessitates a playful process of re-imagining and re-negotiating identity and finally, that there is no evidence that audiences around the world watched spaghetti westerns as if they were genuine American movies.

The Searchers, Ringo and Django

IT IS CLEAR then that in terms of the production process and marketing strategies the spaghetti and the American western are closely related. As the previous discussion demonstrates, this relationship is by no means simple and it does not unproblematically follow the logic of a conflict between the hegemonic power of Hollywood's global cinema and the opportunism of a commercial national cinema. In what follows, I shall challenge the assumption that in terms of formal characteristics the spaghetti is nothing else but a counterfeit by analyzing in detail short sequences from the films *The Searchers* (John Ford, 1956, USA), *Johnny Oro/Ringo and His Golden Pistol* (Sergio Corbucci, 1966, Italy) and *Django* (Sergio Corbucci, 1965, Italy/Spain).

A number of methodological issues require clarification before the analysis. What the latter aims to achieve is not a definitive, authoritative and all-inclusive definition of the spaghetti western as a genre; instead, the objective is to identify textual aspects of the relationship between the spaghetti and the American western. The usual caveats required when one works within the constraints of genre also apply here. Not all the films that are possible to classify as spaghetti westerns conform to the findings of my analysis—however, the vast majority of the more than one hundred films viewed do so. The analysis does not offer an exhaustive list of formal characteristics exclusive to spaghetti westerns, but highlights certain aspects that are crucial for understanding both the relationship between the spaghetti and the American western and the questions around national identity and national cinema that this relationship raises. My analysis is based on a working definition of the American western that follows André Bazin's suggestion that the genre is the "American film *par excellence*." The films are chosen not necessarily for their typicality but because of the clarity that they offer to the argument. *The Searchers* is a classic text in critical discourse. Corbucci's films were chosen for pragmatic and tactical reasons. His work is increasingly becoming appreciated and he is gradually achieving the (rather rare for European commercial directors) status of a minor *auteur*. At the same time his work is more alien to Anglo-US critics than the films of the now canonized Sergio Leone, whose subsequent work in Hollywood (as well as that of his chief collaborators Clint Eastwood and Ennio Morricone) has brought him within mainstream critical discourse.

The Searchers

WHEN BAZIN WROTE his seminal essays on the western,[37] and for at least another decade, Hollywood was producing more westerns than any other kind of film (from 1926–67 a quarter of all films produced were westerns). Bazin, rather surprisingly, expresses astonishment for the global appeal of the genre:

> Its world-wide appeal is even more astonishing than its historical survival. What can there possibly be to interest Arabs, Hindus, Latins, Germans or Anglo-Saxons, among whom the western has had an uninterrupted success, about evocations of the birth of the United States of America, the struggle between Buffalo Bill and the Indians, the laying down of the railroad, or the Civil War![38]

This might sound a bit naïve today, given the understanding that we have of Hollywood as global cinema, but what Bazin seems to suggest is that the western is not just a form of film but the essence of American cinema. The western is the American film *par excellence* because it is linked to America in two crucial ways. It is made in Hollywood and follows the formal conventions of its mode of production. It is also about American history, the reworking of that history through mythical and symbolic structures and the moral and cultural values and conflicts that constitute a certain powerful version of American national identity. The American western can be defined as an epic narrative set in the American West between 1866 and 1914 and structured around the binary civilization/wilderness. This is a consensual, working definition, but important for my argument is Bazin's suggestion that the western is best understood as a relation:

> It would be hopeless to try to reduce the essence of the western to one or other of the manifest components . . . The western was born of an encounter between a mythology and a means of expression . . .[39]

This understanding of the American western as a particular form of relationship between historical events, ideological operations, cultural meanings and aesthetic forms is arguably most evident in westerns directed by John Ford. Bazin is unambiguous about that:

John Ford struck the *ideal balance* between social myth, historical reconstruction, psychological truth, and the traditional theme of the western mise en scene. *None of these elements dominated any other.*[40] [my emphases].

Without having any intentions to add to the considerable volume of scholarship on Ford and on *The Searchers*, I shall use the credit sequence of the film and the short sequence that follows to offer examples of Bazin's notion of an "ideal balance" of various elements. While there has been a long debate around *The Searchers* (regarding the place that it occupies in Ford's oeuvre, its classification as a classic or an unorthodox western, its handling of the ideological contradictions of the genre), there is critical consensus that the film is about the crucial antinomy civilization/wilderness and the position of the (male) hero in relation to it. Whether *The Searchers* reinforces or deconstructs the history/ideology/form compound is not important for my argument. What is important is the fact that the film makes the defining relation between elements its central concern.

Credit sequences (especially those appearing at the very beginning of a film) can be seen as transitional. They function as a connection, or a bridge, between brightness and darkness (in the theatre), between the "real world" (real people such as actors, producers, directors but also the historical reality) and the film (characters, pictures and stories), between the general (genres, star careers and images, cultural contexts) and the particular (the film with its own world), between the abstract (graphics and sounds) and the concrete (visual and musical motifs). They also very often offer the "essence" of a film, a condensed, abstract and emotive representation of what the film "is all about."

The credit sequence of *The Searchers* (1'22" long) is very simple in visual terms: the credits appear against a backdrop of a red-brown brick wall. After 20" of dramatic music it changes to a "cowboy ballad":

> What makes a man to wander?
> What makes a man to roam?
> What makes a man leave bed and board
> And turn his back on home?
> Ride away, ride away, ride away

The lyrics of the song suggest that the central issue of the film is a question concerning male identity. Furthermore, the music places this questioning within the historical and cultural parameters of the American West. The enigma unfolds against the backdrop of a wall, which in this context is a particularly meaningful symbol. A wall is what separates civilization and wilderness, what protects, encloses and shelters, and as such it is a frontier, a border that splits inside and outside, domestic and public. The wall captures rather than resolves the tension between these spheres, and is a sign not only of safety but also insecurity, of the celebration of the colonization of the West as Americans build the new settlements, villages and towns, and of a lamentation of the destruction of wilderness and innocence. The credit sequence, then, places the hero and his contradictions within more general, historical, national and cultural tensions. The hero is simultaneously an individual ("a man who wanders") and a general position that encapsulates and expresses the ideological tensions of the western. Ethan (John Wayne) occupies precisely this position, that of a unique individual who experiences the conflicts that American history, ideology and generic conventions place upon him. "What makes a man leave bed and board and turn his back on home?" is a formulaic question which finds its unique expression as Ethan turns his back on the open door in the closing shot of the film. Similarly, the wall from the symbolic abstraction of the credit sequence becomes a visual motif, the fragile wall of Martha (Dorothy Jordan) and Aaron's (Walter Coy) home.

The opening sequence of the film, 1'33" long is described in Table 1.

Shot 1, Intertitles, 6" fade out	"Texas 1868."	Music continues with the credits theme and fades out.
Fade in, Shot 2, 18" medium shot that becomes long shot	From complete darkness, a door opens and we see through it a desert land-scape (Monument Valley). Martha stands at the door and walks outside as the camera tracks following her. Once outside the camera stays behind Martha who stands at the porch looking out of frame.	The music changes to an orchestral version of the song "Lorena" that carries out throughout the sequence but with changing volume.

Shot 3, 6" medium/close-up shot, frontal	Martha raises her hand to her forehead and looks intensely.	
Shot 4, 6" extreme long shot, Martha's point of view, reverse shot	Ethan rides his horse moving towards the camera.	
Shot 5, 10" medium shot, frontal	Aaron enters the frame from the left, walks off the porch and stands in front of Martha looking out of frame.	Aaron to Martha: "Ethan?"
Shot 6, 10" long shot, from the side	Martha and Aaron stand at the porch looking off frame as first Debbie with a dog and then Lucy enter the frame taking positions on either sides of their par- ents; finally, Ben carry- ing wood enters the frame and stands on the porch.	Dog barking.
Shot 7, 3" long shot, frontal	Debbie with her dog holding a doll and look- ing out of frame.	Dog barking. Debbie to dog: "Quiet!"
Shot 8, 10" long shot, reverse shot	Ethan rides closer, gets off his horse as Aaron enters the frame to meet him.	
Shot 9, 3" medium shot, frontal	Lucy and Ben standing and looking.	Lucy to Ben: "That's your uncle Ethan!"
Shot 10, 6" medium shot, reverse shot	Ethan approaches Aaron and shakes his hand; we see Ethan's uniform and sword.	
Shot 11, 5" long shot, frontal	The whole group in the shot as Ethan with his back turned to the cam- era approaches Martha.	
Shot 12, 12" medium shot, frontal	Ethan kisses Martha on the forehead.	Martha to Ethan: "Welcome home, Ethan!"
Shot 13, 4" long shot, frontal	They all enter the house through the open door.	

Table 1. The opening sequence of *The Searchers*

It can be argued that the whole problematic of the film is established in these opening shots. The various positions to be occupied by the characters in the progression of the narrative are set, the binary domesticity/wilderness is established through the *mise-en-scène* and editing, the ambivalence of the binary is registered through the use of audio-visual codes, the historical time and space are clarified. It is worth paying closer attention to some of these elements.

Shot 1 defines the specific time and space of the narrative that the credit sequence only vaguely defined as the American West. Shot 1 is linked both to the credit sequence (through the continuation of the music) and to Shot 2 (it matches the blackness that the opening of the door disrupts). Through Shot 1 the transition from the general, abstract sphere of the credit sequence to the specific diegetic world of the film is smoothly accomplished.

Shot 2 is the visual representation of an opening, the opening of the door, and the opening move in a narrative. This is also the only shot in the whole sequence in which the camera moves, as it follows Martha from the darkness of the inside to the brightness of the outside. Shot 2 neatly introduces a series of visual binaries that are loaded with symbolic meaning in the American western: inside/outside, domesticity/wilderness, culture/nature, enclosure/exposure, safety/danger, feminine/masculine, movement/stasis. It is important to note that the binaries exist in tension and in mutual capture, not only because the dark inside frames the bright outside which in turn gives the former its shape and form, but also because the camera movement makes it possible to represent in this shot both the inside (in the first part of the shot) and the outside (in the second part of the shot). There is a profound ambiguity about the binaries as the outside, the spectacular desert landscape of the Monument Valley, is at the same time incredibly exciting (especially compared to the dull darkness of the inside) and menacing as the wind sweeps the landscape. Registering this ambiguity, Shot 2 begins to suggest possible answers to the question "what makes a man to wander?"

Ethan only appears in the sequence in Shot 4 as a response to Martha's look in Shot 3. His appearance is mediated through the point of view of the character that initiates the film's narrative. Crucially, Ethan's entrance occurs *after* the film introduces a comprehensive context for his character: ideological and cultural through the credit sequence and the binaries of Shot 2, historical and geographical through Shot 1, narrative through Shots 2 and 3, and again cultural and historical through the use of the soundtrack ("Lorena" was a favorite song of soldiers from both sides during the Civil War and refers to the lovers that they left back home).

The shot/reverse shot structure of the sequence further emphasizes the binaries that Shot 2 introduced by dividing the scene of action into two spheres: the civilized sphere of domesticity and family life (Shots 3, 5, 6, 7, 9, 11, 12 and 13) and the sphere of wild nature where the lone male roams (Shots 4, 8 and 10).

There are two conclusions that I want to draw from this brief analysis. First, that the sequence demonstrates an economic, smooth and efficient strategy of integrating cinematic codes with ideological and cultural values and the historical context. Second, that the (male) hero of the film is also fully integrated within such structure. Furthermore, while the symbolic sphere and narrative space that he occupies are marked as different and in opposition to that of the community, the editing links them through the use of point of view shots. No matter how the film works with (and possibly even explodes) the contradictions of the relationship between the hero and the community, the two exist in mutual dependency and they are only meaningful in relation to each other.

Ringo and His Golden Pistol

THE HERO OF spaghetti westerns, on the other hand, is profoundly an outsider, not in the narrative sense of being somebody who comes from outside the community (which in most cases he is), but in terms of existing in a relationship of mutual exteriority in terms of cinematic codes and ideological values. The credit sequence of *Ringo and His Golden Pistol* (2'06" long) consists of two shots of a black-dressed cowboy riding his horse as he wanders through hills and valleys. Movement, both of the man and the camera, marks the shots, and the combination of the two is disorienting, as the direction constantly changes with the man approaching and then moving away from the camera, moving from left to right and right to left, and the camera tracking, panning, zooming and tilting continuously. While the object of the two shots is undoubtedly the travelling man, and despite their considerable length (each one of them is over a minute), perfect access to his image is teasingly withheld as the image is never still or fixed, and we cannot see his face. A song (of the "cowboy ballad" genre) accompanies the image:

I knew a man once down in Texas called Johnny Ringo
A man's best friend he said is his pistol . . .
. . . He didn't care about loving, the man called Johnny Ringo
Only the gold which was due him for a man with a price on his head
He only loved the glitter and power of gold
And love was a thing he thought could be bought and sold
Now you have heard the tale I told you of Johnny Ringo
Yes, he still rides the hills and plays down in Texas
And though a man's best friend he says is his pistol
In his loneliness he has only gold . . .

In marked difference with the song of the credit sequence of *The Searchers*, here the lyrics pose no central question that the narrative explores, neither do they introduce the hero as the embodiment of a fundamental, culturally and historically specific tension that will inform his actions and motivation in the film. Instead of an epic and tragic figure who captures the conflicts of American masculine identity ("what makes a man to wander?"), we have a unique individual, Johnny Ringo, whose actions and desires are already defined. What appears to be significant about the hero is just his presence in the film—not his presence in the middle of dramatic conflicts saturated with ideological and historical significance, but simply his physical presence, in his black clothes, golden pistol and his love for gold. The only question that the lyrics seem to pose and answer concerns his presence: "Yes, he still rides the hills and plays down in Texas." The main curiosity that the credit sequence excites (through the song and the orchestration of movement) concerns Ringo's appearance and presence in the scene of action, a desire to see what he looks like and to enjoy the things that he does.

The sequence that follows (described in Table 2) further elaborates this theme.

| Shot 1, 35" long shot | Against lush vegetation of olive trees Ringo on his horse slowly approaches the camera to a close-up of his face. As he turns to the left of the frame the camera pans right and tilts down to a close-up of his golden pistol. The camera then pans left to show Ringo entering a dusty village. | The musical theme from the credits continues. Dramatic bars of strings accompany the close-up of the pistol. The music merges with the sound of a church bell ringing and it stops |

Shot 2, 21" long shot	Inside a church a wedding is taking place. As Paco (the groom) turns right, the camera pans right to show Juanito standing by the door. Outside the door and in the distant background Ringo appears and starts to dismount.	Distant bell ringing. The musical theme restarts with Ringo's appearance.
Action match to Shot 3, 14" long shot	Ringo dismounts and turns his head to the camera. Fast zoom in to Ringo's face in close-up. The camera pans right to follow Ringo as he ties his horse.	The musical theme continues.
Shot 4, 5" long shot	Inside the church, Paco, Manuela (the bride) and four gang members stand in front of a priest and an altar boy.	Paco: "Come on, padre, I haven't got all day. Juanito, the ring!"
Shot 5, 3" medium/close-up shot	Juanito next to the door. We see Ringo in the distant background.	
Shot 6, 8" long shot, same as Shot 4	Inside the church, the wedding.	Priest (off screen): "Paco Perez, do you take Manuela Rodriguez to be your lawful wedded wife?" Paco: "Sí, that is a stupid question to ask. What do you think I am here for? Get on with it!"
Shot 7, 6" medium/close-up shot	The priest with the altar boy.	Priest: "Manuela Rodriguez, do you take Paco Perez as your lawful wedded husband?"
Shot 8, 8" medium/close-up shot	Paco and Manuela.	Paco to Manuela: "Say a nice yes or we will have your father's funeral here tomorrow." Manuela (reluctantly whispers): "Yes." Priest (off screen): "What?" Paco: "She said yes . . .

Shot 9, 5" long shot, same as Shots 4 and 6	Paco grabs the ring and puts it in Manuela's finger.	". . . She is very proud to be a Perez."
Shot 10, 3" medium/close-up shot, same as Shot 7	The priest gives his blessing.	Priest: "I now pronounce you man and wife . . ."
Shot 11, 4" long shot, same as Shots 4, 6 and 9	Paco puts an end to the wedding and he moves to the right of the frame towards the door of the church, followed by Manuela and his gang.	Paco (interrupts): "All right! That's enough! Vamos muchachos!"
Shot 12, 3" long shot	Outside the church Ringo polishes the golden plate of the horse's bridle.	A whistling variation of the musical theme begins and continues until Shot 20.
Shot 13, 2" medium/close-up shot	Ringo continues polishing the plate; we can see his reflection in it.	
Shot 14, 5" long shot, wide angle and low camera	Paco with Manuela and his gang leaving the church.	
Shot 15, 1" medium/close-up shot, same as Shot 13	Ringo sees the reflection of the gang on the plate.	
Shot 16, 3" extreme close-up	In the golden plate Ringo sees the gang approaching from behind.	
Shot 17, 1.5" long shot, low camera	The gang walk towards Ringo.	
Shot 18, 1.5" medium/close-up shot	Ringo continues polishing as the camera zooms in the plate were we see Ringo's eye.	
Shot 19, 1" long shot	Paco pushes Juanita away and goes for his gun.	
Shot 20, 1" close-up shot	The camera zooms out of the golden gun as it is raised and reveals Ringo firing.	The sound of gunshots drowns the music

Shot 21, 1" long shot, same as shot 19	Paco and his men get shot.	Gunshots.
Shot 22, 1" medium shot	Paco going down.	Gunshots.
Shot 23, 0.5" long shot	Ringo shooting. The camera zooms in on his gun.	Gunshots.
Shot 24, 0.5" close-up shot	Pigeons scatter away.	The sound of gunshots is now mixed with dramatic bars of instrumental brass music.
Shot 25, 0.5" medium shot	Ringo firing.	Music gets louder and continues until the end of the sequence.
Shot 26, 0.5" long shot	A member of the gang falls dead outside the church at the feet of Juanito.	
Shot 27, 3" medium shot	The camera tilts up from the golden pistol to show Ringo ceasing to shoot.	The music gets very loud and more melodic.
Shot 28, 1" long shot	Juanito stands at the door of the church with bodies scattered around him.	
Shot 29, 0.5" long shot	The dead bodies.	
Shot 30, 2" medium/close-up shot	Juanito looks up.	
Shot 31, 1" medium/close-up shot	Ringo returns the look.	
Shot 32, 1" medium/close-up shot, same as Shot 30	Juanito looks at Ringo.	
Shot 33, 2" long shot	Ringo moves to the left of the frame towards Juanito.	
Shot 34, 1" medium/close-up shot, same as Shots 32 and 30	Juanito looks scared.	

Shot 35, 10" long shot	Ringo, golden pistol in his hand, walks slowly towards the camera and stands next to the dead bodies in the foreground.	
Shot 36, 8" medium shot	Ringo polishes his pistol.	Ringo: "It's OK Juanito, you can go. I don't want you."
Shot 37, 6" long shot	Juanito walks away as the priest comes out of the church.	
Shot 38, 1.5" close-up shot	Ringo smiles as he says . . .	Ringo: "Not until you've got . . .
Shot 39, 1.5" long shot, same as Shot 37	Juanito walks away.	". . . a price on your head."
Shot 40, 0.5" close-up shot, same as Shot 38	Ringo's face as he says . . .	Ringo: "See you!"
Shot 41, 4" close-up shot	Juanito walks away to his horse.	
Shot 42, 1" close-up shot, same as Shots 40 and 38	Ringo watches Juanito.	
Shot 43, 3" long shot	Juanito rides away.	
The sequence concludes with Ringo letting Manuela go but he keeps the golden wedding ring. Ringo who gets "forty gold pesos" for the heads of the killed Perez brothers welcomes the arrival of Mexican army.		

Table 2. The opening sequence of *Ringo and His Golden Pistol*

Shot 1 is the longest in the opening sequence and one of the longest in the whole film. After the teasing shots of the credit sequence, Ringo's (Mark Damon) body and face are on full display as he slowly moves towards the camera with his eyes looking straight out. As Ringo's head floats closer and closer we can see his dark eyes and hair, his perfect moustache and the golden chain on his jacket in an amazing soft focus shot that places Ringo's body and his immaculate black clothes against the simmering foliage of olive trees.

Whatever question the credit sequence might pose is answered here as Ringo presents himself and his appearance initiates the narrative.

The first shot also represents Ringo in two different narrative spaces: the beginning of the shot shows Ringo in the "wilderness" and the end in a village road as he enters "civilization." Effortlessly, without a cut or through the mediation of point of view, the film moves the hero from the one pole of the binary to the other. What links the two spheres in the film is not a tension loaded with symbolic meaning and laboriously stylized through the *mise-en-scène* and editing, but a fast movement of the camera down and across Ringo's body that momentarily centralizes the golden pistol. Ringo's physical presence, the materiality of his body and weapon, offers the means of a visual continuity that through his presence overcomes what in the American western is the fundamental antinomy civilization/wilderness.

In a similar fashion Ringo's presence offers a visual anchor that connects Shots 2 and 3, as the danger of disorientation inherent in cutting from inside to outside the church without altering the direction of the camera is overcome through the action match that dismounting the horse enables. Ringo's image (the immaculate black clothes against the dusty, white village) is a point of connection between the two shots. Once again the film connects two distinct narrative spaces (inside/outside, the space of Ringo and that of his enemies) without dividing them through shot/reverse shot structures and the use of point of view. A similar strategy is used to connect Shots 16 and 17 as the golden plate of the horse's bridle is used as a reflective surface that links what Ringo sees with what is behind his back. Until Shots 30 and 31 where Ringo and Juanito (Franco Derosa) exchange looks, the sequence progresses without a single point of view shot. In this sense Ringo is endowed with a considerable degree of autonomy, his presence in the film unmediated visually by any of the other characters.

Particularly interesting is the zoom-in that the camera performs in response to Ringo's direct look at it in Shot 3. The camera and Ringo exist in a relationship of mutual attraction so powerful that it overcomes formal conventions of economy and motivation of movement, so self-sufficient that it stretches beyond the symbolic barriers of ideological binaries. This is further facilitated by the systematic undermining of such binaries by the film. In Shot 1 the connotations of garden/desert that underpin the civilization/wilderness opposition are totally reversed as the village is a dusty deserted area marked by the ominous bell-ringing of the soundtrack, whereas "wilderness" is overwhelmingly green and dominated by the confident, well-groomed Ringo. Shots 4–11 make a mockery of the values of domesticity, the family and religion, as the church is used for the staging of a caricature of a wedding.

Equally important is the way in which the opening sequence and the film in general, work with objects. While in the American western clothes, guns and horses are key iconographic elements linking specific representations with cultural and historical contexts, in *Ringo and His Golden Pistol* objects are detached from such significance and presented mainly for their pure visual qualities. In this sequence the black clothes against the white background, the glitter of gold and the reflectiveness of the horse's plates are used for their visual effects. They add glamour to the *mise-en-scène* but also function as points of reference for a mode of editing that does not depend on the interactive exchange of point of view between characters.

Let us examine a bit closer the golden pistol that is Ringo's "trademark." The emphasis placed on the gun's form (what the gun is made of and what it looks like) appears to detract from its function (to shoot and kill). In a sense such a pistol is suitable for a film that centralizes the hero's presentation and appearance and is expressive of his vanity and obsession with gold. But Ringo uses his gun excessively as his greed for gold can only be satisfied through the effective use of the pistol. In a sense, there is no subordination of function to form but a mutual dependence—as Ringo says about his gun: "the more I shoot it the prettier it gets." The significance of the golden pistol is that it links looks and actions: to be pretty is to shoot well and vice versa. The gun, then, becomes relatively independent of narrative function and of moral or ideological codes: its function is to shoot, and if this looks good everything is fine. The camerawork in the gunfight of the opening sequence is orchestrated around Ringo's golden pistol: the fast zooming and tilting in Shots 20, 23 and 27 make the action visually explosive, centralize the gun and link it to effective, deadly shooting. By contrast, the shots of the Mexicans trying to fire their guns and dying are visually chaotic and disorganized, resulting in their ugly death. Looking good in this scene entails power, efficiency and *de facto* justification.

Django

DJANGO APPEARS TO be different. Here Django (Franco Nero) is motivated by the single-minded desire to avenge his lover's death at the hands of Colonel Jackson (Eduardo Fajardo). Furthermore, an element of depth and a narrative enigma revolve around his motivation. The credit sequence of the film (2'45" long, consists of three shots of Django, carrying a saddle on his back and dragging a coffin over extremely muddy paths) is accompanied by a song (a rather poppy version of a "cowboy ballad" using a lot of electric instruments) whose lyrics refer to the past of the hero and his inability to deal with the present and future:

> Django have you always been alone
> Django have you never loved again . . .
> . . . For you cannot spend your life regretting
> Django you must face another day . . . .
> When there are clouds in the sky and they are gray
> You may be standing and remember the little one that passed away
> For Django after the showers the sun will be shining . . .

This not only sets up the possibility that a change might occur in Django's life but also suggests a symbolism that permeates the *mise-en-scène* of the film. The omnipresent mud can be seen as an expression or extension of Django's state of mind and psychology. But while this links a certain aspect of the *mise-en-scène* with the hero, it also erases the oppositions involved in the iconography of the American western. As in *Ringo and His Golden Pistol,* the hero in *Django* is an outsider, whose singular obsession with revenge detaches him from the tensions that the antinomies of the American genre establish. The extreme, self-sufficient individualism of Ringo and Django is not placed in any meaningful comparative context but simply offers the background for their actions. They are in this respect drastically different from Ethan, who, according to John Tuska:

> is both hero and anti-hero, a man riven in two by his passions, radically estranged from his community and yet driven to act in its name. His strengths and failings, like the promise and danger of the land around him, are inextricable.[41]

Django also involves a playful use of props, which liberates them from the burden of heavy symbolism and iconographic conventions. The coffin that Django drags everywhere can be seen as possessing symbolic qualities (perhaps the memory of the dead lover or the promise of death for Django's enemies), but any symbolism is eventually undercut by the film: the coffin is used not as a symbol of Django's emotions, but as a purely functional object, a hiding place for his machine gun that mows down Jackson's and Rodriquez's (Jose Bodalo) men and for the treasure that he takes from the Mexicans. The lasting memory from the film is the purely visual effects of the coffin, the absurdity of watching the cumbersome gray box endlessly dragged through paths and streets covered with mud. Equally absurd (given Corbucci's communist affiliations) is the use of red scarves and hoods together with the other Ku Klux Klan iconography around Jackson's men. Again these are used beyond any textual or extra-textual symbolism: just for the stunning effect that they accomplish by luridly standing out against the grayness of the mud and the costumes.

What *Ringo and His Golden Pistol* and *Django* demonstrate is a different relationship between elements than the one that, according to Bazin, makes the western the American film *par excellence*. Both films take the mythical aspect of the West as well as the legacy and the conventions of the American western as raw material that they process and transform. This process (essentially an act of transculturation) shatters the particular relationship between historical events, ideological operations, cultural meanings and aesthetic forms that defines the American genre. In the films analyzed here, this involves first a weakening of the historical referent by structuring the films around the presence of unique heroes who transcend historical and cultural specificity; second, a disengagement of the *mise-en-scène* from the ideological and iconographic values of the American western; and, finally, a detachment of the heroes from a point of view system that could place them in an interactive relationship with other characters. For the purposes of the present argument, the most important effect of this process is the autonomy of the hero, his emotional, moral and visual separation from the values of the community and the defining antinomies of the American western. Ringo's obsession with gold is also a testimony of his contempt for the community—he is not even willing to enter into a basic relationship of exchange involving the shared value of money.

This is reinforced by the particular way in which cycles operate within the spaghetti western. There is clear emphasis on heroes whose names are used to construct series of films: Django, Ringo, Sartana and Trinita (Trinity) are the central characters in around one hundred films. The names of the heroes are used in order to market and sell spaghettis,[42] but this is not accompanied by any consistency in the way that the heroes' identities are constructed and represented. The actors portraying Django, Ringo or Sartana vary from film to film: Django has been played by Franco Nero, Anthony Steffen/Antonio de Teffé, George Eastman/Luigi Montefiori, George Ardisson/Sean Todd, Terence Hill/Mario Girotti (who later became famous as Trinita), George Hilton, Tomas Milian and many others. Similarly, Mark Damon's Ringo follows the footsteps of the Ringo introduced by Montgomery Wood/Giuliano Gemma in *A Pistol for Ringo* (Duccio Tessari, Italy/Spain, 1965) and *Return of Ringo* (Duccio Tessari, Italy/Spain, 1966). The confusion around nationality and the difference in physical appearance and defining characteristics of the heroes renders them autonomous even within cycles constructed under their name!

Spaghetti Western, National Identity and Questions of Genre

IN THE CONCLUSION of this chapter we need to return to the questions that the spaghetti western poses to conventional conceptions of national identity and cinema and to issues of generic classification.

The important methodological and conceptual issue that requires clarification is the exact nature of the "national" aspect of the spaghetti and where to locate it. With reference to European westerns, there have been less than a handful of critics who attempted to address the issue. We have already discussed (and criticized) Christopher Frayling's attempt to discover Italianness in the spaghetti westerns. Motivated by his admirable desire to challenge notions of authenticity and cultural superiority that surround the American western, Frayling discovers an Italian essence in the themes, the plots and the characters of the spaghettis and the peculiarity of the studio production in Italy. On the other hand, Tassilo Schneider, discovers a new *Heimat* in the German western of the early 1960s which, he argues, "offers a neatly organized narrative and social Utopia where everything is out in the open, plain to see, and under control."[43] Schneider, while still looking for and identifying a central core of distinctly German concerns in the films that he examines, is doing so with direct reference to both the American and the spaghetti western as well as the prevalent genres in Germany at the time. The comparison to the spaghetti is particularly interesting:

Despite the similarities, the ironic or even parodic quality that this generic "self-consciousness" (or self-reflexivity) takes on in many Italian Westerns is missing from the May adaptations. While the "spaghetti Western" might be said to "deconstruct" the genre, the German films may be said to *reconstruct* it. If the Italian films might be said to be interested in "demythologisation," the May adaptations seem to pursue the opposite objective: to construct, or reconstruct, a viable generic mythology.[44]

Although this is probably an accurate account of the German westerns and their relationship with the spaghettis, and offers a description of the latter that is reasonably compatible with the one suggested here, it relies on a conceptualization of the national that is problematic for the spaghetti. The latter are defined in negative terms ("deconstruction," "demythologization"), and in contrast with their German counterparts, which in the process of reconstructing the genre can be seen as expressive parts and constituent components of German nationhood. This leaves the spaghetti western's relationship to national identity marked by a similar negativity, or rather a gap, a place beyond the reach of the discourse of national cinema.

A way to overcome this impasse is by revising the conceptualization of the "national" both in terms of identity and in relation to cinema. The spaghetti western involves a re-imagining of identity that takes place beyond the boundaries of the nation and must be conceptualized in terms of a transcultural and transnational understanding of national cinema. The Italianness of the spaghettis does not reside in hidden national cultural references, plots, themes and underlying value systems, but in the very ability of this type of film to weaken (if not erase) the national as its referent. Two of the most obvious ways in which this happens is through the erasure of the national identity of the heroes and in terms of co-production as the main mode of spaghetti production.

The heroes of the spaghettis are never Italian (although there could have been plausible historical grounds for that) and rarely American. In most cases they are "transnational," either by defining themselves as "half American, half Mexican" like Ringo, or by avoiding to commit themselves to an identity: when Django is asked whether he is a Yankee he replies that he "fought for the North." If one also adds the confusion around the identity of the actors portraying the heroes, fixing a national identity for the hero of the spaghetti becomes a very problematic affair. The disjuncture of the history/ideology/form compound and the mutual exclusivity between hero and community makes it impossible to have the Great American Hero in the center of a spaghetti—but it also makes it impossible to have a Great Italian Hero or, indeed, any national hero. The spaghettis are fundamentally about men with no name, no place and no nation. This is in marked contrast with the Hollywood approach. Hollywood dissolves the national into the universal, as American cinema becomes just cinema without a hint of national peculiarity. The spaghetti, on the other hand, is classified as national by definition (simply by not being American), irrespective of the exact label attached to it (even if you substitute the adjective "spaghetti" for the more respectable "Italian" or "European"). In order to claim the universality envisaged by the Italian industry, the spaghetti has to negate the national.

Co-production, on the other hand, is a mode of production that is clearly transnational but one that also challenges the constructed unity and narrative of a national cinema. In the context of popular European cinema in the 1950s and 60s, Tim Bergfelder has explored the contradictions involved in the way that co-productions were viewed by critics and national and pan-European bodies.[45] Despite the ability to compete with Hollywood and to expand international markets, co-productions were often viewed with hostility as undermining "the project of re-centring the definition of national cinemas through critical discourses and national film policy."[46]

The weakening or erasure of the national in the spaghetti entails a rethinking of the "national" of the national cinema. This must involve an understanding of national cinema that does not seek to discover ways in which national film cultures are defined in unique national terms, but explores the ways in which such cultures engage with and transform other film cultures. It also involves the realization that on a general, structural level such processes might characterize many different national cultures. Indeed, the outward orientation of the Italian film industry in the 1950s and 60s is by no means unique to Italy, as similar tendencies are evident in the film industries of Germany, France and Britain. But it is also important to identify the specific ways in which the spaghetti operates within this general outward look—this inevitably leads to a return to issues around genre criticism.

One can be intentionally iconoclastic and argue (following Charles Musser's pioneering work on the origins of the American western[47]) that the spaghetti western is closely related to a genre historically prior to the American western. Like *The Great Train Robbery* (Edwin Porter, USA, 1903) spaghettis make better sense examined in terms of their relationship to the "travel genre." Let us briefly reconsider the conclusions of the analysis of *Ringo and His Golden Pistol* and *Django*. The detachment of the hero from the community, the importance attached to the physical presence of the hero (a simple "being there") rather than the way he embodies and resolves ideological tensions and contradictions, and the presentation of a system of objects detached from their cultural and historical specificity can all be interpreted as fundamental components and essential characteristics of the travel genre. The mythical setting of the West, the landscape, clothes, horses and guns, the characters and the stories simply offer an exotic background and location for the travelling outsiders of the spaghetti.

The suggestion that the spaghetti western as a generic category is more meaningful in its relation to the travel film is supported by examining closer the European and Italian context. As Bergfelder notes, a variety of popular European genres in the 1960s (all subcategories of what he calls the "adventure film") demonstrate a "shrinking of the world" in their perception of space:

> Amidst increasingly international casts globe-trotting through convulated global intrigues, the notions of national and cultural identity became dispersed or reduced to empty clichés . . . Despite their nostalgic references to old-fashioned narrative traditions, the popular genres of the 1960s suggested to their audiences the possibility of a cosmopolitan and classless identity in a new world, made accessible and commodified by tourism, leisure and lifestyle consumption.[48]

The disjuncture of the history/ideology/form compound makes it possible to approach the spaghetti western as a form of "fantasy tourism" or "pauper's travelling," in which the non-American explores the mythical and exotic Wild West in an entertaining journey that pays no respect to local codes of authenticity. Of course the irony is that Italy itself (as well as many other European countries) became in the 1950 and 60s an attractive, exotic destination for many wealthy American tourists.

The credit sequences of *Ringo and His Golden Pistol* and *Django* are marked by movement, by the travelling of the heroes to the location of their adventure. Obviously, as Jane Tompkins notes,[49] many American westerns have similar openings, but in most cases movement is located within the wilderness/civilization antinomy. The first shot of *Ringo and His Golden Pistol* can be read as emblematic of the kind of movement involved in the spaghetti western (in clear opposition to the opening shot of *The Searchers* which is emblematic of movement in the American western). Ringo is placed against a background that has no connotations whatsoever of wilderness, the peaceful, simmering olive trees bring to the mind Mediterranean landscapes. The contrast of this background to the scene of the adventure, the dusty, desert Mexican village, is extreme. The shot can be read not as failed attempt to construct meaningful binaries but as a self-conscious, ironic representation of the hero moving from his Mediterranean background to the exotic landscape of the Wild West. The fact that the hero is played by an American actor reinforces rather than undermines the irony, a quality that Sergio Corbucci was renowned for.

A similar sense of travelling informs many of the popular Italian films and genres of the period and the condition of the national film industry. The mythical adventures of the peplum are obvious examples of travelling in space and time. The exploitation documentaries fashioned after *Europe by Night* (Alessandro Blasetti, Italy, 1958)— with films such as *World by Night* and *World by Night II*, *America by Night*, and *Universe by Night*—the documentary series initiated by *Mondo cane* (Paolo Cavara and Gualtiero Jacopetti, Italy, 1962), the comedies of Franco Franchi and Ciccio Ingrassia (with films such as *I Due della legione straniera*, 1962, and *Due samurai per cento geishe*, 1964) and the various spy films all involve exotic locations and travelling around the world either as the setting for adventures or as material for (pseudo)documentaries. At the same time the Italian films themselves travel as they access new international markets, establish international partnerships through co-productions and shoot in Spain, Portugal or Yugoslavia.

These manifestations of real or imaginary travelling find a particular articulation in the spaghetti western. The textual practices of the genre disentangle the position of the hero from the context of American cultural and historical specificity and by liberating this position they are able to offer it as a place from which you can experience the Wild West without buying into the American myth. Spaghettis do not produce shared national self-representations but offer imaginings of the world that transcend the boundaries of the nation.

This is a process that is simultaneously inclusive and exclusive: it extends the appeal of the fantasy to transnational audiences but it articulates it in purely masculine terms. Even more than the American western, which at least maintains and dramatizes the tensions between civilization/wilderness, domestic/public, masculine/feminine, the spaghettis offer unparalleled mobility to the male hero, while condemning women to occupy a fixed objectified place in the exotic landscape of the Wild West. The spaghettis (together with other examples of the travel/adventure genre) can be seen as a reaction to the comedies and melodramas of the 1950s that dominated the Italian film culture. Interestingly the one obvious involvement of women in the outward orientation of Italian cinema is the international popularity of stars such as Sophia Loren (*It Started in Naples*, Melville Shalvelson, USA, 1960, starring Clarke Gable), Gina Lollobrigida (*Trapeze*, Carol Reed, USA, 1956) and Claudia Cardinale (*The Pink Panther*, Blake Edwards, USA, 1963). But in most cases, as the above examples demonstrate, their roles in international productions are stereotypical and clichéd representations of exotic, Latin beauties.

The domesticity of the melodramas and comedies of the 1950s (set in Italy and concerned with the domestic life of the family) is rejected for the cosmopolitanism of the travel genre, of the "fantasy tourism" that takes male heroes to spectacular adventures around the world. This is remarkably similar to the interpretation, offered by Jane Tompkins, of the American western as a negation of the domesticity of the nineteenth-century sentimental novels. Indeed her analysis resonates with meaning in relation to the spaghetti:

> The Western *answers* the domestic novel. It is the antithesis of the cult of domesticity that dominated American Victorian culture. The Western hero, who seems to ride in out of nowhere, in fact comes riding in out of the nineteenth century. And every piece of baggage he doesn't have, every word he doesn't say, every creed in which he doesn't believe is absent for a reason. What isn't there in the Western hasn't disappeared by accident; it's been deliberately jettisoned.[50]

This not only illuminates the (even more amplified) masculine orientation of the spaghetti, but also connects to the approach of the genre as fantasy tourism. We can summarize the engagement of the Italians with the Wild West and the American Western by using the vocabulary of tourism. The textual eclecticism of the genre is not unlike the holiday photographs of tourists. There the messy, ugly bits, all the internal affairs of the locals are carefully eliminated from the frames that record the attractive, glorious views of the place with the visitors on the foreground making a spectacle of their good time. And perhaps the wrath and contempt of the American critics can be compared to the similar emotions that overcome the locals when the tourists produce their own souvenirs.

Notes

1. See Christopher Frayling, *Spaghetti Westerns: Cowboys and Europeans from Karl May to Sergio Leone* (London: Routledge, 1981), p. xi.
2. For an early identification and discussion of the problem see Andrew Tudor, *Theories of Film* (London: BFI/Secher and Warburg, 1974); for a more detailed critique of genre classification see Rick Altman, *Film/Genre* (London: BFI, 1999).
3. Altman presents and criticizes this thesis, ibid, pp. 14–15.
4. See Frayling, op. cit.; Marcia Landy, *British Genres: Cinema and Society, 1930–1960* (Princeton: Princeton University Press, 1991).
5. See Rosie Thomas, "Indian cinema–pleasures and popularity," *Screen*, vol. 26, nos. 3–4; Vijay Mishra, "Towards a theoretical critique of Bombay cinema," *Screen*, vol. 26, nos. 3–4; Ravi Vasudevan, "Addressing the spectator of a 'third world' national cinema: the Bombay 'social' film of the 1940s and 1950s," *Screen*, vol. 36, no. 4.
6. Pam Cook and Mieke Bernink (eds), *The Cinema Book* (London: BFI, 1999), p. 154.
7. Steve Neale, *Genre* (London: BFI, 1980), p. 48.
8. See Ginette Vincendeau, "France 1945–65 and Hollywood: the *policier* as international text," *Screen*, vol. 33, no. 1, 1992; Tim Bergfelder, "The Nation vanishes: European co-productions and popular genre" in Mette Hjort and Scott Mackenzie (eds), *Cinema and Nation* (London and New York: Routledge, 2000); Christopher Wagstaff, "Italian genre films in the world market," in Geoffrey Nowell-Smith and Steven Ricci (eds), *Hollywood and Europe: Economics, Culture, National Identity 1945–95* (London: BFI, 1998).
9. For example, Jan Nederveen Pieterse, "Globalization as hybridization" in Mike Featherstone, Scott Lash and Roland Robertson (eds), *Global Modernities* (London: Sage, 1995).
10. For example, Saskia Sassen, *Cities in a World Economy* (Thousand Oaks: Pine Forge Press, 1994).

11. Marshal McLuhan, *Understanding Media: The Extensions of Man* (London and New York: Ark Paperworks, 1987).

12. Donna Haraway, "Manifesto for cyborgs: science, technology and socialist feminism in the 1980s," *Socialist Review*, no. 80, 1985.

13. Mikhail Bakhtin, *The Dialogic Imagination: Four Essays by M. M. Bakhtin* (Austin: University of Texas Press, 1981).

14. For example Ireneusz Opacki, "Royal genres" in David Duff (ed), *Modern Genre Theory* (Edinburgh: Longman, 2000).

15. Stuart Hall, "New Ethnicities," in *Black Film, British Cinema*, ICA Documents 7 (London: Institute of Contemporary Arts, 1989).

16. Homi K. Bhabha, *The Location of Culture* (London and New York: Routledge, 1994).

17. Frayling, op. cit.

18. Ibid, p. 42.

19. Will Wright, *Sixguns and Society: A Structural Study of the Western* (Berkeley: University of California Press, 1975).

20. Frayling op. cit., especially pp. 39–53.

21. Mary Louise Pratt, *Imperial Eyes: Travel Writing and Transculturation* (London and New York: Routledge, 1992), p. 6.

22. Ibid, p. 4.

23. Ibid, p. 143.

24. See for example Gian Piero Brunetta, "The long march of American cinema in Italy from fascism to the cold war," in David Ellwood and Rob Kroes (eds), *Hollywood in Europe: Experiences of a Cultural Hegemony* (Amsterdam: University of Amsterdam Press, 1994); Thomas H. Ghuback, "Hollywood's international market," in Tino Balio (ed), *The American Film Industry* (Madison: University of Wisconsin Press, 1985); Ian Jarvie, "The postwar economic foreign policy of the American film industry: Europe 1945–1950," in *Film History*, vol. 4, 1990; Pierre Sorlin, *Italian National Cinema 1896–1996* (London and New York: Routledge, 1996).

25. Thomas Guback, op.cit., p. 479.

26. *Statistics on Film and Cinema 1955–1977* (Paris: Unesco, 1981); the figure for France is an approximation based on figures for previous and following years.

27. Wagstaff, "Italy in the post-war international cinema market," in Christopher Duggan and Christopher Wagstaff (eds), *Italy in the Cold War: Politics, Culture and* Society (Oxford: Berg, 1995), pp. 108–9.

28. *Statistics on Film and Cinema 1955–1977*, op. cit.

29. Wasgstaff, "Italy in the post-war international cinema market," op. cit., p. 100.

30. *Statistics on Film and Cinema 1955–1977*, op. cit.

31. Colin Haskins, Stuart McFadyen and Adam Finn, *Global Television and Film: An Introduction to the Economics of the Business* (Oxford: Oxford University Press, 1997), pp. 102–6.

32. Wasgstaff, "Italy in the post-war international cinema market," op. cit.
33. Ibid and also Christopher Wagstaff, "A Forkful of westerns: industry, audiences and the Italian western," in Richard Dyer and Ginette Vincendeau (eds), *Popular European Cinema* (London and New York: Routledge, 1992).
34. Frayling, op. cit., p. 50.
35. Geoffrey Nowell-Smith with James Hay and Gianni Volpi (eds), *The Companion to Italian Cinema* (London: Cassel and BFI, 1996), p. 67.
36. Edward Buscombe and Roberta E. Pearson, "Introduction" in Edward Buscombe and Roberta E. Pearson (eds), *Back in the Saddle Again: New Essays on the Western* (London: BFI, 1998), p. 5.
37. André Bazin, "The western: or the American film *par excellence*" and "The evolution of the western" both in *What Is Cinema?* vol. 2 (Berkeley: *University* of California Press, 1971), written in 1953 and 1955 respectively.
38. Bazin, "The western: or the American film *par excellence*," op, cit., p. 141.
39. Ibid, p. 142; for the civilization/wilderness antinomy see Jim Kitses, *Horizons West* (London: Secker and Warburg/BFI, 1969).
40. Bazin, "The evolution of the western," op. cit., p. 149.
41. Jon Tuska, *The American West in Film: Critical Approaches to the Western* (Westport and London: Greenwood Press, 1985), p. 148.
42. See Christopher Wagstaff, "Italian genre films in the world market," in Geoffrey Nowell-Smith and Steven Ricci, *Hollywood and Europe: Economics, Culture, National Identity 1945–95*, op. cit.
43. Tassilo Schneider, "Finding a new *Heimat* in the Wild West: Karl May and the German western of the 1960s," in Edward Buscombe and Roberta E. Pearson (eds), op. cit., p. 155.
44. Ibid, p. 146.
45. Tim Bergfelder, "The Nation vanishes: European co-productions and popular genre formula in the 1950s and 60s," op. cit.
46. Ibid, p. 139.
47. Charles Musser, "The travel genre in 1903–04: moving toward fictional narratives, Iris, vol. 2, no. 1, 1984; Musser's argument is also considered and developed by Rick Altman, op. cit. and Steve Neale in "Question of genre," *Screen*, vol. 31, no. 1, 1990.
48. Bergfelder, op. cit., p. 150.
49. Jane Tompkins, *West of Everything: The Inner Life of Westerns* (Oxford and New York: Oxford University Press, 1992).
50. Ibid, p. 39.

6 ISSUES OF AUTHORSHIP AND THE CASE OF LINA WERTMÜLLER

The Difficulties of Authorship

DESPITE THE DECISIVE defeat of the *auterists* in the critical debates of the seventies, the author has not died. While the critique of the romantic individualism involved in positing a singular creative source in film has been successfully challenged for its theoretical weakness and its politically suspect methodology and critical values,[1] the concept of the author (of the director as the most obvious and powerful organizing principle in the production of film) has undoubtedly survived in the pragmatics of cinema culture and scholarship. Film courses are still structured around "important" or "typical" directors and their films (especially so in the study of national European cinemas), the director still remains an extremely valuable commodity in the marketing and promotion of films,[2] and it is often the director's name and reputation that decides applications for funding by various national and transnational bodies. For a number of reasons, however, the category of the *auteur* is particularly problematic for the study of popular European cinemas. I shall briefly address some of these difficulties and suggest ways in which the organization of research around directors can add to rather than inhibit our understanding of popular films.

The most obvious of these obstacles is the historically limited application of the label *auteur* to either directors working within the Hollywood studio system or those great "art directors" who exist in the epicenter of national cinemas. The lists are well known, on the one hand, Hitchcock, Ford, Sirk and Minnelli, on the other, Eisenstein, Renoir, Bergman, Ozu, Ray, Antonioni. In either case, the canon was initially created by European critics and is informed by ideological and aesthetic values of European origin. The debates around the status of individual *auteurs* undertaken in issue after issue of *Cahiers du cinéma* in the fifties revolve around the values of aesthetic universality and individual creativity as discussed in previous chapters. Furthermore, the practice of *auteur* criticism is largely

responsible for the creation of the unwieldy and questionable binary Hollywood/Europe that not only renders popular European cinema an "out of bounds" area for film studies but also creates an
exclusive canon of European directors and films considered to be
worthy of serious critical attention.

This kind of binarism depends on an understanding of the director's function and role in two different modes of production/con-
sumption. On the one hand Hollywood, with its established studio
practices, genres and marketing strategies, offers the background
against which an individual director's work is analyzed and evaluat-
ed. On the other hand, the "art cinema" mode of production is less
clearly defined but is generally perceived as more liberal offering the
freedom required by art directors in their pursuit of aesthetic excellence. This leaves popular European cinemas and the directors
working within such contexts in an unknowable position, once
again. This is reinforced by the lack of critical attention (with a few
rare exceptions[3]) to commercial modes of production within
Europe. Furthermore, as we have seen in previous chapters, the construction of national canons is, in many cases, based on the assumption that it is through the discursive category of the art director that
national European cinemas achieve distinct and stable identities.[4]
This, in turn, leads to a stubborn critical reluctance to engage with
directors working within a commercial national (and even more so
in a transnational) context.

Additional difficulties arise around the marked heterogeneity of
the commercial modes of production within and across national film
industries and historical periods in Europe. This is further aggravated by the relatively short life span of many of the popular genres
developed in Europe compared to the longevity and stability of
generic conventions that characterizes Hollywood production. This
makes the identification and study of individual *auteurs* working in
the commercial European sector not only politically undesirable[5] for
national critical establishments, but also profoundly laborious even
for favourably inclined researchers.

Approaching the question of authorship in a way that pays
attention to the pragmatics and the power invested in, as well as the
effects of, critical categorizations can shift the frame of reference
from theoretical deliberation to pedagogic and cultural politics. A
desirable implication of such a conceptual shift is the translation of
the question "how theoretically useful and accurate is the category

of the *auteur*?" into "what are the effects of the use of authorship for the study of popular European cinemas?"

Obviously, one of the effects is the creation of an alternative canon that places popular films on the critical and academic agenda. In reality such a canon is already under creation but it operates under the aegis of the "cult" paradigm: obvious examples of such a tendency are directors such as Mario Bava, Sergio Corbucci, Dario Argento and Franco Manera/Jesus Franco.[6] An engagement with popular European directors that goes beyond the arbitrary assertion of personal taste or the celebration of "Eurotrash kitsch," usually involved in "cult" criticism can offer valuable insights into the history of genres, industrial practices and socio-cultural contexts, as well as the formal properties of popular texts.

Clearly there is no intention here to retreat to a discourse of authorship that conceptualizes the director as an all-powerful, ahistorical category that transcends contextual conditions and imposes a unified creative identity in the texts. On the contrary the "author" must be approached as a fundamentally historical entity. The analysis of the works of directors in the context of popular European cinema should therefore address questions that foreground the complex, interconnected and dynamic relationship relations between texts and contexts. For example, why are directors popular at certain times, what constitutes their popularity, how do film theory and/or criticism establish and utilize directors as authors, what types and levels of institutional investment revolve around certain directors at given times, how are directors implicated in the marketing and promotion of films and how does one account for textual, thematic or ideological continuities and discontinuities in the films of certain directors in relation to the genres and the national or transnational context within which they work?

Lina Wertmüller: A Director of the Seventies

IT IS WITH these questions in mind that this case study approaches the work of the Italian director Lina Wertmüller. Her films as well as her career seem to blur some of the most rigid binarisms that inform *auteurist* criticism and tend to marginalize popular texts. By focusing on the films made in the 1970s (the period of her career that attracted considerable critical attention) I shall argue that "impurity" is a term that seems to aptly describe Wertmüller as a director: her films are undeniably preoccupied with questions of form but they also heavily rely on familiar generic conventions and stars; they deal with sophisticated political debates but also adopt an often vulgar comedic form. Furthermore, the films that Wertmüller directed in the 1970s are inextricably linked to discourses and practices that existed in explosive conflict at the time. These include different critical approaches to political cinema, debates on the relationship between art and politics as well as between action and theory, Italian and American approaches to feminism, and so on. Wertmüller's 1970s films do not offer orderly and distanced artistic/ideological reflections of the political "messiness" of the period, but instead surrender themselves to the confusing political emotions that inform their narratives and motivate the characters. My intention in revisiting these (now almost totally forgotten) films is not to reclaim them as the products of a misunderstood genius but to explore the historical specificity of the encounter between their textual politics and the critical reception that they attracted.

Wertmüller's Career

WERTMÜLLER WAS BORN in Rome in 1928 and her real name was Arcangela Felice Assunta Wertmüller Von Elgg Spagnol Von Braurich. She studied drama, was interested in choreography and became a puppeteer and a well-known theatre director, before working as assistant director to Fellini in 8½ (Federico Fellini, Italy, 1963). She was very active in Italian politics and a member of the Communist Party of Italy until 1958, when she left in disagreement over the Soviet intervention in Hungary. She later became a prominent member of the Socialist Party and was involved in the Italian feminist movement, but has always resisted descriptions of her work as "feminist" and of herself as a "woman" filmmaker:

> I reject that entirely . . . I am a filmaker who happens to be a woman. A human being at work. Of course I always try to show the woman's situation in my films. I become very passionate when I think of the plight of many women. But I am also passionate and worried about the situation of many men.[7]

Her first film *I basilischi/The Lizards* (Italy, 1963) was a sociological and psychological study of life in a small Italian town. She then directed two musical comedies (primarily for TV) which capitalized on the popularity of pop star Rita Pavone (*Rita la zanzara*

(Italy, 1966) and *Non stuzzicate la zanzara* (Italy, 1967) and also introduced Giancarlo Giannini, who became the big star of her films in the seventies. Part of her work for television was the western *Il mio corpo per un poker/The Belle Starr Story* (Italy, 1967). Her career breakthrough came with *Mimì metallurgico, ferito nell'onore/The Seduction of Mimì* (Italy, 1972), which introduced Mariangela Melato as Giannini's partner and attracted international critical attention.

Wertmüller became one of the most celebrated and controversial directors of the 1970s but her success was limited to that decade. Very much a director "of the moment," she addressed key political issues of the period in a series of films that were extremely successful, both critically and commercially. Most notable were *Film d'amore e d'anarchia, ovvero stammattina alle 10 in via dei Fori nella nota casa di tolleranza/Love and Anarchy* (Italy, 1973), *Travolti da un insolito destino nell''azzuro mare d''Agosto/Swept Away* (Italy, 1975), and *Pasqualino Settebelezze/Pasqualino: Seven Beauties* (Italy, 1976). With *Pasqualino* she became the first woman to be nominated for an Academy Award as the best director and the film was ninth in the box office in Italy.[8]

The success of the film prompted Warner Brothers to offer her a contract for four English-language, Hollywood-produced films, the first of which was *La fine del mondo nel nostro solito letto in una notte piena di pioggia/Night Full of Rain* (Italy/USA, 1978), which starred Candice Bergen opposite Giannini. Wertmüller, initially thrilled with the opportunity to produce high-budget and well-distributed films was ultimately bitterly disappointed with the experience. It is paradoxical that for her major commercial venture she chose to make what is arguably the most "arty" of her films of the seventies. Warner Brothers withdrew the contract and Wertmüller's response was *Fatto di sangue fra due uomini per causa di una vedova—si sospettano moventi politici/Blood Feud* (Italy/UK, 1979), set in Sicily in the early 1920s and starring three legends of Italian cinema: Giannini (appearing for the last time in a Wertmüller film), Marchello Mastroianni and Sophia Loren. Both *Night Full of Rain* and *Blood Feud* proved unpopular with the critics and although Wertmüller's career continued into the eighties and the nineties she never again enjoyed the critical attention that she commanded in the seventies. Some of the better known films of her more recent career include *Sotto, sotto/Softly, Softly* (Italy, 1984), *Un complicato intrigo di donne, vicoli e delitti/ Camorra* (Italy/USA, 1986), *Notte de'estate con profilo greco, occhi a mandorla e odore di basilico/ Summer Night, with Greek Profile, Almond Eyes and Scent of Basil* (Italy/Spain, 1987), *Io speriamo che me la cavo/Ciao, Professore!* (Italy, 1993).

In the following two sections I shall offer an outline and an evaluation of the critical controversy that Wertmüller's films caused in the seventies by referring extensively to critical writings of the period, and then identify some of the textual strategies that articulate very complex and often explosive relationships between the historically specific context of the films and the personal dramas of the characters that populate them.

Critical Reception

IN THE 1970s Wertmüller's films were widely distributed and exhibited across Europe, as well as shown in many of the international festivals, but it was in the USA that she became a celebrated if controversial director. *The Seduction of Mimi* initiated a very passionate critical engagement with Wertmüller and her films that culminated with *Swept Away* and *Pasqualino: Seven Beauties* and lasted less than a decade, with a number of prominent film critics involved in the debate.[9] It seems to me that both friendly and hostile criticism revolved around the political and formal impurity of her work—a glimpse of which we get from the examination of a career that encompasses a multiplicity of audio-visual forms (television programmes, documentaries, comedies, western, musicals) and modes of production (from television companies to small independent outfits, from the Warner Brothers and Silvio Berlusconi Communications to marginal theatre groups).

The "Wertmüller phenomenon" was very much an enigma for American critics (and the question marks at the end of many of the articles about her is an obvious indication of that) who were amazed by the combination of political radicalism of her films and the appeal to the "general American public":

> The paradox of Lina Wertmüller rests within the seeming contradiction of her politics and her success among the general public, a contradiction that is heightened because it emerges among one of the most depoliticized populaces in the advanced industrial West. For this is a populace which views culture as entertainment, and a culture in which politics is defined as casting a vote for a presidential candidate.[10]

But while the above quotation expresses fascination with the mixture of politics and entertainment, the most obvious and controversial manifestation of impurity in Wertmüller's work revolves precisely around politics. Many of the films explore the intersection between class and gender politics, and they were exposed to the scrutiny of feminist critics. Her films have been praised for their engagement with such complex issues but they have also been attacked for offering an impure mixture that combines a critique of Italian patriarchal structures with offensive, stereotypical and objectifying images of women:

> [I]n Wertmüller's vernacular, man usurps the classic female "receptacle" role in his relationship with the bullish lust of the political system. Women in turn are portrayed as either instruments or ornaments of that system. They are sirens . . . and frustrated sybarites . . . waiting only to be loved into motherhood and marshmallowy submission. The "ornaments," on the other hand, tend to be mole-branded leviathans like the gargantuan-thighed adulteress of *Mimi* or Shirley Stoler's titanic love object of an SS Guard in *Seven Bauties*.[11]

But the controversy around Wertmüller's politics is not limited to feminist critics—she also infuriated Marxist critics for the perceived lack of a positive and clear political "message" in her films. Commenting on the ending of *Pasqualino: Seven Beauties*, Richard Astle, somewhat didactically, suggests that:

> For in the final scene in the prison camp, with the pistol in his hand, Pasqualino *could* have rebelled, could reasonably have been fed up enough to rebel, and the prisoners *could* have been shown rising with him. It would have been, no doubt, suicide, but not as empty as Francesco's or the anarchist's (and it would have made their gestures less empty by completing them). The problem with Wertmüller's film as it stands is that, whatever its intentions, it leaves its audiences only with a sense of overwhelming despair. And this, it should be clear, is not politically productive.[12]

Some critics compare her unfavourably with the other political director "of the moment," Costa-Gavras, whose films are treated as exemplary documents of revolutionary struggle.[13] The political impurity of her films is seen as existing in parallel with a number of generic, stylistic, textual and thematic impurities. Wertmüller is often criticized for mixing comedy with tragedy, realistic settings with improbable situations and events, ordinary characters with exaggerated characterization, stories rooted in the everyday with historical processes. But most of the hostile criticism of her work seems to return to the iconoclastic mixing of popular forms and conventions with "serious" politics. I quote extensively from one of the most caustic and all-encompassing denouncements of Wertmüller's themes and aesthetics, where Brooks Riley argued:

> At the heart of it all is formula—a very popular one, but a formula all the same . . . The ingredients—politics, buffoonery, hubris, nemesis, pathos, bathos, comedy, tragedy, melodrama, psychodrama, Giancarlo Giannini, misplaced convictions, mismotivated sex, displaced honor, dialogue permeated with the comparisons of religion and politics, to the remotest banalities—are all dumped in varying quantities into the vat and cooked just long enough to produce the sweet smell of excess. Wertmüller's timing isn't off; *there is simply too much of everything* . . . Her vehicle is a comic bathosphere bulging with ideas, some good, some bad, some screaming to be edited out. An overeager synthesizer, she's gotten something from everyone: characters and comic grotesques from Fellini, theatrical lighting from Visconti, satire from de Filippo, the concentration-camp blue from Cavani. But the overriding influence is her own past. A former puppeteer, she's made living, breathing puppets, and tried to fit them into the naturalistic world of cinema. Her *commedia dell'arte* figures appear as incongruous in the settings they stalk as the first astronauts on the moon: and the result is imaginative artifice disguising itself as art.[14] [emphasis mine]

It is obvious that the impurity of Wertmüller's films was a cause for considerable anxiety for the American film critics, whose demand for political and aesthetic clarity led to either vitriolic attacks or theoretically and politically naïve attempts to offer politically meaningful, definitive readings of her films.[15] What is strikingly absent, however, from every critical approach presented here is an attempt to contextualize the films with references to the specific Italian historical and political context. It is precisely this inability (symptomatic of a mixture of political naïveté and cultural arrogance) to address the films in Italian rather than American and/or universal terms that leads to such (mis)interpretation of her work.

Although both Wertmüller's films and the American film criticism of the seventies were closely linked to radical politics they also belonged to dramatically different historical and political moments. Despite the apparent similarities it is more than an ocean that separates the politics of Italy and the USA in the seventies.

The post-'68 period in Italy is marked by an incredible complexity (easily mistaken for impurity) of political discourse and practice. While the Italian Communist Party (PCI) steadily increased its political influence to an impressive 35 percent of the popular vote in the 1976 general elections, it also faced a series of theoretical, ideological and practical crises. The seventies were a key period for most European communist parties, who found themselves discredited politically after the events of 1968.[16] The debates within the PCI involved a thorough revision of the tactics and ideology of the Party, which embraced "Eurocommunism" and proposed the notorious "historic compromise" in its commitment to power-share with the Christian Democrats. Furthermore, there was an ongoing political debate within the Italian and European Left involving a variety of theoretical perspectives (from the Freudian Marxism of Marcuse to the Lacanian revisionism of Althusser and the Foucauldian rethinking of power and sexuality). These debates centered on the thorny issues of the relationship between class and sexual politics, between the personal and the political, as well as on the role of power structures in political organizations and sexual relationships.

This intricate political and cultural formation was marked by a considerable emotional investment for millions of Italians whose commitment to the Left was in many cases fundamental to a sense of identity. The complexity of the politics was complemented by an emotional complexity. The loss of faith in the political meta-narratives went hand-in-hand with a sarcastic and humorous deconstruction of the mythologies of the Left that in turn gave rise to a sense of betrayal and failure. The sense of powerlessness in front of the enormous machinery of the system was matched by the exhilarating feeling of sexual emancipation, and the excitement about the empowering possibilities of direct action was followed by despair in the face of the ultimate futility of extreme versions of activism, such as terrorism.

At the same time Italian feminists developed distinct (if constantly changing) political practices, diverging from both the Italian Left and the American feminist movement. Giuliana Bruno and

Maria Nadotti explain the more fragmented, experiential and experimental (rather than theoretical and academic) nature of the Italian feminist movement:

> To grasp the Italian experience one should be aware that it is different from what produced "Women's Studies," the experience of knowledge which has played and still plays such a major part in the direction of women's intellectual and political research in the United States. The path pursued by American feminism, that of acquiring the status of a formal discipline, a field of "scholarship," a path which has generated "feminist film theory," has no parallel in Italy where feminist theory and criticism are not identified in the same way as an academic field or option . . . The dramatic growth of feminism in Italy historically followed, was generated within, and, at the same time, set to surpass the massive political movement of 1968, of which feminism was a subversive product. Consequently the confrontation with Marxism, with both Marxist theory and political praxis, was more painful for Italian women and was undertaken as an unavoidable commitment.[17]

Importantly, Bruno and Nadotti stress the centrality for the Italian feminism's encounter with the forms of organization, practices and ideologies of the Left. It is not surprising, then, that despite the fact that Wertmüller's work was problematic for some Italian feminists she was always seen as dealing with issues crucial for the feminist movement and as contributing to the strengthening of women's filmmaking in Italy—there is no doubt that together with Liliana Cavani she was an inspirational figure.[18]

The unwillingness of the American film critics to address the context of Wertmüller's work leads to evaluations and analyses of her films that blatantly ignore the political, cultural and emotional complexity of the historical moment within which they surface. This is further aggravated by the fact that the textual practices of the films constitute elaborate and intricate systems of interaction between the protagonists and diegetic and non-diegetic contexts.

The Films: "Too Much of Everything"

INDEED, THE DEFINING characteristic of Wertmüller's films of the seventies is the textual construction of a dense and crowded discursive and emotive environment whose dynamic relationship with the characters is explored in a multiplicity of ways. Furthermore, this textually constructed environment is overwhelmingly informed by the political historical context of the period. This stylistic and thematic feature is nowhere more clearly demonstrated than in *Night Full of Rain*, though with startling complexity.

Wertmüller was aware of (and worried about) the unique circumstances surrounding the production, distribution and exhibition of the film, and in particular with the unprecedented scale of the encounter with American audiences that the contract with Warner Brothers envisaged. Unlike the American film critics who stubbornly ignored the relevance of the context for the analysis of her films, Wertmüller was very attentive to the difficulties around the cultural encounter with a foreign public—"I wanted to create a bridge between Italy and America," she explains in an interview.[19] Not only is the narrative of the film structured around the encounter between the Italian communist journalist Paolo (Giancarlo Giannini) and the American feminist photographer Lizzy (Candice Bergen), but the film also fully integrates cultural difference within its discursive/emotive environment. The film opens with a close-up shot of a detail from a Giorgio de Chirico painting (*The Great Automaton*, 1925), and the camera tilts up to explore the surface of the print in which various disfigured and convoluted mechanical and organic parts form a kind of statue in the middle of a dark, empty and enigmatic landscape. The shot that follows shows a room lit by the moonlight coming from a window, through which we can see rain falling. The camera tracks out along a long, dark and empty corridor as the uneven light forms mysterious shadowy patterns on the walls. The shapes and the colors (grey, black, silver) of the scene as well as the emptiness of the space recall the empty landscapes of many of the paintings of de Chirico's "metaphysical period."[20]

With the opening shots the film establishes clear visual links with a painter whose work has been very much analyzed in terms of the metaphysical tension between humans and their surroundings, and the foregrounding of alienated and lonely figures placed within impressive but devastatingly stark and empty spaces. This is further emphasized by the shots that follow: a very brief shot of a room crowded with objects (where we get a glimpse of a girl sleeping) and then a series of lingering explorations of the objects on the walls of yet another room (a fireplace, books, another de Chirico painting, photographs). We finally meet Lizzy (initially through a reflection of her image on a window, and then) in a close-up as she moves her face from side to side, lit by the flickering light of a television set. We then see Paolo typing away madly. Paolo and Lizzy are totally absorbed in their separate activities and completely oblivious of each other's presence in the room.

While this opening suggests alienation similar to that expressed by de Chirico it also rejects the romantic nostalgia that saturates his work. The tranquillity and emptiness of the scene is disrupted by the exuberant energy of the Neapolitan folksong that dominates the soundtrack, whose lyrics express the erotic thoughts of washerwomen while they are doing their washing.[21] As the song fades away, an ominous voice emanates from the television set, talking about "catastrophes" in the form of the continuous rain and flooding caused by the destabilization of the "ecological equilibrium." As more shots of the apparent isolation of the couple follow, a strange chorus of voices begins commenting on the scene: "And once the TV's off? Silence"— "But this is not silence. This is marriage." This introduces a startling feature of the film, the recurring appearence of a group of men and women "friends" of the protagonists. These friends have several functions. They offer a level of meta-discourse with their commentary, they are involved in the actual story, they surrealistically appear out of nowhere in the diegesis of the film, they surface in the dreams and thoughts of the protagonists, and in general they surround Paolo and Lizzy with a presence that is simultaneously real and imaginary, diegetic and non-diegetic, internal and external.

The opening scene of *Night Full of Rain* articulates the thematic and stylistic complexity of Wertmüller's films. Paolo and Lizzy are visually, dramatically and symbolically placed within a very crowded context: the rain that falls throughout the film is linked to the ecumenical environmental catastrophe, the space that surrounds them is loaded with symbolic meaning (from the de Chirico paintings to the photographs invested with personal emotional value), the friends around them knot a dense discursive web that comments and debates on every single aspect of their lives (significantly, the commentary comes from clearly identifiable, culturally and historically specific discursive positions: Italian/American, communist/feminist, man/woman). At the same time the camerawork is hectic, exploring every detail of this complex environment, moving constantly from face to face, object to object and space to space, caressing in its movement the surfaces that surround the protagonists.

The sequence that follows is a flashback of the first meeting between Paolo and Lizzy. The voice over of an Italian male friend gradually fades out: "It was in '68 and she was fresh—fresh from Paris with a lot of shit in her head, with Marcuse, the servant of Mao . . ." while the film shows a religious procession in a small Italian town. The sequence functions as a representation of their first encounter but it also fully explores the different ways in which positions are constructed in relation to the eventful procession. Paolo, surrounded by his friends, notices Lizzy and her friend watching with amazement the religious ceremony. As a violent argument between a man and a woman ensues, Lizzy intervenes and knocks out the man with her bag; Paolo finds the intervention obviously funny while Lizzy seems nervous, scared and out of place. As violence turns against Lizzy, Paolo abandons his inaction and tries to help her and everybody gets embroiled in the fight: the religious fanatics are fighting Paolo, his friends and the two Americans, from a balcony the local communists play the tune of the revolutionary song "Avanti popolo!" while the Christians reply with their own music, as the *carabinieri* arrive at the scene and Paolo and Lizzy flee in panic. Not only does the first meeting between Paolo and Lizzy take place in a well defined historical and cultural context, it also occurs in conflict and in a way that delineates different attitudes and positions: communists versus Christians, Americans versus Italians, men versus women, the police versus the crowd. It seems that Wertmüller's anxieties about the reception of the film in America are reflected in the obvious effort to locate the encounter between Lizzy and Paolo within a wider context and to foreground the multiple levels of difference involved in their relationship.

As is the case with the previous sequence, the film places the "personal" level (emotions, desires, fears) in a dynamic and inescapable relationship with the broad political, cultural and historical context. This is also articulated in a variety of different ways in most of the films that Wertmüller directed in the seventies.

In *The Seduction of Mimi*, Mimi (Giancarlo Giannini) is involved in a process of constant political transformation (from indifferent to communist to right wing) and in constant emotional flux (from dissatisfied husband to amorous bigamist to defender of male honour). The hero's demise grows out of his inability to articulate a personal position in relation to the many conflicting political, institutional and cultural practices and discourses that surround him. Here the contextual web assumes absolute and destructive control over the destiny and desires of Mimi. The film clearly refers to a landmark film in the history of Italian cinema, *Divorzio all'italiana/Divorce Italian Style* (Pietro Germi, Italy, 1961), and a brief comparison between the two is illuminating. Ferdinando Cefalú (Marchello Mastroianni) is a Sicilian nobleman who sets out to eliminate his wife by exploiting the lenient treatment of "crimes of honor" by the Italian legal system. *Divorce Italian Style* is a humorous account of his plotting, which involves a sophisticated (if hilarious) manipulation of the legal discourses surrounding marriage, unfaithfulness and the code of honor. In *The Seduction of Mimi*, however, the hero is captivated by the legal and masculine discourses and his personal happiness is ultimately destroyed by his inability to distance himself from them. Instead of the simplicity of Ferdinando's articulation and pursuit of personal desire, in Mimi we witness the complex but systematic alienation of the hero from his emotions by the inexorable power of the discursive formation of the period.

Love and Anarchy further elaborates on the theme of "man in disorder," an idea articulated explicitly in *Pasqualino: Seven Beauties* and identified by Wertmüller herself as key to her cinema.[22] The film traces the emotional conflicts that Tonino (Giancarlo Giannini), a peasant who wants to assassinate Mussolini, experiences during his brief stay in a brothel in Rome. Tonino, driven to despair about the lack of control over his life (pushed to the limit through the witnessing of the brutal murder of his anarchist friend Michael by fascists), decides that a final act of defiance (the assassination of Mussolini) is the only way to regain some pride. The strength of his political beliefs, based on a spontaneous act of rebellion rather than organized struggle, are seriously challenged by the emotions of love, security and pleasure that he experiences in the brothel and through his involvement with Salomé (Mariangela Melato) and Tripolina (Lina Polito).

Through the conflict between "love and anarchy" the film offers a powerful deconstruction of the romantic (and male) myth of the revolutionary hero. It offers a powerful exploration of the role that pleasure and desire play in the revolutionary process and investigates the double movement involved in the personal/political relationship. This is reflected by a startling visual opposition between the scenes in the brothel and the outdoor scenes (mainly in Rome), between the set where sexual desire unfolds and the public sphere of politics. The *mise-en-scène* and camera work create in the brothel a warm, sensual and secure environment (with the camera gently lingering on object after object in tones of red, pink and brown). The public scenes on the other hand are dominated by the hard, angular and geometrical shapes of the buildings, squares and ornaments of the city shot in grey, blue and white.

Interestingly, Tonino expresses the passion that motivates his political objective in terms of a desperate assertion of male pride: "This action is what I need to feel like a man," and in clear negation of his love for Tripolina: "You are the best thing that's happened in my life." As Tonino's plot fails pathetically, the hero, in a state of obvious disorder displays emotions of rage, self-pity, denounces his love ("I'm worse than dead now. Like a worm sleeping in the whores.") and then begs for protection, until, completely crazed, he shoots some policemen, gets arrested and ultimately murdered by the fascists. The futility of Tonino's terrorism (and the overwhelming sadness of the final scene) offers an understanding of the desirability of personal survival even in the face of fascist oppression, while at the same time questioning the value of such survival.

While *Love and Anarchy* offers a sympathetic (albeit essentially ambiguous) view of survival by killing the desperate, incompetent, crazed but romantic Tonino, *Pasqualino: Seven Beauties* questions the value of survival at all costs by constructing a protagonist who survives the most appalling and obscene manifestations of power. Developing one of the important themes of the political films of the seventies, *Pasqualino: Seven Beauties* is an interrogation of the complacency of individuals in the rise of fascism and a study of the structures of power involved on both the political and the personal level. By placing Pasqualino (Giancarlo Giannini) in a position of both subject and object of power the film echoes some of the most sophisticated theories of power developed in the sixties and seventies, notably those of Michel Foucault.[23] Here the complexity of the film lies in the complex interplay of power involving both the macro political level of state goverment and the micro political level of the individual.

Similar concerns are articulated in *Swept Away,* which, after carefully defining the specific social and political background and context of the two protagonists, Gennarino (Giancarlo Giannini) and Rafaella (Mariangela Melato), proceeds to isolate them as castaways in a desert island. But the spectacular removal of the context in terms of the story's setting does not get rid off of the inescapable grip of power and discourse. The film explores the complex ways in which power operates on a personal level, while at the same time it exposes them as constructed around power structures that exceed the individual and invade the safe haven of the island. In this sense the film is a detailed (but not necessarily subtle) study of how the political permeates the sphere of the everyday. Significantly, it is the communist proletariat Genarino who is committed to the idea of constructing an alternative power structure that places him in total control and mastery over Rafaella. Rafaella's survival strategy, however, involves an idealization of their love that elevates it beyond the specificity of their class difference: "Why be part of the system? Of that monstrous machine that cripples us all?" However, after they are rescued, it is Genarino who wants to recreate the glorious isolation that made their relationship possible by inviting Rafaella to return to their island. And it is Genarino (yet another man in disorder) who after her rejection is left crying and shouting, "Rotten capitalist slut, deserting me like this," before eventually following his wife home, totally defeated.

This brief examination of some of the key films of the seventies outlines the variety of ways in which close links are constructed between the protagonists, the diegetic context and the general discursive and political context of the period. In order to achieve this, the films utilize a startling repertoire of visual techniques, thematic concerns and narrative structures. The result is a set of incredibly complex but rich and extremely dynamic texts that offer a comprehensive survey of some of the most pressing political questions of the period.

It is very unfortunate, then, that the American film critics who eagerly engaged with Wertmüller's work demonstrate such blatant insensitivity to the context of the films and to the significant differences between the American critical discourse and Italian political and cultural practices. The demand for political and stylistic purity seriously overlooks the complexity of the seventies in Italy—commenting on the relationship between films, social processes and politics, Mirco Melanco concludes:

> What emerges from this overview of forty years of cinematic production is that Italian filmmakers have long denounced institutions and practices which have contributed to such modern phenomena as alienation from the political process, unbridled greed, loneliness, urban crimes and undermining of family life . . .

Movies are neither treatises of moral conduct, nor sociological studies. If the most pressing challenge Italy has to face today is the quest to reconcile individual demands and collective principles, it is not the cinema which will provide all the answers.[24]

Indeed, Wertmüller's films (as the American critics note) do not offer explicit political solutions but a messy web of connections, contradictions and conventions. But her films are undoubtedly political and historical: not only because of their historical and political narratives but also because they are intensely preoccupied with the political and ideological discourses of the time and saturated with the passion, uncertainty and anxiety of the struggles around them. Wertmüller's films place her within these conflicts not as a superior director with ready-made aesthetic solutions but as somebody deeply engrossed in the context within which her texts exist. The study of her films makes the encounter with such contexts inevitable and thus decisively shifts the frame of reference of such auteurism from the creative genius of the director to the materiality of the historical conditions within which she operates. Furthermore, the "impurity" of her films poses serious challenges to the coherence and validity of critical classifications (art/popular, politics/entertainment) and categories (stylistic unity attributed to the unified creativity of the auteur) that have been traditionally used to marginalize popular texts. If we follow Foucault's reconceptualization of the author as a discursive "function"[25] it seems that the usefulness of studying the Wertmüller films of the seventies lies in the ability to bring into critical attention the limitations of the categories routinely involved in the study of both directors and national cinemas, as well as in the foregrounding of the text/context relationship that such a study entails.

Notes

1. Perhaps the most effective critique was offered by John Caughie in his brilliantly deconstructive edited collection of essays on authorship, *Theories of Authorship: A Reader* (London and New York: Routledge/BFI, 1988).
2. For a discussion of the function of the author as a discursive category within marketing and publicity practices see Catherine Grant, "www.author.com?" *Screen*, vol. 41, no. 1, 2000.
3. For example studies of Ealing studios Charles Barr, *Ealing Studios* (London: Cameron and Tayleur, 1977) and Cinnecitá Christopher

Frayling, *Spaghetti Westerns: Cowboys and Europeans from Karl May to Sergio Leone*, (London: Routledge, 1981).

4. For an early diagnosis of this tendency see Steve Neale, "Art cinema as institution," *Screen*, vol. 22, no. 1, 1981.

5. It is important to remember that the critical engagement with directors was fundamentally a polemical discourse, hence the designation *la politique des auteurs* offered by Truffaut in 1954.

6. There are, however, instances of a more productive engagement with their work: for example, in the case of Bava, Jean-Paul Torok, "La cadavre exquis," in *Positif*, July 1961, and Jean-Luc Moullet, "La peur et stupeur," in *Cahiers du cinéma*, no. 486, December 1984, to mark the occasion of the Mario Bava retrospective at the *Cinémathèque*.

7. quoted in John J. Michalczyk, *The Italian Political Filmmakers* (London and Toronto: Associated University Presses, 1986), p. 263.

8. *Catalogo Bolaffi del cinema italiano no. 3: tutti if film della stagione 1975/76* (Torino: Giulio Bolaffi editore, 1976).

9. For example, Molly Haskell, "Swept away on a wave of sexism," *Village Voice*, 29 September 1975; Pauline Kael, "Seven Fatties," *New Yorker*, 17 February 1976; Tania Modleski, "Wertmüller's women: swept away by the usual destiny," *Jump Cut*, June 1976; Ruth McCormick, "*Swept Away*," *Cinéaste*, Spring 1976.

10. Henry A. Giroux, "Film and the dialectic of alienation: the paradox of Lina Wertmüller," *Film Criticism*, vol. 1, no. 1, 1976, pp. 13–14.

11. Diane Jacobs, "Lina Wertmüller: the Italian Aristophanes?" *Film Comment*, vol. 12, no. 2, 1976, p. 48.

12. Richard Astle, "*Seven Beauties*: survival, Lina style," *Jump Cut*, July 1977, p. 23.

13. Ibid and also Jacobs, op. cit.

14. Brooks Riley, "Lina Wertmüller: the sophists' Norman Lear?" *Film Comment*, vol. 12, no. 2, 1976, pp. 49, 51.

15. The most obvious example of this tendency is offered by Giroux in his eulogy: "Lina Wertmüller has translated to film a message and a foundation for a political strategy that qualifies her as one of the most sophisticated Marxist filmmakers in the West. Beneath the subtle dynamics that flow from her films is a call to 'awaken the dreamers from their reified sleep. ' Therein lies the seed of Wertmüller's genius," op. cit., p. 17.

16. For a detailed account of the events of May 68 and the debates that followed see Sylvia Harvey, *May '68 and Film Culture* (London: BFI, 1980).

17. Giulian Bruno and Maria Nadotti, "Off screen: an introduction" in Bruno and Nadotti (eds), *Off Screen: Women and Film in Italy* (London and New York: Routledge, 1988), pp. 9–10.

18. See Annabella Miscuglio, "An affectionate and irreverent account of eighty years of women's cinema in Italy," in Bruno and Nadoti, ibid.

19. Quoted in Michalczyk, op. cit., p. 259.
20. This refers to the period 1915–1925 when de Chirico concentrated almost exclusively on "dreamscapes" featuring classical statues, mannequin figures and everyday objects in empty Italian piazzas with sinister shadows.
21. Michalczyk offers the following revealing anecdote in relation to the song that comes from the play *La gata Cenerentola (Cinterella the Cat)*: "Someone from the Warner Bros. Production company took it for a modern rock song, which indicates the great cultural abyss between America and Italy, says the director," ibid, p. 284.
22. Characteristic is another anecdote provided by Michalczyk: "Lina Wertmüller told Jerry Tallmer of the *New York Post* (27 January 1978) that the U.N. wanted to give her an award for 'Woman of the Year,' and asked her what phrase she wanted inscribed on it. She told them, 'Man in disorder, that's the only hope.'" ibid, p. 283.
23. Michel Foucault, *Discipline and Punish* (London: Penguin, 1977) and *The History of Sexuality, vol. 1* (London: Penguin, 1979).
24. Mirco Melanco, "Italian cinema, since 1945: the social costs of industrialization," *Historical Journal of Film, Radio and Television*, vol. 15, no. 3, 1995, p. 391.
25. Michel Foucault, "What is an author," in *Language, Counter-Memory, Practice* (Oxford: Blackwell, 1977).

7 GENDER, SEXUALITY AND MEDITERRANEAN FAMILIES

IT IS A widespread belief that popular European films offer stereotypical, oppressive and often offensive representations of gender and sexuality. Such a belief is reinforced through the rampant misogyny of the spaghetti western and the sexist clichés of the *Gendarme* cycle (as discussed in Chapters 4 and 5) and the various exploitation films (adventures, comedies, documentaries or pure pornography) of European origin. In what follows I shall attempt to challenge this belief through the examination of three case studies that demonstrate profoundly ambivalent tendencies in the representation and function of gender and sexuality. I shall first consider the star image of the Greek actress and politician Melina Mercouri and investigate the ways in which qualities originating in her melodramatic roles in the 1950s informed her political persona in the following decades. The second case study is a close examination of the ambivalence around gender, sexuality and the family in the film *La Cage aux folles* (Edoard Molinaro, France/Italy, 1978), one of the biggest commercial successes of European cinema. Finally, the work of the Spanish director Bigas Luna, and in particular his "Iberian trilogy" (*Jamón, jamón*, Spain, 1992, *Huevos de oro/Golden Balls*, Spain/Italy/France, 1993, and *La teta y la luna/The Tit and the Moon*, Spain/France, 1994), will be analyzed in relation to the critical claim that it deconstructs traditional definitions of Spanish masculinity.

It is beyond the scope of this chapter to engage in detail with theorizations of gender and sexuality which, in the last thirty years of film studies, have occupied a central place and contributed to some of the most important and invigorating debates. However, it is necessary to outline the rationale of my approach. I have elsewhere explored the limitations of psychoanalytic models of gender and sexuality for the study of non-Hollywood cinemas and films.[1] The universality of the psychoanalytic approach not only reinforces the assumed universality and normative position of Hollywood constructions of gender and sexuality but also overlooks the specificity that informs alternative constructions. The films, stars and representations discussed here are closely linked to historical, cultural and political contexts that provide the background against which they surface and circulate. Gender and sexuality are approached in a "relational" way rather than through eternal and universal categories.[2]

The choice of the case studies (necessarily limited) reflects the emphasis placed on historical and cultural specificity, differences and similarities insofar as the family's importance in gender construction in Mediterranean cinema and social life is concerned. While it is not my intention to impose a unity on the sexual and family politics of Southern European countries, it is important to highlight three shared characteristics: first, the key place that the extended rather than the nuclear family occupies; second, the presence of women in apparently powerful positions within the extended family which lead to descriptions of such structures as matriarchal. This may explain the recurring presence of strong matriarchal figures in the cinemas of Mediterranean countries; finally, the existence of a system of male "honor" that regulates sexual behaviour and is strikingly similar across borders in southern Europe, as the anthropologist Sara Delamont notes:

> There does seem to be a difference between the Mediterranean parts of Portugal, Spain and France and southern Italy and Greece where a man's status *does* seem to be related to the respectability of "his" women, especially in the working and middle classes, and northern Europe where the status of a man is more dependent on his own behaviour and possessions than on the virginity of his daughters and the faithfulness of his wife.[3]

As the quotation suggests and Delamont further explores, there are significant regional and class variations, as well as a factor of historical change of social relations that we need to take into account. The three case studies are chosen because they highlight difference as well as similarity.

However, the family is an institution that offers concrete and specific manifestations of the complex ways in which gender and sexuality intersect with political discourses and practices. Furthermore, in many southern European countries (Italy, Spain, Portugal, Greece but not to the same extent France) in the post-World War II period, crucial debates around the rights of women, the relations between men and women and the public perception and regulation of sexuality have focused on the role, structure and function of the family. This was further intensified by the impact of processes of urbanization and structural and legal modernization of the social role and cultural meaning of the family. The fall of the authoritarian regimes in Spain, Portugal and Greece in the 1970s was followed by the rise to power of socialist governments who in the 1980s introduced legislation that revised the traditional patriarchal framework of the family. Similarly, as Marcia Landy notes, in Italy

> [l]egislation in the 1970s "marked the end of an era in which the governance of family life had been a matter entirely for the family itself: now the silence and secrecy of the domestic sphere were broken." Laws contested the husband's place as legal head of the family and provided for the equal rights of conjugal partners in relation to each other and to their offspring.[4]

As numerous critics note, at various periods in the post-World War II period the family became a central theme in the cinemas of Italy, Spain, Portugal and Greece. Particularly interesting is the link between political and familial oppression that surfaces in many films and in different contexts. For example, Barry Morgan and Rikki Morgan-Tamosunas, following Marsha Kinder's pioneering work,[5] suggest that the "prominence of sexual thematics" in recent Spanish cinema can be interpreted as a reaction to "Francoism . . . [which] operated on the basis of highly traditional and retrograde concepts of gender and sexuality. This led to the conflation of sexual and political repression in the cultural life of the dictatorship."[6] This necessarily makes representations of the family significant instances of the intersection of political discourses, moral values, cultural traditions and cinematic codes, and is closely linked to historically specific national (and regional) formations.

Within such an overdetermined and complex structure, constructions of gender and sexuality are fundamentally ambivalent and often profoundly contradictory. As Marcia Landy explains in the context of Italian cinema:

> Portraits of *la famiglia* seem bilateral at best: The family appears ideally to be a source of order and stability, and a force for national unity. On the other hand, it also appears a tenuous haven from the depredations of the social order; a signifier for social fragmentation; a critique of gendered and sexual roles;

and a myth in need of demystification. The numerous representations of family in the Italian cinema are largely characterized
by conflict, ambivalence, and by reference to a larger social fabric that exceeds the domestic sphere.[7]

The case studies that follow are explorations of the ambivalence
around gender and sexuality as well as the role and function of the
family. They belong to different historical moments and cultural
formations, and they vary in terms of methodology and scope.

Melina Mercouri: From "Scarlet Woman" to "National Symbol"

IN MARCH 1994, WHEN Melina Mercouri died at the age of seventy,
hundreds of thousands of people from all over Greece thronged the
streets of Athens to attend her funeral, many in tears of genuine
grief. The press described her death as a tragedy for Greece in which
the "nation lost its soul." The profound impact of her death on
Greeks (or rather the "meaning" of her life and her film and political career) can be culturally and historically understood with reference to another death, a fictional one that concluded her debut film
Stella (Michael Cacoyannis, Greece, 1955). The role of Stella, the
tragic victim of oppressive patriarchal practices and conventions,
provided Mercouri with a certain type of iconic and symbolic cultural significance that accompanied her throughout her life.

Mercouri's filmography is surprisingly short—she appeared in
fewer than twenty films, most of them between 1955 and 1966, with
the majority of them directed by Jules Dassin, whom she married in
1966. The early films of her career (especially *Stella*, *The Gypsy and
the Gentleman* (Joseph Losey, UK, 1958), and *Pote tin Kiriaki/
Never on Sunday* (Jules Dassin, Greece, 1960)) were by far the most
memorable. When a military dictatorship staged a successful coup in
1967, Mercouri was declared an enemy of the state and had her cit-
izenship revoked, her passport confiscated and was forced into exile
abroad. She was particularly active and effective in worldwide campaigns against the dictators, and her political activism took up most
of her time and energy, practically bringing an end to her film career.
In 1974, with the fall of the dictatorship, she became a founding
member of the Greek Socialist Party (Pasok) which, since it came to
power in 1981, has governed Greece almost uninterruptedly.
Mercouri, a member of the historic leadership of the Party, was a

key player, extremely popular both inside and outside Pasok, known as and referred to by everybody as simply "Melina." She was particularly influential as Minister for Culture, a post that she held from 1981–1989 and from 1993 until her death. She initiated the movement for the return of the "Parthenon marbles" and her ceaseless campaigning has identified her with the issue. Mercouri was also central in the establishment of the pan-European initiative "Cultural Capital of Europe," held for the first time in Athens.

What was extraordinary about Mercouri was that her glamorous career as a film star was surpassed by the even greater success of her political career. In what follows I shall explore the ways in which her star image intersects with and informs her political persona to articulate an extremely complex and contradictory icon who occupies an important position in Greek discourses of gender and nationhood.

Mercouri's character and performance in *Stella* was particularly important and defined a set of connotations that informed the public perception of her image until her death. The film is the story of Stella (Melina Mercouri), a taverna singer who shows total disrespect for the strict patriarchal conventions of Greek society in the 1950s. She rejects her middle class, young and handsome lover Alekos (Alekos Alexandrakis), who dies heart-broken, and starts a passionate affair with Miltos (Giorgos Foundas), a man from the working class suburbs of Piraeus who plays football for the local team Olympiakos. When Miltos proposes to her, she feels trapped but accepts, only to realize later that marriage and the family will kill their love and take away her freedom. On the day of her wedding instead of attending the ceremony she spends the day with a young student. In the final sequence of the film the outraged (and "dishonored") Miltos kills her while Stella kisses him passionately.

The film was heralded by most film critics as a powerful indictment of patriarchy and was called the "best Greek film ever made"; it was also internationally acclaimed (it won the 1956 Golden Globe for Best Foreign Film). The film's heroine represented a type of female identity virtually "alien" to Greek society at the time. The historian Yiannis Soldatos writes:

> Stella is not an ordinary heroine. Although she expressed the secret desires of many Greek women very few followed her example and even less managed to realize it. And even the latter never did so with the confidence of Cacoyannis' heroine, otherwise the whole of Greece would still remember them. Stella was

the symbol of a type of women's freedom that was not even discussed in Greece at the time. There were such restrictions of
political freedom then that what Cambanellis [the scriptwriter]
and Cacoyannis created appears to be a science fiction film.[8]

Clearly the historian speaks from a historical perspective, recog-
nizing the social and cultural challenge that the film posed.
However, the contemporary critical reception was somewhat different, as the film was praised for its portrayal of "diachronic" values
and forms and for its moral and structural resemblance to ancient
Greek tragedy. As Soldatos points out, it was only left-wing critics
who addressed the film in its contemporary context and were unambiguous in their condemnation. Kostas Stamatiou, for example,
wrote: "Do you think that by giving freedom to women to go with
whoever they like they can get independence? I am afraid that there
are going to be many victims of Cacoyannis' folly."[9]

The film lends itself to both readings: while *Stella* explicitly and
implicitly articulates specific and contemporary challenges to patriarchy, the characters seem to be trapped within a rigid system of
morality that propels them with fatalistic force towards a tragic destiny. The ending of the film reinforces the second reading. After failing to turn up for the wedding ceremony Stella wanders in the street
of Athens with the young student, while Miltos waits for her in the
taverna. Miltos gets drunk and dances, and Stella dances maniacal-
ly and passionately with her partner. The sequence is edited as a fast
and accelerated montage of shots of the dancing protagonists, who
are, in this sense, inescapably and inextricably linked. It is obvious
that there is no way out for either of them, and as the pace finally
slows down they face each other across a public square in the middle of Stella's neighborhood. Miltos pleads with Stella to run away,
that he's got a knife and will kill her, but she walks steadily and fear-
lessly towards him. When Miltos stabs her she asks him to kiss her,
which he passionately does, and she dies in his arms. Soon the empty
square fills with neighbors who, forming a circle around the
embraced protagonists, resemble an ancient Greek chorus as they
mourn the tragic fate of the heroes.

Like heroes of tragedy, Miltos and Stella personify the conflict
between two unwieldy and uncompromising moral codes: on the
one hand, the code of honor and shame and the family structure that
it safeguards and on the other, a sexual passion that cannot survive
within such structure. This positioning and resolution of the

conflict, however, has important ideological implications. Removing the two conflicting systems of value from their concrete historical context transforms them into eternal and abstract categories. As a result they are represented as equal (and equally responsible for the tragedy) when they are not: textually, because it is Stella who dies, and contextually because Miltos' morality is also the dominant morality of a culture and society that violently oppresses women. The code of honor and shame is not an ahistorical, neutral moral system but has specific causes, agents and effects. As Sara Delamont notes in relation to Greek society:

> . . . in the culture where the honour-shame system operates a man gets status by being out of his home with other men, and displaying the behaviours that are of value in men to other men. The ideal is that a man controls "his" women, if necessary by violence, but it is also the case that the woman is in control of the home, and she can ruin the reputation of her husband (but only at the cost of her own).[10]

Stella openly rejects the shame-honor system by resisting one after another of its powerful effects and implications. In numerous occasions in the film she delivers outspoken rebuttals of male authority and marriage: she calls Miltos "an owner, like the rest of them" for wanting to marry her, and she declares that "marriage will drown and kill all her passion and love for life." Interestingly, Stella shows more contempt for the women who perform their expected roles rather than for the men who make such demands. What makes her decide not to marry Miltos is the visit of his mother who on the day of the wedding lays down the rules: Stella has to give up her job and move out of her neighborhood to a new house that Miltos is buying for them. This is very much in line with the representation of strong matriarchs in the Greek films of the period, their position and power as head of the family rarely challenging patriarchy, instead offering concrete examples of what a "good" wife and mother should be like.

The character of Stella and Mercouri's presence and performance in the film defined the star's iconicity in a profound way that, despite shifts in the relative importance of the connotations attached to it, has changed very little with time. Mercouri as Stella and Stella's persistence in Mercouri's persona created the image of a powerful and passionate woman who celebrated her sexuality and rejected male authority, with her screen role and public role complementing each other, overcoming in the process crucial ideological and social contradictions. Stella is forever an outsider, a "scarlet woman," whose sexual freedom cannot be accommodated within traditional patriarchal structures. The roles that Mercouri was offered in the 1950s were rather unimaginative versions of Stella. She was the gypsy Belle in *Gypsy and the Gentleman*, and the prostitute in both *Celui qui doit mourir* (Jules Dassin, France/Greece/Italy, 1957), where she played Katerina, and in *Never on Sunday*, as the happy-go-lucky Ilya. While the Dassin films treat her with some sensitivity and seem to celebrate as well as exploit her sexuality, *The Gypsy and the Gentleman* is doubly offensive. Mercouri is caricatured as a gypsy, the appeal of her presence based on nothing else except her exotic, wild looks. Dressed in a red dress for most of the film, Belle goes around gesticulating wildly and uttering incomprehensible sounds—incomprehensible that is unless you happen to understand that some of these expressions (both words and gestures) are actually Greek!

But Stella offered to Mercouri much more than the scarlet woman quality. Stella's passion (for life, love and happiness) and her defiance of any kind of authority became, as we will see later, fundamental aspects of her image (both as a star and as a politician). Furthermore, Stella was clearly associated with working class values, and there are at least three scenes in the film in which Stella is followed or surrounded by adoring crowds of "ordinary hard-working" people. It is a very similar sequence that opens *Never on Sunday*, where groups of men working at the shipyards of Piraeus celebrate Ilya's arrival. This image of spontaneous rapport with the "masses," as if she was one of them, was in marked contrast with Mercouri's upper class background—her father was an influential politician and mayor of Athens.

Furthermore, Stella was seen not only as a woman of her time fighting for her right to freedom but also as a diachronic heroine of tragedy, and in this sense her image linked the past with the present and the future. Mercouri's performance as Stella was praised for its freshness and energy as well as her ability to make her face a "mask of passion and suffering." The association of Mercouri with tragedy was reflected by her roles in *Phaedra* (Jules Dassin, Greece, 1962) and *A Dream of Passion/Kravgi Ginekon* (Jules Dassin, Greece/Switzerland/USA, 1978), which feature her as an ancient heroine in contemporary settings. Her last acting performance was in the ancient theatre of Epidaurus in 1980 when she appeared as Klytaemnistra in *Orestia*.

In addition, Mercouri's image also bridged national characteristics and international recognition, a Greek icon with transnational currency. At a time when the number of famous Greeks was depressingly small, Mercouri's film career was seen as a precious representation of national culture abroad. The fact that Mercouri's international success was not seen as based on a "betrayal" of her origins gave her a privileged position in comparison to the other two stars of the period, Nana Mouscouri and Maria Callas—unlike them, "Melina" was always perceived to be committed to Greece and her people.

Mercouri used her star image effectively as a powerful weapon that helped her succeed in political campaigns and objectives. The campaign against the dictators, which was carried out in exile, was facilitated by both her reputation and the image of the outsider suffering for her love of freedom. Political campaigns of broad social and cultural implications became associated with her personally, became Melina's issues. The passionate, emotional mode of address that she adopted then became the main characteristic of her political rhetoric. Of course this is most clearly evident in her campaign for the return of the Parthenon marbles. In 1982 she addressed the World Conference on Cultural Policies on the issue:

> We see ancient cultural chains broken, past traditions crumble and wonderful special characteristics wither away. Our common memory is threatened, our soul shrivels, our creativity is stifled, our present becomes rootless . . . This past must emerge from the museums in order to become a source of inspiration and creativity, to become the instrument and the joy of the people.[11]

And a few years later in her speech to the Oxford Union she started by declaring:

> You know, it is said that we Greeks are a fervent and warmblooded breed. Well, let me tell you something—it is true. And I am not known for being an exception. Knowing what these sculptures mean to the Greek people, it is not easy to address their having been taken from Greece dispassionately, but I shall try.[12]

Mercouri was fully aware of the significance of her image. In 1991, when she unsuccessfully stood for mayor of Athens, her advertising campaign was outrageously minimalist: a photograph of her face against the Parthenon with the caption "Melina for Athens." The strength of her candidacy became the self-evident love for the city, with her face functioning as an emblem of change and action, as well as expressive of an "essence of Greekness" as old and genuine as Stella's mask of passion and suffering.

But Mercouri was far more successful in real life (both personal and public) than Stella. A socialist and a feminist dedicated to social modernization, she was part of the movement that campaigned against the patriarchal system that supported the code of honor that gave Miltos the right to murder. Indeed, one of the major achievements of the socialist governments of the 1980s was the total overhaul of the legal framework that defined gender relations in general and family structures in particular, putting Greece in line with other European countries in terms of women's rights. Mercouri's marriage to Dassin was also seen as a rare example (for Greek society) of a partnership that did not subordinate the aspirations of the woman—the public perception was that Dassin gave up his promising career to be with Mercouri.

The political image of Mercouri exploited certain aspects of her star image but abandoned some of the most challenging features of it. Indeed in many ways the early image of Melina as a scarlet woman rebellious and marginal, with an uninhibited sexuality and uncompromising independence, a husky-voiced cigarette smoking adventurer, was used by her opponents in order to discredit her political positions. On numerous occasions the right-wing tabloid press used lines (like the notorious "I am a nymphomaniac" in *Topkapi* (Jules Dassin, USA, 1964)) or incidents from her films in order to ridicule her. Mercouri consciously and gradually transformed this image to a more acceptable one that valorized unifying aspects: the passion for love, freedom and social change, the international reputation, the combination of the diachronic and the modern, and of middle class background and populist appeal. For most of her life, however, her image (reinforced by her political success and influence) remained a threat to male power and control, and at the same time an inspiration for many Greek women struggling for emancipation.

It is ironic, then, that after her death Mercouri became such a unifying symbol, an emblematic expression of Greek nationhood. And, as suggested at the beginning of this section, such cultural meaning is based on a re-appropriation of her star image as established in *Stella*, rather than her personal and political achievements. The particularity of the historical circumstances in Greece enabled a selective re-working of her image that was seen as faithfully expressing the "soul of the nation" at the moment.

In the early 1990s hegemonic and long established notions of Greek national identity were doubly and fundamentally challenged. The arrival in the country of hundreds of thousands of immigrants and refugees after the collapse of the communist governments in Eastern Europe threw simplistic (and extremely oppressive) notions of what it meant to be Greek into deep crisis. This gave rise to a paranoid, aggressive and exclusive nationalism, unprecedented racism and rampant xenophobia, which were further intensified by the controversy around the name of Macedonia, with the vast majority of Greeks believing that naming the neighboring country after an area historically belonging to Greece represented a threat. Unsuccessful in their attempts to make the "international community" understand their fears, Greeks felt betrayed and deeply isolated. This gave an emotional and passionate tone to nationalism and xenophobia and led to dangerous attempts to define Greek national identity in terms of historical continuity. Mercouri's image gave a powerful and unique expression to such nationalist sentiments. Her international campaign to get back the marbles (this powerful and unambiguous emblem of Greek culture) obtained a totally new meaning that was reinforced by the "Stella" aspects of her image: the marginal, defiant independence, the suffering and passion, the resistance to authority and injustice. And if the reading of *Stella* as tragedy deprives the heroine of any contemporary social relevance, the image of Mercouri as a national symbol of unity conveniently overlooks the radical threat posed by the scarlet woman to a still deeply patriarchal Greek society.

It becomes clear, then, that Mercouri's image is not only complex but also contradictory. She was very successful at manipulating her image to further her political interests, and in the process she helped to introduce social reforms that eased the burden of patriarchy in Greece. At the same time some of the most challenging aspects of her star image (both at the beginning and at the end of her career) were subjected to appropriations that placed them within unifying, often nationalistic discourses and frames of reference.

La Cage aux folles and the Liberalism of the 1970s

THE FRENCH-ITALIAN CO-PRODUCTION *La Cage aux folles*/(Italian title *Il vizietto*), is one of the greatest commercial hits in the histories of the Italian and French cinemas. The film was successful both nationally and internationally, and this was probably helped by the fact that the French partners, Les Productions Artistes Associés (the Italian producers were Da Ma Produzione) were in reality the French branch of United Artists. In Italy in 1978/79 it attracted 1.4 million viewers and topped the list of the most popular films of that year by some margin (the second film in the list *Amori miei* (Stefano Vanzina/Steno, Italy, 1978, starring Monica Vitti), which was watched by 0.7 million viewers).[13] In France it was one of the most successful films of the 1970s,[14] while in the USA it grossed $17 million in 1979 (one of the top five foreign language films of all time),[15] and in the same year in Germany it attracted half a million viewers.[16] The film inspired two sequels (*La Cage aux folles II*, (Eduard Molinaro, France/Italy, 1980) and *La Cage aux folles III: "elles" se marient*, (Georges Lautner, France/Italy, 1985)), a Broadway musical, and one American remake (*The Birdcage*, (Mike Nichols, USA, 1996)). Particularly interesting for the concerns of this chapter is the popularity of the film with both straight and gay audiences: while the film's prime target was clearly the "family" audience, it also achieved legendary cult status[17] and became a regular feature in gay film festivals.[18] In the following analysis of the film I shall explore the profound ambivalence that surrounds the film's attitude in relation to traditional, heterosexual and patriarchal family structures and fixed, essentialist gender roles, and identify some of the textual strategies through which the film constructs and manages its dual mode of address and popularity.

The narrative of the film explores the comedic potential of the conflict in moral codes, socio-cultural conventions and style, between two different family structures. The romance between Renato's son Laurent (Rémi Laurent) and Andrea (Luisa Maneri) brings into contact the diametrically opposite worlds of an ultra-conservative and patriarchal family, whose patriarch Charrier (Michel Galabru) is the deputy leader of the political party "Union for Moral Order," and that of the "alternative" family of the trans-vestite nightclub, with the gay middle-aged couple Renato (Ugo Togniazzi) and Albin (Michel Serrault) as its central unit. This conflict, initially constructed through parallel editing between the two households, culminates with the visit of the Charrier family at the St. Tropez night club.

One of the functions of such a narrative structure is that it contextualizes and possibly deconstructs the normative position of the heterosexual, nuclear family. The film does not treat the two spheres of action equally, as the narrative space of the nightclub occupies what is clearly a privileged position. The Charriers household is an austere, serious space where only "essential" narrative events occur. The nightclub, on the other hand, is thoroughly explored by the film, with particular attention given to the *mise-en-scène* as well as the interaction between the characters that populate the nightclub. Not only does the film spend considerably more time at the nightclub, it also provides the stage for most of the comedic incidents of the film and its climax.

The structure of the community of the nightclub, nevertheless, is itself riddled with contradictions. While the Charriers are represented as a nuclear unit, literally besieged by outsiders, Renato and Albin's intense relationship is part of a far more interactive, communal world. Indeed, the film constructs a utopian world that celebrates the caring, warm and imaginative interaction between Albin, Renato, Jacob (Benny Luke), Laurent and the transvestite performers, and places them within a surrounding community that accepts the different sexuality of the protagonists. The sequence of the doctor's visit at the beginning of the film, as well as the one that shows Albin doing his shopping and cheerfully socializing with the shopkeepers, are particularly enjoyable examples of that.

However, the scope of such a utopia is limited. The important relationship between Renato and Albin is both structured along stereotypical heterosexual roles and deprived of any display of sexual desire. Renato and Albin are in many ways portrayed along a masculine/feminine division that mirrors the structure of a "normal" heterosexual family: Renato manages the club and is active and rational and a "father" to Laurent while Albin is the star of the show and is fundamentally re-active, overwhelmingly emotional (if not "hysterical") and acts as an "auntie"; the language and body language used during the numerous (and violent) arguments between the two is reminiscent of bickering middle-aged heterosexual couples.

But the lack of demonstrations of explicit sexual desire between Albin and Renato is the most serious challenge to the gay utopia of the film. Only Jacob in his half-nakedness, his outrageously sexy clothes and the poses that he strikes against the lavish, over-the-top *mise-en-scène* becomes an object of erotic contemplation. The sexual attraction between Renato and Albin is never openly acknowledged, and in this sense the basis of their relationship becomes the management of their crises.

It is Renato's "masculine" position that is particularly problematic. On the one hand, as we will further explore later, the film brilliantly foregrounds performative elements of his gendered identity, but on the other, it also seems to suggest that he has access to some form of primordial essence of masculinity. The two scenes in the film that Renato directly or indirectly expresses sexual desire are profoundly incoherent. Early on, after dealing with Albin's exhibition of a *prima donna* temperament, Renato is preparing to receive a mysterious guest. The tone of the scene is heavily suggestive of a sexual encounter, as it has been prefaced by Albin's jealous questioning and is accompanied by a softening of the music, the lowering of the lights and Renato's attentiveness to his clothes and appearance. This is further intensified when a young, handsome man (fetishized by the camera that lingers on parts of his white-dressed body as he approaches the door) arrives and an intimate, physical exchange of affectionate gestures and comments ensues. However, when the visitor's identity is revealed (he is Laurent, Renato's son), the sexual undertones of the relationship are exchanged for expressions of paternal concern and love. This is a pivotal scene, which, by first building the encounter as sexual and then transforming it into a family relationship, negates the position of "lover" for Renato and fixes him in the role of "father."

The other scene in the film that allows the expression of sexual desire is the visit to Simone (Claire Maurier), Laurent's biological mother. The scene offers an explanation of the "mystery" of how Laurent came to existence in the first place, but more intriguingly, connects Renato's fatherhood with a mysterious, irresistible sexual attraction that he feels towards his ex-wife (their intimate embrace is interrupted by Albin who, overwhelmed by jealousy, bursts into the room). The significance of this is that the locus of sexual desire is shifted away from the relationship between Renato and Albin and placed in the context of a biological, "natural" family. This is further emphasized by the narrative resolution that affirms the latter as the "normal" institution, through the wedding of Laurent and Andrea.

The closing scene of the wedding offers the ceremonial spectacle of a symbolic reconciliation of two extremes: the moral order of the Charrier family and the sexual disorder of the nightclub family. The film represents both family set-ups as problematic. The Charrier family's sense of moral order is represented as unbearably dull and is exposed as hypocritical, as they use the opportunity of the wedding in order to manipulate public opinion for political and careerist purposes. The negation of sexual interaction between Renato and Albin, as discussed earlier, undermines the credibility of their relationship and their ability to function as a family unit. The film suggests a renewal of the family through the marriage of the young offspring of these two equally (but differently) problematic set ups. In this sense the film is informed by a post '68 liberal view of social relations and interaction, characterized by tolerance and moderation very much in line with the liberal rhetoric of Giscard d'Estaing's presidency. The wedding scene becomes a spectacle of social tolerance as both the heterosexual and the gay community are accommodated within the church, an institution of unparalleled moral conservativism and normative power. This happy cohabitation (further emphasized by the strong suggestion that the priest himself is gay) inoculates any subversive or unsettling aspects of sexual difference and non-patriarchal models of family and ultimately demonstrates the strength of the social bond that an inclusive and permissive liberalism provides. The cosmopolitan St. Tropez (and French and Italian societies in the late 1970s) establish a liberal setting that is in this sense very different from the oppressive patriarchy of *Stella* and, as we will see later, the crisis of the traditional family in 1990s Spain.

The movement of the narrative of the film, with its resolution celebrating tolerant heterosexuality, works against the more challenging aspects of the film that exist in the periphery of narrative importance. In a sense, the film, duplicating the narrative binaries, constructs a universe of alternative pleasures (around mannerisms, the *mise-en-scène*, Jacob's outrageous spectacle and so on) that runs parallel and against the liberal moral order of the narrative. But the film is not incoherent (despite a couple of "difficult" scenes) and it does not push the possibility of a (gay) reading to the margins. The film manages to reconcile this dual mode of address by centralizing performance.

The credit sequence of the film makes performance the essence of the film not only by offering numerous shots of performers and dancers before an audience, but also by introducing binaries that refer to a broad spectrum of connotations attached to perform-ance: from outside the club the camera follows the spectators inside, there the editing and the camerawork divide the space of spectacle into stage and backstage, and this enables us to observe the dancers preparing for their routine or shedding off the "instru-ments" of their performance (wigs, dresses, etc). Additionally, per-formance is emphasized in *La Cage aux folles* in a variety of ways and on many levels: the story is set predominantly in a nightclub, a space of spectacle and performance where Albin performs; the plot (through the visit of the Charrier family) dictates that Albin and Renato perform the roles of a "normal" heterosexual couple; this in turn leads to numerous debates around the performance of normality as well as a thorough satire of various performed ver-sions of masculinity/femininity; finally, the success of the film depends on the entertaining and convincing performances of Michel Serrault and Ugo Tognazzi.

The film has been critically acclaimed internationally for its per-formative aspects, with Ambra Danon and Piero Tossi nominated for an Academy Award for their costume design and Michel Serrault winning a César prize for best actor. Tognazzi and Serrault's per-formances were seen as demonstrations of skill testifying to the broad range of acting of these two straight actors—they are, in this sense, comparable to the celebrated performances by Dustin Hoffman in *Tootsie* (Sidney Pollack, USA, 1982—Hoffman was nominated for an Academy Award for his performance) and Robin Williams in *Mrs. Doubtfire* (Chris Columbus, USA, 1993, for which Williams won an American Comedy Award). Like Hoffman and Williams, Tognazzi (who was clearly more established and better known internationally than Serrault) had the reputation of a versa-tile actor. As *The Companion to Italian Cinema* suggests:

> [Tognazzi was] a very skilled actor, he gained the esteem of his directors, was encouraged by the critics and adored by the pub-lic . . . His considerable range overlapped with that of the other great comic actors of his generation: he could be Sordi's mean "average" Italian, Gassman's ostentatious braggart, Nino Manfredi's well-behaved "everyman," and Mastroianni's tor-mented bourgeois, but he always succeeded in adding some qualities of his own.[19]

But at the same time, the film explores performance on a deeper and more interesting level. Renato and Albin offer concrete examples of masculine identities based on a dislocation of the normative alignment of sex, gender and sexuality. Indeed, the film constructs their identities in anti-essentialist terms and in constant flux and transformation. The play between the two different notions of performance involved in the film is perhaps most clearly demonstrated in the scene in the bar when Renato and Albin discuss, analyze and perform different versions of masculine identity. At the end of the scene first Renato and then Albin try to imitate the "John Wayne walk." Here, on one level, masculinity is portrayed as double performance (the performance of a star's mythologized performance), whereas on another level the scene displays the performance of a straight actor pretending to be a gay character who is pretending to be straight.

Furthermore, on numerous occasions (albeit not with absolute consistency) the film defines masculine identity in terms of performance, as a set of learned and acted codes of body language, social behavior and cultural conventions. Of course, this is an understanding of identity that has become politically and critically important in queer theory and most evidently so in Judith Butler's theorization of gender as relating to performance (through the fragmented, discontinuous enactment of roles) rather than to an essential identity.[20]

The "Iberian" Trilogy and the Trials of Spanish Masculinity

THE FILMS THAT comprise what Bigas Luna himself defined as the "Iberian trilogy"[21] can be seen as visually impressive explorations of Spanish masculinity. Not only do the stories of the films locate the action in various places and regions of Spain of historical importance to Spanish identity (from North African Melilla to Hispanic Miami, and from Benidorm to Los Monegros and Catalunya), they also knit a dense web of specifically Spanish cultural references: dreams constructed like Dali paintings, shots pastiching *Un Chien andalou* (Luis Buñuel, France, 1929), mechanical bulls reminiscent of Picasso's *Guernica*, Julio Iglesias songs, huge billboards advertising Osborne brandy, numerous gastronomical specialties and so on.

The films were very successful commercially (*Jamón, jamón* made $7 million from international exports and $1.5 million in the home market,[22] the others had similar runs) and won accolades in international festivals: *Jamón, jamón* won the Silver Lion at the

1992 Venice Film Festival, *Huevos de oro* the Special Prize of the Jury at the 1993 San Sebastián International Film Festival, and *La teta y la luna* won the Golden Osella at the 1994 Venice Film Festival. However, the critical reception of the films has been much more ambivalent.[23] The films have been criticized both for the hyperbolic demonstrations of Spanish machismo and for their lack of coherent narrative and comprehensible characters that the powerful imagery fails to compensate for.

However, other critics have identified the humorous exploration of masculine identities as a powerful deconstruction of traditional masterful and domineering Spanish masculinity, as well as an exposition of the failings of patriarchal family structures. Javier Bardem (whose status as the biggest male star of contemporary Spanish cinema owes a lot to *Jamón, jamón* and *Huevos de oro*) has been identified as a star whose iconicity suggests a new definition of masculinity that corresponds to a Spain that has moved beyond the culture of the immediate post-Franco years.[24]

In what follows I shall explore the scope of the deconstruction/redefinition of masculinity and question its radicalism by paying equal attention to representations of both masculine and feminine identities in the three films. Indeed, I shall argue that examining masculinity in isolation and in itself is analytically flawed and politically misleading. It is within a relational approach to masculinity that we can fully understand and evaluate the critique of gender and the family that the Iberian trilogy undertakes.

There is no doubt that the films painstakingly explore various aspects of Spanish masculine identity and that in the process they challenge many of the conventional ways in which regimes of representation have been historically constructed around the male body. From the beginning of the first film to the end of the last, fantasies of male power and domination are consistently and in a variety of ways undermined and/or delivered to parody and satire.

The trilogy ends with a stage show of the now reconciled love triangle of *La teta y la luna*. There Estrellita (Mathilda May), surrounded by her lovers Miguel (Miguel Poveda) and Maurice (Gérard Darmon), perform a ludicrous act accompanied by the Edith Piaf song "Les mots de l'amour." The happiness of the male characters consists simply in being able to perform next to Estrellita, who wears ballerina clothes. The masculine identities displayed in the sequence are unambiguously farcical. Miguel, dressed in cyclist's white lycra and waving his white feathered wings hovers over a racing bike as he sings the Piaf song, while Maurice, the fire king, whose impotence is compensated by his ability to blow fireballs from his bottom, poses on his immobile motorbike wearing a shiny leather suit decorated with flames. The quest of the rivals comes to a happy conclusion in this scene, which, although spectacularly choreographed, fails to connect with any conventional definition of male power, mastery and control.

In the conclusion of the credit sequence of *Jamón, jamón*, the black background is revealed to be an enormous billboard advertising brandy and representing a bull. As the field of vision opens to reveal the space of narrative action (a desert scarred by a busy motorway) a final circular patch of blackness—the testicles of the bull—remains dominant in frame and provides the backdrop for the director's name. In the most obvious, even vulgar, way the film defines its perspective and interest to be the relationship between the story, the actions, the place and various (symbolic and/or iconic) representations of masculinity.

And if irony here is suggested by the location of the "director Bigas Luna" credit, the sequence that follows offers a more thorough and powerful demystification of traditional Spanish masculinity. A long (70") and slow crane shot explores a beautiful but hard and dry landscape (Bigas Luna describes it as "The Monegros; a sea of land where everything is accentuated by aridity.")[25] that is basking in the golden sunlight of the setting sun. As the music of the credit sequence (a gentle but powerful *adagio*) fades out, we hear exerted, inarticulate male voices, which the camera finally reveals as coming from two young men in an empty football pitch on a plateau involved in a bizarre form of bullfighting practice. A rapid succession of close-up and medium shots follows: shots of parts of a mechanical bull with wheels pushed by a young man on the cracked, dry earth are intercut with shots of parts of Raúl's (Javier Bardem) body. Raúl wears tight blue shorts and a gray sleeveless vest and the close-ups reveal both his muscularity and his big penis bulging against the clothes.

The juxtaposition of the hard and beautiful landscape and the male bodies involved in the "fake" bullfighting works on several levels. It links the protagonist with the land and in this sense defines Raúl's identity in regional/national terms. The empty landscape and the appearance of the male figures in it also suggests a more universal, transnational connection between men and nature ("packaged" in films as landscape). The function of the desert landscape is explored in relation to westerns (ironically, the deserts of Spain offered the setting for many spaghettis) by Jane Tompkins in a way pertinent to the film, despite its obvious geographical and historical difference:

> So the desert is the classic Western landscape, rather than the rain forests of the Pacific Northwest or the valleys of California, because of the messages it sends. It does not give of bird or bush. Fertility, abundance, softness, fluidity, many-layeredness are at a discount here. The desert offers itself as the white sheet on which to trace a figure. It is a tabula rasa on which man can write, as if for the first time, the story he wants to live . . . The apparent emptiness makes the land desirable not only as a space to be filled but also as a stage on which to perform and as a territory to master.[26]

But in *Jamón, jamón*, the destiny of Raúl, this Spanish man of the deserts of Southern Spain, is on a lesser scale, and his assertions of mastery are miniscule, as the childish caricature of bullfighting becomes a masculine adventure grotesquely disproportionate to the celebrated size of his penis.

As is clear from the above scene, the films, far from being reluctant or uncomfortable with the exploration of the male body, a tendency that Steve Neale identifies in relation to "mainstream" cinema ("the male body cannot be marked explicitly as the erotic object of another male look"),[27] they offer an abundance of images of men on display. Even in *La teta y la luna*, in which the body of the protagonist/narrator nine-year old Tete (Biel Duán) is carefully shielded, the bodies of Miguel, Maurice and Stallone (Genis Sanchez) are generously offered as a spectacle in various forms, from close-ups that fragment and fetishize their image to soft focus idealistic representations.

Significantly, female characters in the films are not excluded from the privileged point of view and in many occasions it is their look that reveals and fetishistically fragments the body of the male characters. All three films provide examples of point of view structures that place women in control of the exchange of looks and objectify the male body, but the most obvious one is witnessed in *Jamón, jamón* in the scene in which Conchita (Stefania Sandrelli) chooses the best "endowed" man (Raúl) to use as a model for the advertising campaign of the Sanson underpants. After a number of shots of women working in the factory, the film moves to the company's headquarters and we see Conchita in total control of the narrative space, moving across the room as she is followed by the camera and her male advisers to whom she explains her marketing strategy: "I won't tire of saying . . . Who buys men's shorts? Women do. And a good basket sells." The following shot is a close-up of a man's crotch in blue underpants. A male voice asks: "Name?" to which the faceless man replies "Raúl González." The viewer of a video camera is visible in the shot and as the camera tilts up and pulls back we see the face of the protagonist, Raúl, as his image gets recorded by a video camera carried by an anonymous man. The shot concludes with the camera moving away from Raúl, who follows its movement (somewhere lower and to his left) with his eyes. The next shot reveals that Raúl is part of a line-up of men in underpants being questioned by the video operator, who moves his camera from man to man and from crotch to face. As the image of the face of a third man in close-up concludes the shot, the film cuts to a television screen that displays not his face but his crotch intensely inspected by Conchita. The scene concludes with a close-up of her face looking at the screen as the "audition" continues off frame.

In this scene Conchita's control over men is made explicit and is expressed on many levels. She runs the factory and thus controls not only production but also the process of decision making. She uses her power over her male employees to stage and control the impressive line-up of men—both the cameraman and the men on display are at her control, and in this sense, she controls the whole field of vision (the viewing, recording and display of the images). In the process she reduces the male protagonist to a faceless crotch, an object not only of her look, but also in a literal sense as the best basket to be used for the promotion of her products. Ironically, men are not even considered as the buyers of these products, as the promotional images are aimed at women. Finally, the last shot lingers on Conchita's face as she expresses curiosity and pleasure in what she sees, legitimizing, thus, both her active control of the image and the desire involved in the process.

Furthermore, the films offer sharp and humorous parodies of the invariably failing attempts of the men to define themselves in terms of a masterful, controlling and hyperbolic masculinity. In *Jamón,*

jamón, Raúl's attempt to stage a nocturnal bullfight in which he and his friend will fight the bull "naked and with a hard on" ends in total disarray being chased by the caretaker, and they run naked and with sore feet to Silvia (Penélope Cruz) for protection and comfort. *La teta y la luna* shows Maurice trying to compensate for his sexual impotence by his tremendous farting abilities, Stallone dreaming of a Californian lifestyle and Miguel expressing his passion for Estrellita through moronic and repetitious flamenco singing.

Huevos de oro, however, is by far the richest source of representations of failed hyper-masculinity. The film centers on Benito's (Javier Bardem) ambition to build the highest tower in Benidorm, a project that ends in multiple disaster, with the hero temporarily paralyzed and permanently impotent. Benito's desperate efforts to obtain and assert masculine power are directed towards the acquisition of material wealth and sexual mastery of the women in his life. The hyperbolic, consumerist nature of his ambitions lends itself to scenes in which the spectacle of his hyper-masculinity is juxtaposed with actions that clearly lack in substance. This is often articulated in terms of obvious excess in the *mise-en-scène* that provides the background for his actions. The apartment where he meets Claudia (Maribel Verdu) for their erotic encounters is decorated from top to bottom in lurid shades of red, lit with stroboscopic disco lights, and features in the center of the living room a sofa in the shape and color of an enormous mouth. In the middle of this "cave" that exhumes passion, sitting on the sofa with Claudia, Benito's sexual pride suffers severe blows as his suggestion to tie Claudia up is met with rejection and when he anxiously commands her to "relax" she replies: "I can't if you talk." The emotions involved in their lovemaking are constantly expressed in clichés heavily informed by either pornography or consumerism.

This play between form and content, artificiality and reality provides an alternative, camp definition of Benito's masculinity. In a pivotal scene of the film Benito holds a roof garden party, during which he hopes to launch Claudia's career as an actress. The American Wolberg (Thomas Lusth), chosen as the male lead, performs bodybuilding poses throughtout the party, first next to Benito and later next to Claudia. Benito, dressed in swimming costume, leopard skin jacket, red fez, with gold chains on his chest and a Rolex on each hand, gets increasingly nervous and jealous of Wolberg's physical perfection and exhibitionism. When the latter performs a karaoke version of "Only You" to the admiring Marta (Maria De Medeiros) and Claudia, Benito becomes enraged. He grabs the microphone and confronts the American with a karaoke performance of his signature song, the Julio Inglesias hit "Por el amor de una mujer." As he stands next to the television screen that displays the words of the song and the accompanying images, he offers the spectacle of his body and the passion of "his" song as the self-evident proof of his superior Spanish masculinity, oblivious to the camp absurdity of his image.

This is just a singular instance of what is one of the defining characteristics of the Iberian trilogy—the play between symbolic representations of an absolute, idealized, all-powerful, controlling masculinity and the manifestations of the real masculine identities of the male heroes. As the symbols of hyper-masculinity offer the back-drop against which the actions of the characters are measured, fail-ure is always guaranteed and becomes a rich source of comedy. In this sense, the films are extremely lucid demonstrations of Lacan's suggestion that the phallus is an unattainable ideal that is always beyond the reach of specific articulations of male identity.[28]

The above discussion suggests that the films of the Iberian trilo-gy undertake a successful critique of traditional models of dominant masculinity. However, this will to deconstruct male power is not consistent, as the regime of representation of female sexuality and of the female body is clearly structured in ways that conform rather than challenge male fantasies of mastery, control and objectification. A clear indication of the films' determination to have it both ways is offered in the brief shot that follows the opening scene of mock bull-fighting in *Jamón, jamón*. The display of childish but undoubtedly phallic masculinity is followed by the close-up of a power-tool, a sharp blade that cuts through sheets of white cloth, operated by a woman's hand (as the bright red nail varnish suggests). The symbol-ic castration clearly suggested by the editing is nevertheless dis-avowed by the fetishistic representation of the hand. As the blade softly moves to the right of the frame and the camera gently pans with it we notice that two of the fingers are clad in shiny, metallic armour. Later in the scene, an identical shot of the hand and the blade is shown intercut with close-ups of the face of its owner, who is revealed to be Silvia. As the camera slowly tilts down to visually link the face and the hand, it fully explores her body and constructs it as the object of erotic contemplation—in a dramatic shift of power, the symbolic castration is replaced by a fragmented, fetishized image of the female body.

This is emblematic of the way in which all three films treat the female body. There are numerous scenes and shots that blatantly objectify women and in the process not only align the "look" of the camera with male spectatorial positions and pleasures but often verge on the pornographic. While the films' narratives seem to attribute such representations to the entrapment of the male characters within reified discourses of sexuality, they also wholeheartedly relish the objectification of the female body. Indicative of this tendency is the discrepancy between the verbal discourse that Tete's narrative provides in *La teta y la luna* and the images of the film: while the former utilizes a pre-adolescent vocabulary preoccupied with notions of nurturing, the latter offers unambiguous fetishistic sexual representations.

Regarding *Jamón, jamón*, Marsha Kinder suggests that ". . . this parodic fast-paced melodrama and its hyperplotted narrative are driven by female desire,"[29] namely, that of the powerful matriarch Conchita. It is important, however, to note that her desire is not only defined in relation to the phallus but that the narrative progressively diminishes her power. While Raúl's masculinity is initially just a basket that sells her products, he later becomes functional, as he seduces first Silvia and then Conchita herself, who eventually surrenders control and becomes enslaved to her obsession for him. In this case, as in all three films, the deconstruction of dominant Spanish masculinity does not entail a reversal or a transgression of the uneven power relations between men and women and it is, thus, only a limited critique of patriarchal structures.

Similarly, the critique of the family that the Iberian trilogy undertakes is poignant but extremely narrow. The failure of the male heroes to live up to the impossible phallic standards that the films set up for them leads to the destruction of any meaningful alternatives. Even in *La teta y la luna*, where the narrative seems to suggest that Tete overcomes his jealousy and anxiety as the family's harmony is reinstated, the resolution of the films depicts Tete regressing to an age of breast-feeding in an imaginary triangle with Estrellita and his mother (Laura Mana) that excludes both his father (Abel Folk) and his baby brother. But, as is the case with the deconstruction of masculinity discussed earlier, the destruction of patriarchal structures that the films envisage does not have any emancipatory effect for the women.

The ending of *Jamón, jamón* is particularly illustrative of this. As the film moves towards the climactic fight between Raúl and Jose Luis (Jordi Mollá), the female characters seem to lose all control over their actions and emotions, which become increasingly dominated by men. First Silvia becomes inexplicably attracted and attached to her lover's father Manuel (Juan Diego), and then Conchita surrenders herself to Raúl, trying to buy his love by offering him a Mercedes. The final sequence of the film has all the elements of tragedy: passion, conflict, death, mournful music and choreographed, immobile groupings of despairing characters. The display of raw masculinity in the deadly fight between Raúl and Jose Luis, motivated by and carried out in the name of phallic power, is thus shown to have tragic consequences. The realization of male destiny brings destruction and death. But the film is ambiguous about what is the possible cause for such a tragic mess, as male access to power is repeatedly limited by the film's deconstructive images and, more importantly, through the presence of strong women.

The last two shots of the film feature all the main characters in a tableau of suffering as the sun sets and a flock of sheep surrounds them. In placing the characters against the landscape of Los Monegros these shots evoke memories of the opening shots. But the difference between the two and the transformation involved are significant. The display of a caricature of Spanish masculinity that opens the film is clearly contrasted with the tragic spectacle of doomed relationships, personal failure and profound unhappiness that engulf everybody at the end. The parody of the bulging shorts and the critique of phallic power that the film initiates is concluded with motionless bodies frozen in incomplete (and impossible) embraces, with the women as the most tragic figures. Conchita holds in her arms Raúl who killed her son; Carmen (Anna Galiena) caresses the dead body of Jose Luis; and Silvia is offered the affection of Manuel. Here, like in the collapsing human towers of *La teta y la luna*, the failure of men to realize their phallic destiny brings everybody else tumbling down and leaves the men and women in a mess.

The critique that the Iberian trilogy undertakes is seriously limited by the inability of the films to perceive and articulate a holistic view of masculinity and the family that fully takes into consideration the power structures that underlie representations of gender. Similarly, Melina Mercouri's star image and the alternative pleasures of *La Cage aux folles* exist within frames of reference that restrict and compromise their radical potential. All three case studies, however, offer examples of cinematic constructions of gender and sexuality that are at least as complex and ambivalent as those routinely explored by film theorists in the context of Hollywood cinema.

Notes

1. Dimitris Eleftheriotis, "Questioning totalities: constructions of masculinity in the popular Greek cinema of the 1960s," *Screen*, vol. 36, no. 3, 1995.
2. For a dicussion of relational approaches to gender and sexuality see Andrea Cornwall and Nancy Lindisfarne, "Dislocating masculinity: gender, power and anthropology," in Andrea Cornwall and Nancy Lindisfarne (eds), *Dislocating Masculinity: Comparative Ethnographies* (London and New York: Routledge, 1994).
3. Sara Delamont, *Appetites and Identities: An Introduction to the Social Anthropology of Western Europe* (London and New York: Routledge, 1995), p. 140.
4. Marcia Landy, *Italian Film* (Cambridge: Cambridge University Press, 2000), pp. 206–7.
5. Marsha Kinder, *Blood Cinema: The Reconstruction of National Identity in Spain* (Berkeley, Los Angeles and London: University of California Press, 1993).
6. Barry Jordan and Rikki Morgan-Tamosunas, *Contemporary Spanish Cinema* (Manchester and New York: Manchester University Press, 1998), p. 112.
7. Landy, op. cit., p. 207.
8. Yiannis Soldatos, *Istoria tou Ellinikou Kinimatografou (History of Greek Cinema)*, vol. 1. (Athens: Aigokeros, 1988), p. 180, my translation.
9. Stamatiou quoted in Soldatos, ibid, p. 181.
10. Sara Delamont, op. cit., p. 189.
11. Melina Mercouri, Mexico City, July, 1982, World Conference on Cultural Policies,organized by UNESCO.
12. Melina Mercouri, Speech to the Oxford Union, Oxford, June 1986.
13. Gianni Rondolino (ed), *Catalogo Bolaffi del cinema italiano 1978/1979* (Torino: Giulio Bolaffi Editore, 1979).
14. Susan Hayward, *French National Cinema* (London and New York Routledge, 1993), p. 30.
15. Tino Balio, "The art film market in the new Hollywood," in Geoffrey Nowell-Smith and Steven Ricci (eds), *Hollywood and Europe: Economics, Culture, National Identity 1945–95* (London: BFI, 1998), p. 64.
16. Joseph Garncarz, "Hollywood in Germany: the role of American films in Germany, 1925–1990," in David Ellwood and Rob Kroes (eds),

Hollywood in Europe: Experiences of a Cultural Hegemony (Amsterdam: University of Amsterdam Press, 1994), p. 132.

17. Susan Hayward, op. cit., attributes the phenomenal uninterrupted run of the film for nineteenth months in New York to its "camp" element.

18. Guy Austin, *Contemporary French Cinema: An Introduction* (Manchester and New York: Manchester University Press, 1996), p. 75.

19. Geoffrey Nowell-Smith with James Hay and Gianni Volpi, *The Companion to Italian Cinema* (London: Cassell and BFI, 1996), p. 117.

20. Judith Butler, *Gender Trouble: Feminism and the Subversion of Identity* (London and New York: Routledge, 1990).

21. Jordan and Morgan-Tamosunas, op. cit., p. 78.

22. Martin Dale, *The Movie Game: The Film Business in Britain, Europe and America* (London: Cassell, 1997) p. 327.

23. See for example, the reviews of the films in *Sight and Sound*, vol. 3, no. 6 (June 1993), vol. 4, no. 7 (July 1994) and vol. 6, no. 7 (July 1996); Jordan and Morgan-Tamosunas, op. cit.; Marsha Kinder, "Spain after Franco," in Geoffrey Nowell-Smith (ed), *The Oxford History of World Cinema* (London and New York: Oxford University Press, 1996); Celestino Deleyto, "Motherland: space, femininity, and Spanishness in *Jamón, Jamón*," in Peter William Evans (eds), *Spanish Cinema: The Auteurist Tradition* (Oxford: Oxford University Press, 1999).

24. This comes from Jose Arroyo's unpublished paper on Javier Bardem delivered in May 2000 at the University of Glasgow as part of the *Identities* series of seminars; for a discussion of Javier Bardem's star image see also Santiago Fouz-Hernández, "All that glitters is not gold: reading Javier Bardem's body in Bigas Luna's *Golden Balls*," in Rob Rix and Roberto Rodriguez-Saona (eds), *Spanish Cinema: Calling the Shots* (Leeds: Trinity and All Saints, 1999).

25. "Notes on the project by Bigas Luna," on the cover of the video of the film, Tartan Video, 1993.

26. Jane Tompkins, *West of Everything: The Inner Life of Westerns* (Oxford and New York: Oxford University Press, 1992), p. 74.

27. Steve Neale, "Masculinity as spectacle," *Screen*, vol. 24, no. 6, p. 8.

28. Jacques Lacan, "The mirror stage as formative of the function of the I," in Jacques Lacan, *Écrits: A Selection* (London: Tavistock, 1977).

29. Kinder, "Spain after Franco," op. cit., p. 601.

8 EXHIBITION: THE APPARATUS MEETS THE AUDIENCE

THIS CONCLUDING CHAPTER focuses on the much neglected concept of film exhibition. An initial historical outline of the theorization of spectatorship in Anglo-US film studies will demonstrate that the dominant theoretical models of the 1960s and 70s (apparatus and text-based theory) not only overlooked the social construction of the audience but also depended on a certain type of exhibition practice that was thus defined as universal and normal. While the political and theoretical questioning of such models led to detailed studies of spectators as social subjects relating in more complex and active ways with the text and the apparatus, there was precious little consideration of the actual organization of the viewing experience around the venue. In both cases, albeit in varying degrees, exhibition is "bracketed out."

Popular European (and other) films, however, were (and still are) shown and viewed in a variety of ways, often in conditions that contrast dramatically with those taken for granted by the dominant models. I shall consider in detail one of those "deviant" practices, the open-air cinema, in the specific context of Greek cinema in the 1960s, in order to investigate the complex ways in which the venue relates to both the texts exhibited and the audiences attending.

A film that represents a viewing experience comparable to that of the Greek open-air cinema is *Nuovo Cinema Paradiso* (Giuseppe Tornatore, Italy/France, 1988) despite its geographically, culturally and historically different setting. I shall analyze the film in terms of its perception and celebration of attending and viewing films. I shall identify and explore two types of "cinéphilia" that inform the sensibility of the film: one that involves a passion for cinema perceived as a "text-delivering apparatus" and another that is structured around the pleasures of communal viewing. I shall argue that the two types of cinéphilia are hierarchically perceived and represented by/in the film and that the terms of such hierarchy relate on the one hand to theoretical models of spectatorship and on the other to perceptions of the "essence" of cinema that are specifically European. In the final section of the chapter I shall examine how the recent crisis around exhibition has forced pan-European organizations and bodies to rethink cinema as an institution, and has led to surprising conclusions that seem to contradict the rhetoric that informs dominant definitions of European cinema.

The Viewing Experience in 1970s Film Theory

SPECTATORHSIP WAS ONE of the key concerns of 1970s film theory, informed by psychoanalysis, semiotics and Althusserian definitions of ideology. The investigation of how the spectator is constructed as a "subject of the text" was of paramount political and theoretical importance. Defining the spectator as a "position" constructed by the cinematic apparatus and/or the film as text, and describing the mechanisms that produce such positioning was one of the major theoretical achievements of the film theory of the period. Despite the obvious limitations of such definitions the usefulness of challenging an understanding of cinema that excluded or ignored the spectator is beyond any doubt. By deliberately attacking any notion of the spectator as a self-sufficient, unified entity existing in powerful autonomy outside the text, the theorists of the 1970s not only destroyed liberal understandings of art but also laid down the foundations of a conceptualization of the complex relationship between text and spectator. It is now canonical in film studies to attack the lack of flexibility of such theorizations, as well as the tendency to overlook the relevance of social, cultural and historical contexts and the condemnation of the spectator to occupy inescapable, ideologically suspect positions. Indeed, from the late 1970s an influential strand of film theory has developed around the interrogation and rejection of such models and the search for other more interactive frameworks.

While it is beyond the scope of the present work to explore these theoretical debates, it is crucial to identify the ways in which the early theoretical works defined the physical environment within which the relationship between texts and spectators occurs. This is particularly important given that the almost unchallenged dominance of such descriptions of exhibition venues is one of the most enduring legacies of the 1970s theory. The defining characteristic of these accounts of exhibition is their negativity. The structure of the film theatre is meaningful only in terms of its self-effacement as a dark, silent and non-descript background that does not interfere with the intense, all-absorbing, one-to-one relationship between spectator and screen. A standard move in many of the pioneering works of the 1970s involves the justification of the exclusion of any physical reality external to that relationship.

In the extremely influential essay "Ideological effects of the basic cinematic apparatus," Jean-Louis Baudry established the classic comparison between Lacan's account of the "mirror stage" and the viewing experience:

> The arrangement of the different elements—projector, darkened hall, screen—in addition to reproducing in a striking way the *mise-en-scène* of Plato's cave (prototypical set for all transcendence and the topological model of idealism), reconstructs the situation necessary to the release of the "mirror stage" discovered by Lacan . . . But for this imaginary constitution of the self to be possible, there must be—Lacan strongly emphasizes the point—two complementary conditions: immature powers of mobility and a precocious maturation of visual organization (apparent in the first few days of life). If one considers that these two conditions are repeated during cinematographic projection—suspension of mobility and predominance of the visual function—perhaps one could suppose that this is more than a simple analogy.[1]

A similar account of the viewing experience is offered by Christian Metz in his attempt to address the specific textuality of cinema in psychoanalytic terms. Contrasting cinema to theatre in terms of acting, Metz highlights the refusal of cinema actors to acknowledge the existence of viewers witnessing their performance. He likens the actors to fish in an aquarium, constantly observed and never looking back:

> In any case, there are fish on the other side as well, their faces pressed to the glass, like the poor of Balbec watching the guests of the grand hotel having their meals. The feast, once again, is not shared—it is a furtive feast and not a festive feast. Spectator-fish, taking in everything with their eyes, nothing with their bodies: the institution of the cinema requires a silent, motionless spectator, a *vacant* spectator, constantly in a sub-motor and hyper-perceptive state, a spectator at once alienated and happy, acrobatically hooked up to himself by the invisible thread of sight, a spectator who only catches up with himself at the last minute, by a paradoxical identification with his own self, a self filtered out into pure vision.[2]

This description of the spectator as "pure vision" in an environment that is only notable for its ability to reduce the physicality of the body and the interaction between viewers to an absolute minimum informs some of the most influential theoretical arguments of the 1970s: both Laura Mulvey[3] and John Ellis,[4] for example, offer accounts of the viewing experience that are strikingly similar. Of course film theory in recent years has paid particular attention to the relationship between texts and subjects and has challenged psychoanalytic models of spectatorship by asserting the importance of the historical, cultural and social specificities of both texts and subjects. There still remains, nevertheless, a lack of study into the actual viewing experience attentive to the different modes that have developed at different times and in different societies. Despite the extremely important theoretical rethinking of models of spectatorship it seems that the importance of the venue is largely ignored and the assumption persists that the viewing experience unfolds in the darkened, quiet immobility that Baudry, Metz, Mulvey and Ellis describe.

Of particular importance for the present argument therefore is Robert C. Allen's article "From exhibition to reception: reflections on the audience in film history,"[5] which proposes the opening up of spectatorship to a historical investigation of different viewing experiences. Crucial for Allen is "the enlarging of the notion of exhibition and the audience to encompass a more general historical concern with reception."[6] This involves the investigation of histories of modes and practices of exhibition as well as the revision of the concept of exhibition itself. Allen's argument is supported by examples of historical research of exhibition in the USA, but there are other cases of film scholarship that explore exhibition in the context of other cinemas.

Christopher Wagstaff, in his analysis of spaghetti western audiences, describes the different experiences offered by *terza visione* cinemas in Italy,[7] while Rosie Thomas notes that

> Indian cinema audience behaviour is distinctive: involvement in the films is intense and audiences clap, sing, recite familiar dialogue with the actors, throw coins at the screen (in appreciation of spectacle), "tut tut" at emotionally moving scenes, cry openly and laugh and jeer knowingly.[8]

It is important that both Wagstaff and Thomas, in their attempts to account for the specificity of their respective objects of study (the spaghetti western and popular Indian films), are confronted with the difficulty of explaining the peculiarity of the texts as well as of the viewing experience. The otherness of the forms of cinema that they study consists not only of strange texts but also of strange ways of relating to them. The fact that they both chose to refer to exhibition in order to map out the differences between their objects of analysis and the dominant paradigm is not a coincidence. Exhibition as a practice that is undertaken within specific spatial and temporal structures binds together texts and audiences, institutional and legal frameworks and entrepreneurial initiatives, universal pleasures and specific constituencies/communities, individual experiences and public sensibilities. As Allen suggests,

> [e]xhibition here designates the institutional and economic dimensions of reception—that is, the nature of the institutional apparatus under whose auspices and for whose benefit films are shown; the relationship between exhibition as that term has been used within the industry and other segments of the film business; and the location and physical nature of the sites of exhibition.[9]

In the expansion of the framework that defines the viewing experience, Allen also includes "audience," "performance" ("the immediate social, sensory, performative context of reception") and "activation" (how particular audience groups relate to texts). In the next section I shall consider in detail a specific venue, the Greek open-air cinema, and describe certain aspects of the viewing experience that it provided at a specific historical period.

Interruptions in the Open-air Cinemas: Greek Culture and Cinema in the 1960s

Venues are historically and culturally specific sites where texts meet audiences. The exploration of the open-air cinema, therefore, involves a close investigation of the structural characteristics of the venue as well as the films exhibited there, the audiences attending and the cultural context that they both inhabit.

Interruption is a term that describes very aptly the main characteristics of the viewing experience in the open-air cinema. It can be used to make sense of the textual practices of many of the popular Greek films of the period. It can function as a representational shorthand that accounts for the dynamics of the national film culture and more generally of the national culture of the period. Finally, it is also a term that illuminates the "subplot" of this section, namely the interruption of dominant theoretical paradigms of textuality and spectatorship through the consideration of the marginal case of the open-air cinema in Greece in the 1960s.

There are, therefore, three interrelated areas that I shall address in this section. First, I shall attempt a brief and tentative definition of the textual peculiarities of the popular Greek films of the period—while the open-air cinemas were by no means exclusively dedicated to Greek films, the majority of films exhibited there were Greek. Second, I shall examine closely the spatio-temporal structures of the open-air cinema and the place that the venue occupies within a genealogy of popular entertainment venues in Greece. Finally, I shall offer a brief and sketchy outline of the national film culture of the period in the context of the overall Greek cultural formation of the period.

Texts

BEFORE ATTEMPTING ANY kind of definition of the textual specificities of the popular Greek films of the 1960s, a word of caution is necessary. What follows is a simplified (even reductive) way of establishing a certain degree of homogeneity in the form of textual characteristics shared by the majority of the popular films of the period. Not all of the films share these characteristics, and these characteristics are not unique to Greek films. Furthermore, what makes them definitive of the textual specificity of Greek cinema depends on the frame of reference. While there are definite variations from what has been described as the "classical Hollywood text," there are startling similarities with other popular cinemas, most obviously so with Hindi melodramas.

David Bordwell, Janet Staiger and Kristin Thompson in their influential account of Hollywood cinema offer a way of analyzing the "classical style" in terms of devices, systems and relations between systems. The basic premise of their argument is that the classical style can be defined in terms of a very specific organization of these elements which in turn leads to a characteristic way in which time and space function within the narrative of the films. "In the Hollywood style," they assert, "the systems do not play equal roles: space and time are almost invariably made vehicles for narrative causality."[10] As

John Caughie explains, Hollywood cinema "develops a chronotope in which time is cut to the economy of narrative causation and motivation, and space is the scene of narrative action."[11]

The popular Greek films of the 1960s do not follow this model, despite the assumption of numerous Greek film critics and historians that they are nothing more than unsuccessful imitations of the classical Hollywood style. The fact that Greek critics consider Hollywood to be the relevant frame of reference for a critical approach to Greek cinema indicates the hegemonic position that Western forms of filmmaking occupy within the critical discourse around Greek cinema. It is indeed very surprising that the formal similarity between certain types of Greek popular films and films made in Turkey or India was never addressed by the critics.

The Greek film industry in the 1960s was organized around the mass production of low-cost films. The huge majority of the films made were melodramas and comedies—these two genres account for 90 percent of the overall production, which averaged around one hundred films per annum (an amazing figure for a country with a population of about 7.5 million at the time). Of these films around two thirds were comedies, by far the most popular genre. The following textual characteristics are more evident in comedies but they are also found in melodramas, musicals and "social" films. They can be seen as the natural outcome of a mode of production geared around the fast completion of inexpensive films and relying heavily for commercial profit on the talent and popularity of the actors:

- The frontal, flat and theatrical composition of shots.
- The extremely long takes—shots lasting over a minute were the norm.
- The static camera. This further intensifies the theatrical nature of many of the shots. Significantly, many of the popular stars of the period had previous or parallel careers in theatre.
- The organization of narrative space around tableaux rather than action.
- The minimal number of sets and locations used.
- Close-ups that tend to foreground comic/melodramatic performance rather than obey the logic of continuity editing.

More important for the purposes of my argument, however, are three additional characteristics of popular Greek films of the 1960s, which in different ways seem to interrupt the coherence, closure, singularity and self-sufficiency of the diegesis: stars, musical numbers and cultural referent.

The majority of popular Greek stars were cast in the same roles again and again. This was undoubtedly dictated by the needs of a rapidly expanding industry with limited resources. As a result some of the leading stars would shoot up to fifteen or twenty films a year. Their performance largely depended on the ability to "play themselves," establishing a powerful link between their star image, style of performance and the characters that they played. In this sense, actors were located simultaneously inside and outside the film, acting as characters but also performing with reference to other roles and other films. Indeed it is true that narratives were in many cases structured around stars rather than characters. Anecdotal evidence suggests that screenwriters were writing scripts only after the casting of certain key actors had been arranged. Characters in films were often named after the actors who played them and in many instances the names of the stars also appeared in the title of the film.

Songs, musical numbers and other "attractions" appear in almost every film made in the 1960s and the early 1970s irrespective of genre, director or production company. There is a standard narrative justification for the appearance of songs/numbers that cuts across genres. The protagonists visit a live music venue (restaurant, nightclub, cabaret or bar), where they watch and often participate in a performance. In most cases the narrative function of the songs is to reflect or heighten the psychological and emotional state of the protagonists. These gestures towards verisimilitude, however, are tokenistic, as the real function of the numbers is the exploitation of the commercial attraction of the singers/performers. This is often evident in the promotional material of the films, where the names of the performers are as prominent as the names of the actors themselves. In the credits (as well as the publicity of the films) the contributors of the spectacular aspects of the films (songs, musical numbers, dance, but also other so-called "attractions" such as trapeze acts and magical tricks) are clearly separated from the other cast and film crew. The numbers, therefore, not only interrupt the narrative flow of the film but also fragment the narrative space of the films through the presentation of popular singers/dancers/performers[12] whose cultural meaning and marketability derives from the non-diegetic world of popular entertainment. The film historian Yiannis

Soldatos is typical of the scornful approach of the critics to such interruptive practices. In *The History of Greek Cinema* and under the heading "musical intervals" he notes with obvious irony: "It is necessary for the commercial success of every film (not just melodramas) to have musical scenes each lasting at least five minutes."[13]

I have argued elsewhere that "the popular Greek films of the 60s are domestic in all senses of the word. They are made for domestic consumption, set in a Greek setting and are usually about domesticity—the troubles and the pleasures of life within the extensive network of family, friends and neighbours."[14] This domesticity, however, is not absolute, as it is interrupted by the constant reference to foreign stars, films and cultures. This is evident in many of the titles of the films: *You Are Better than Marlon Brando* (Orestis Laskos, Greece, 1963), *Doctor Zivegos* (Thanassis Vegos, Greece, 1965,, and the clear 007 references that appear in the titles of a number of films of the period: the film *Bald Agent* (Thanassis Vegos, Greece, 1969) actually opens with a scene from the James Bond film *Thunderball* (Terence Young, UK, 1965). The films of the 1960s demonstrate an awareness of the place that they occupy in an international film market. Furthermore, in many films the domestic world of the diegesis exists in a wider context of cultural practices and references. *In a Crazy, Crazy Family* (Dinos Dimopoulos, Greece, 1965), for example, there are unambiguous references to Italian culture (Venice offers the backdrop for two spectacular sequences of the film) and to English culture (one of the characters has lived in London and speaks English). English, French and Italian words and expressions are regularly used in the film and there are numerous references to Western youth culture, primarily through the portrayal of the younger characters. A recurring theme and concern of the period is modernization (in its economic, political, social and cultural dimensions) and its challenge to what is perceived to be traditional Greekness. The adjective *moderno* (modern) is widely used in the films of the 1960s as a designation of a Western (European or American) lifestyle that becomes increasingly influential and originates outside the Greek system of social and cultural values. The fact that the narrative resolution of many of the films denounces the foreign influences and that traditionalism emerges victorious against the advances of modernization is of crucial ideological and political significance. Equally important, however, is the mere presence of this wider context in the dramatic conflicts of the films as a point of reference and as an invitation to relativize cultural and ideological assumptions and positions.

Open-air Cinemas

APART FROM A handful of air-conditioned theatres in the big cities, open-air cinemas were almost exclusively the only available venue for a summer season that extended from May to September. The number of open-air cinemas in Greece rose sharply throughout the decade and peaked in 1969, when 559 cinemas operated in Athens. A measure of the incredible popularity of the venue is that in 1967, the attendance of open-air cinemas in Athens was over 31 million[15]—an average attendance of once a week. In reality the core audience (families, young people) visited the venue two or three times a week.

The films exhibited in the open-air cinemas were very much a repetition of those shown during the winter months, but they also included selected new releases (almost exclusively of Greek films) and a large number of older films (Greek and foreign). The viewing conditions and the program depended on the physical location of the venue and its place in the distribution network. Central venues were first run, state of the art cinemas and showed recent or new films; suburban ones offered basic facilities and relied on re-runs.

The nature of the viewing experience becomes evident through the consideration of some of the spatio-temporal structural characteristics of the venue. The interval in the projection initiated a hectic movement of people: refreshment sellers appeared, people went to the bar or the toilet, others left or arrived during the break. As a ticket was an admission to all the showings of the evening, spectators often decided to watch the film more than once, or from interval to interval rather than from beginning to end, or to arrive late and catch up with the beginning in the next screening. As most of the films on exhibition during the summer season were repetitions, spectators made informed decisions about what films and even what parts of the film to watch. The interval became a crucial point of reference, as memorable scenes or spectacular numbers were located in terms of the break and films were "mapped" accordingly. Cinemas advertised not only the time that the shows started but also the time of the break. Although the films were exhibited with the break at a pre-determined point, this was not in any sense recognized by the narrative structure of the films, as is the case with Hindi melodramas in which the break has a clear narrative function.[16] Although the intervals in the Greek films were not abrupt, they were more or less arbitrary in terms of their position in the narrative.

The bar/canteen became an important space during the interval: people met there and chatted, sometimes missing the beginning of the next part of the film. This led to more late arrivals, re-organization of the seating arrangements and arguments with annoyed spectators. The buildings adjacent to the cinema were usually the source of more interruptions, as lights came on in the balconies and disrupted the darkness of the screening. The nocturnal activities of the neighbors (visible through their windows or in their balconies) provided a regular source of distraction for the spectators. A cause of friction (and angry exchanges) between spectators and neighbours was the volume of the soundtrack of the film, with some screenings interrupted by the arrival of the police, who ensured that the level of the noise remained within acceptable limits.

The weather played an important role in the viewing experience: unexpected rain caused interruptions or cancellations of screenings, leading to complaints, arguments and refunds. On particularly hot evenings the location of the cinema became crucial, as venues situated in cool places were much preferred by audiences. It was often the case that just to be able to sit outside and enjoy a breath of fresh air and a cold drink was as important as the pleasures offered by the films.

Interruptions from the audience themselves included exclamations, whistling, clapping, laughing or sobbing, reciting well-known lines, and asking or answering questions on behalf of the characters. Members of the audience would regularly volunteer comments on the actions, appearance, intelligence or morality of the characters and the quality of the film. They would also get involved in dialogue with other members of the audience and sometimes into noisy arguments.

Cinema-goers were very knowledgeable about the kind of audiences that frequented various venues and made sophisticated choices in terms of this knowledge. A Greek comedy, for example, was best enjoyed in a third run cinema with the interrupting audience adding rather than detracting from the entertainment; a Hitchcock thriller, on the other hand, demanded a more central or serious venue. In decisions about what to watch, the venues and the audiences that they attracted were as important as the actual films that they exhibited.

It is clear from the above description that in the open-air cinemas of the 1960s the venues, the textual practices and the audiences of the popular Greek films are bound together in a mode of viewing which is not solitary and unified but open to interaction and interruption. Furthermore, the social, cultural and historical context is referenced, not only in terms of the actual viewing experience but also in terms of the films defining themselves in relation to other social and cultural spheres, other films, other cultures and other cinemas.

In Greece there is a strong nostalgia and romanticism involved in thinking of open-air cinemas as liberating spaces where spectators find a voice and passivity is overcome. The numerous popular songs of the 1980s and 1990s referring to open-air cinemas is one of the ways that this nostalgia is articulated in Greek popular culture and critical thinking. But the interrupting voices were usually male and the tone and content of the comments was often oppressively sexist, homophobic and racist. It is interesting to note at this point that after the decline of the popularity of the open-air cinemas this interruptive mode found an outlet in cinemas specializing in pornographic and exploitation movies.

The open-air cinema must be seen as an integral part of a long, and to some extent distinctly Greek, history of popular entertainment. Venues and forms of entertainment that precede and follow the heyday of the open-air cinema in the 1960s—such as the theatrical *revue*, the *café-aman*, various types of live music performance, cabaret shows, street performances, Karagiozis[17] shows and later television—all embraced interruption. Importantly, Karagiozis theatres, tavernas with musical programs and open-air cinemas were equally popular venues throughout the 1950s and shared many architectural features.

The link between Karagiozis and cinema is powerful and persistent in the history and historiography of Greek cinema. Karagiozis is, for cinema-goers and critics alike, not just another form of popular entertainment but a conceptual tool, a way of making sense of the history, the characters and the stories of Greek cinema. Crucial here, however, is the link between Karagiozis theatres and open-air cinemas as venues. In the late 1950s and early 1960s many Karagiozis theatres doubled as open-air cinemas, and in the later part of the 1960s most of them actually converted to open-air cinemas. In Karagiozis shows interruption was an essential feature of the performance: the three-act plays used the intervals imaginatively (to involve the spectators in playing games or even present local singers) while the performers encouraged dialogue with the audience during the performance.

Interruption in performance, text and viewing experience, however, is an important structural characteristic common to most popular forms of entertainment. In a different context John Caughie describes mainstream Hollywood cinema as being "out of line" as "a rupture within the generic tradition of the popular novelistic form"[18] in terms of its uninterrupted singularity and coherence. Clearly this was not the case with Greek popular cinema—the latter is firmly placed within a continuum of Greek popular forms that embraced and exploited interruption.

It is particularly important that Caughie's theorization of interruptions is situated in the context of television viewing. The decline of Greek popular cinema in the 1970s can be understood in terms of the similarity between the television and the open-air cinema viewing experiences. A historical peculiarity of Greece as a European country is that the networking of television on national level did not begin until 1969–70 and was only completed in around 1972–73. There are, nevertheless, specific aesthetic, cultural and sociological reasons for the decline of film audiences in Greece that go beyond the mere arrival of the technology of television. Early Greek television offered a six-hour daily program consisting mainly of news, soaps, musical programs and chat shows. The program content of early television revolves around themes and forms borrowed directly from the popular cinema of the 1960s, and the viewing of television structured around interruptions offered an experience very similar to that of the exhibition of popular films in the open-air cinemas. Furthermore, the domesticity of the family viewing of television is not unlike the contextual, interactive mode of spectatorship in the open-air venues. But the decline of cinema-going is also closely linked to the process of modernization of Greek society that started in the 1950s and 1960s and accelerated considerably in the 70s and 80s and, as discussed earlier, informs the ideological conflicts of many of the films of the 1960s. Crucially, modernization in the Greek context involves a progressive weakening of the role of the extended family and the neighborhood and the emergence of the nuclear family as the basic social unit.

National Culture

THE TERM INTERRUPTION can also be used on a more general level to describe the Greek cultural formation of the period. The 1960s are characterized by a rethinking of popular culture marked by an intensive activity of border crossing of two kinds.

The first refers to an internal border and it is expressed in terms of a re-negotiation of the relationship between high art and popular culture. The most obvious examples are in popular music, where the work of Mikis Theodorakis and Manos Hatzidakis combined the internationally acclaimed, "modernist" poetry of George Seferis, Odisseas Elitis, Nicos Gatsios and Yiannis Ritsos with traditional musical forms. Equally important is the rediscovery and appreciation of various popular and often marginalized forms such as the *rebetika* in music, the paintings of Theofilos, the writings of Makrigiannis, and the elevation of Karagiozis into the status of official cultural heritage.

At the same time, the cultural sphere is marked by an intense internationalization, which is manifested by the strong public interest in world-wide popular cultural production going well beyond the obvious instances of Hollywood cinema and rock and roll music. A few arbitrary and selective examples illustrate the point:

- The emergence of magazines (such as *Vendetta*, *Romanzo*, *Domino*, *Pantheon*, *Fantasio*) covering at length foreign popular entertainment news, as well as the popularity of children's fiction magazines (such as *The Young Hero*, *The Young Serif*, *The Young Superman*, *Gaur Tarzan*) which were structured around the fantastic adventures of young Greeks around the world.
- The star status that Italian singers/actors such as Al Bano, Romina Power, Adriano Celedano enjoyed in Greece, a measure of which is provided by the fact that the annual Italian music festival of San Remo was transmitted live on Greek radio.
- The huge success of the comedies of the Sicilian duo Franco Franchi and Ciccio Ingrassia which were generally considered unexportable beyond the South of Italy.
- The extremely popular serialization of Wilkie Collins's *The Woman in White* by Greek radio; fifteen minute long episodes were broadcast daily for over three years.
- The star status of the Turkish singer and actress Hulya Kocyigit whose films were massively imported in the 1960s.

- The popularity of Hindi melodramas and of stars such as Nargis and Madhubala—one of the most commercially successful popular songs of all time is dedicated to the latter and sung by the "king" of popular music Stelios Kazantzidis.
- In general the fascination with Indian popular music (familiar to the public through the movies) and the circulation of hundreds of Indian songs with Greek lyrics.

It is particularly interesting that such an opening to foreign cultural forms takes place in a period when the domestic cultural industries are particularly strong. In 1970 Greece imported over 700 films (of which 50 were Turkish and 120 Italian) while at the same year it produced 112 films.[19] This strongly suggests that for a brief period of ten to fifteen years Greek culture had the confidence to open itself up to what was perceived to be a non-threatening international context. This led to the production of a phenomenal variety of cultural forms offering numerous competing models of national identity. This should not be interpreted as a totally polyphonic or even democratic formation: homophobia, racism and sexism were deeply rooted within many cultural forms and profoundly so in the popular Greek films of the 1960s. It is fair to say, however, that the 1960s were a period marked by considerable mobility and flexibility in cultural production. The anarchic culture was certainly a contributing factor to the crisis of political legitimacy in the period. That the answer to the political crisis took the form of a brutal and paranoid nationalistic dictatorship is a testimony to the inability of this remarkable cultural formation to perceive itself in political terms. The destabilizing potential of such a formation was fully understood by the propaganda instruments of the dictators who launched massive (but largely ineffective) campaigns to "purify" Greek culture.

Interruption is a useful way of thinking about texts, modes of exhibition and the socio-cultural context of Greek cinema in the 1960s. However, the critical value of the term is parasitic, depending for its currency on models of textuality, spectatorship, national culture and identity insensitive to difference. The peculiar cultural formation of Greece in the 1960s, as well as the films and venues that are integral parts of this formation, merit a definition that involves more positive terms.

What defines the open-air cinema as well as the films and the general culture of the period is a "looking around," an awareness of surrounding spaces, people, cultures and discourses. What is particularly strange about the conventional venue, as described by Baudry et al., is that it tries so hard to deny the existence of anything outside the screen, any meaningful existence beyond the solitude of the subject. Similarly, the only looking around that hegemonic definitions of national culture and identity allow is a brief outward look that instantly divides the world in "us" and "them."

A clearly more interactive and productive looking around is evident in the Greek open-air cinemas of the 1960s, and it is enabled by a number of factors, some of which are peculiar to Greek cinema of the period, while some others are of more general nature: the genealogy of popular entertainment venues, the textual specificities of the films of the period, the fluid and outward-looking national cultural formation, the international character of the national film culture, the spatio-temporal structures of the venues.

A similar looking around informs the viewing experience as represented in *Nuovo Cinema Paradiso* that I shall discuss in detail in the following section. Although there is no intention to treat the film as a documentary on film exhibition it must be noted that it deals with the venue in a way that is consistent with historical accounts. For instance, Giovanna Grignaffini, notes that in Italy in the 1950s

> [d]ue both to the arrangement of halls and constant interruptions in the flow of images as the audience continually moved about and changed places in the rituals of communication that took place during screening, viewing was subject to a series of intrusions and interferences by the real world that made distraction a significant part of the experience of going to the cinema and rather similar to watching television.[20]

Finally, in terms of methodology, the close consideration of a venue (the open-air cinema) as a conceptually expanded form of exhibition brings to the critical attention this looking around. A discussion of venue interrupts the completeness and unity of the text by asserting the temporal and spatial structures that operate parallel to those of the text, and opens the theorization of the viewing experience to social and cultural spaces outside the text and even beyond the venue itself.

Cinéphilia in *Nuovo Cinema Paradiso*

NUOVO CINEMA PARADISO is a lamentation of the demise of Italian cinema. The death of the projectionist of the cinema of a small Sicilian town initiates a process of remembering in Salvatore (played by three different actors: Salvatore Cascio as a child, Marco Leonardi as an adolescent and Jacques Perrin as an adult) who nostalgically relives a childhood overwhelmingly obsessed with cinema. The film, made in 1988, became an international success (one of the most commercially successful Italian films ever) and won a long list of awards around the world. It is a pivotal film in the history of Italian cinema as it appears as the culmination (and the best-known example) of the thematic exploration of the glory and destruction of the Italian film industry that only a decade earlier was the healthiest in Europe. The list is impressive (but by no means exhaustive): *E la nave va/And the Ship Sails on* (Federico Fellini, France/Italy, 1983), *Ginger e Fred/Ginger and Fred* (Federico Fellini, Italy, 1986), *Intervista* (Federico Fellini, Italy, 1987), *Good morning Babilonia/Good Morning Babylon* (Paolo and Vittorio Taviani, Italy/France, USA, 1987), *Splendor* (Ettore Scola, France/Italy, 1988), and after 1988 *Ladri di saponette/The Icycle Thief* (Maurizio Nichetti, Italy, 1989), *Caro diario/Dear Diary* (Nanni Moretti, France/Italy, 1994), *L'uomo delle stelle/The Star Maker* (Giuseppe Tornatore, Italy, 1995).

The thematic preoccupation of the Italian filmmakers of the period with cinema itself as well as with its relationship to the all-conquering television is well established and remarked,[21] usually in relation to the rapid decline in number of films produced and attendance at the cinema since the mid 1970s. While 230 films were made in 1975, the number for the rest of the 1970s and 1980s fell to around 100–120. The fall of attendance was even more dramatic: the 544.4 millions of 1974 is reduced to 241.9 millions in 1980 and to 90.5 millions in 1990.[22] Although the downward trend in attendance was not reversed until the late 1990s it is probably the case that the tremendous success of *Nuovo cinema Paradiso* initiated a series of Italian produced or co-produced films with impressive international box office returns; *Mediterraneo* (Gabriele Salvatore, Italy, 1991), *Il postino* (Michael Radford, Italy/France/Belgium, 1994) and *La vita é bella/Life Is Beautiful* (Roberto Benigni, Italy, 1997) are the obvious examples. Perhaps the ultimate irony about *Nuovo Cinema Paradiso* is the fact that while the film mourns the waning of the importance of cinema in

Italy it also signals the arrival of a new wave of Italian films with the potential to reach world-wide audiences.

For the purposes of this chapter, however, the film's manifest cinéphilia is crucial (the tagline was: "A celebration of youth, friendship and the everlasting magic of the movies") in that it not only informs its emotional appeal but also offers a powerful description of what cinema itself is. The passionate love of cinema that the film demonstrates necessarily involves a thorough investigation of the essence of the object of love. The film is biographical, with its narrative exploring the life of Salvatore, whose involvement with cinema encompasses many of its institutional aspects: Salvatore as spectator, projectionist, amateur filmmaker and established producer/director. In this sense the story of Italian cinema and the story of the man are interdependent, inextricably linked by the narrative and interlocked in an exchange of cultural values and meanings.

The film also involves an interplay between the present and the past, the latter divided into two different periods: the late 1940s (Salvatore's childhood) and the mid 1950s (Salvatore's adolescence). The temporal tension between past and present, apart from establishing an inescapable mood of nostalgia, also introduces a series of binaries worked into the text that define the personal conflicts of the hero: past/present, south/north (while Rome is difficult to view as "north" in geopolitical terms it is emphatically so in terms of film culture), traditional/modern, childishness/maturity, poverty/wealth, community/individual.

The same binaries map two connected but distinct "loves of cinema," two types of cinéphilia, or, perhaps more accurately, two different aspects of the film's cinéphilia. On the one hand, the film revolves around Salvatore's fascination with cinema as text as well as with the apparatus that delivers it. This involves the fetishization of the films projected in the cinema (a theme of the film is the citation by Alberto (Philippe Noiret) and Salvatore of lines from films), the obsession with the actual materiality of the film as a medium (the young Toto stores fragments of celluloid and re-enacts scenes from films by holding them against the light of a lantern), the projector (Toto's ambition is to become a projectionist) and the actual making of a film (the amateur films that the young Toto makes and the "proper" films that he makes as a successful producer/director).

On the other hand, some of the most memorable moments of the film offer a celebration of cinema as a shared, communal and interactive viewing experience. Numerous members of the audience are identified with their mannerisms studied and their personalities placed in relation to other spectators. Furthermore, the film constructs the viewing experience as substantially integrated with the everyday life of the community of Giancaldo. Indeed the spectators' visit to the cinema is not necessarily an act of withdrawal to a sphere of specialized activity; sleeping, flirting, making love, having arguments and fights, breastfeeding and even dying are all activities that the venue accommodates. Within this kind of cinéphilia the presence of the audience in their messy interaction is a rich source of pleasure and as important as the film itself. The predictability of the spectators is compared to the predictability of the films in the scene when the audience recites the characteristic line ("I will make mincemeat of you"), quoting not of a film star but of a rudely awakened spectator. Here spectatorial participation constructs an idiosyncratic and equally pleasurable text that runs parallel to the film on display.

In many instances these two types of cinéphilia co-exist harmoniously and even complement each other. However, powerful oppositions between the two are also constructed both in terms of narrative structure and representation and in terms of its mode of address.

The splitting of the story time into past and present offers two hierarchically organized narrative enigmas. While the events of the past unfold in the extended flashbacks, a question set in the present dominates the progression of the narrative: "will Salvatore return to Giancaldo?" On the contrary the question "will the young Salvatore leave the village?" that pertains to the past is already resolved by framing the past by the present. In this sense Salvatore's departure is inevitable whereas the possibility of his return drives the narrative.

The film's reliance on flashback has a double function that adds complexity, as it gives the film its nostalgic tone and at the same time investigates the reasons that made Salvatore's departure inescapable. While the emotional power of the film comes from the return to the past it is also clear that Salvatore's social and personal progress depends on the determination to turn his back on the reassuring but backward and ultimately oppressive Sicilian community.

The narrative of the film, then, makes it clear that the pleasures of care-free youth and communal living, as well as the pleasures of Cinema Paradiso that accompany it, need to be firmly separated and controlled if personal and social maturity is to be achieved. The connection between the two is made powerfully by the film: the attachment to Cinema Paradiso and the projectionist's job are not considered to be adequately important for Salvatore's personal development and they have to be left behind together with his youth, family and friends. Alberto's advice is unambiguous: "Life isn't like in the movies. Life . . . is much harder. Get out of here. Go back to Rome. You're young. The world is yours." The hard but necessary decision to leave involves an understanding of the limitations of life in the village and the ability to see beyond what is readily available. Similarly Salvatore's real contribution to cinema is not as a projectionist but as an accomplished and successful producer/director.

The fascination with Cinema Paradiso and its viewing community (and consequently the kind of cinéphilia that it involves) is bound by limitations as a youthful, innocent phase that has ended, while on the other hand Salvatore's love for and involvement with cinema continues in his adult life. During his return visit to Giancaldo not only does he attend Alberto's funeral and the demolition of the cinema but also views in blissful isolation some amateur footage and later, in Rome, Alberto's last offering—the compilation of the censored fragments of the films shown in Cinema Paradiso. Unlike the cinema venue, films and the apparatus survive and are capable of offering a powerful experience attentive to "the everlasting magic of the movies."

Particularly important is the scene in which Alberto reflects a film out of the window of the projection booth and on to the wall of a house across the village square. The scene opens with chaotic shots of cinema-goers angry at the refusal of the owner to let them in. Up in the projection booth Alberto shows Salvatore how the light beam can be diverted to project the film outside the cinema in order to satisfy and pacify the crowd. Salvatore admires the tiny frame of the film as it travels on the uneven walls of the room, bending at the corners, caressing as it floats a variety of objects and surfaces, changing direction and shape, distorted but omnipresent, until it finally rests on the big exterior of a house. The rectangular improvised screen is disrupted by a balcony, and when the inhabitants of the house make an appearance they realize that they "are in a movie."

The scene clearly celebrates the dismantling of the fixed positioning of the apparatus, abolishing and transgressing in the process all the boundaries between inside/outside, private/public, subject/ object, screen/viewer, text/context, film/venue. Significantly, the overall tone of the scene is one of an extraordinary experience, a profoundly "magical" moment. Before the framed image begins its journey, there is a shot of the light beam with clearly visible glittering particles being intercepted (or caressed) by Alberto's extended hand as he says "Get ready . . . Abra cadabra . . . And we pass through walls."

It is worth considering for a moment what makes the projector's light beam such a recurring and enduring image encapsulating the magic of cinema—an image that surfaces in so many references to the cinema in film, constituting one of the most powerful signifiers of cinéphilia. The flickering, simmering light that emanates from the projector (a lion's mouth), in perpetual transformation as it is formed against the background of the auditorium, is a recurring visual theme of *Nuovo Cinema Paradiso*. The strange attraction that this image has offered for countless generations of cinema-goers can perhaps be understood in terms of the film's preoccupation with two types of cinéphilia. The extraordinary quality that the beam possesses is the ability to combine the fascination with the apparatus and the text with the material reality of the venue in one magical omnipotent signifier of the viewing experience. There is something of the magic of the apparatus in the apparent immateriality of the beam, in its ability to bridge the distance between projector and screen and to transform a tiny film frame into the dominating image displayed on the screen. On the other hand, what gives the beam its shape and form is the dust generated by the audience and the venue, a material testimony to the temporal and spatial specificity of the moment and place of projection that intersects with the abstract and detached generality of the text and the apparatus. It is an image that offers a composite sign of the ethereal and eternal qualities of cinema and of the uniqueness of the moment of viewing, of the textual and technological workings of the film and of the performative aspects of the projection.[23]

The scene from *Nuovo Cinema Paradiso* discussed here fetishizes this special, magical quality of the light beam and in this sense offers a moment when the two types of cinéphilia that inform the text work together in a holistic representation of what cinema is as well as of how we relate to it. However, the effect of this exceptional scene is considerably diminished by the narrative context that surrounds it, as the pleasure of the unbounded viewing experience is extremely short-lived. Alberto's transgressive act is destabilizing and dangerous—the ensuing fire not only destroys the theatre but also seriously injures the projectionist who loses both his job and his sight in the incident. Alberto's misfortune can be read as a punishment for his inability to control and contain the film-experience within the walls of the theatre, within the fixed positioning of the apparatus. In this scene the film foregrounds its ambiguity: while it celebrates a love of cinema that is firmly based on the interactivity of the viewing experience it also disavows it by treating it as a dangerous and impossible one time affair. It is significant that before Alberto commits his "crime of transgression" he refers to the viewers with obvious contempt: "A mob doesn't think. It has no mind of its own. Spencer Tracy said that in *Fury*." Mirroring apparatus theories of spectatorship, the film attempts to bracket out, to exclude the audience and the venue from the essence of cinema by constantly reminding us that the interactivity of the viewing experience (like Toto's childhood) must be tamed, restrained and ultimately negated.

Furthermore, the film's narrative is structured around lack, loss and unfulfilled desire. Toto's happiness is always incomplete, always missing something; not only because the film is addressing the lost past (and communal living), but also by offering a plethora of themes and images overwhelmingly determined by loss: Toto's missing father, the separation from Elena, the lack of love in his adult life, the missing kisses. In this sense the film adopts a mode of address and an emotive structure informed by "an Oedipal moment of lack, castration and desire" that John Caughie identifies as characteristic of a cinema (and by extension, of a cinematic viewing experience) that negates the possibility of interruption.[24] In other words, the film places its "heart" not in the love of a cinema of interruption, interactivity and "looking around" but in an all-absorbing (and perpetually incomplete) passion for the text and the apparatus.

Clearly, then, the film creates a hierarchy between the two types of cinéphilia: one is legitimate and everlasting, all-encompassing and worth dedicating your life to, the other is exciting and youthful but also immature and dangerous and needs to be controlled and contained. It is important to note, nevertheless, that the film is deeply ambiguous in its attempt to contain a type of cinéphilia that it also celebrates. Such ambiguity is also evident in representations of cinema and the cinematic experience offered by Italian films in the 1950s (the historical moment that *Nuovo Cinema Paradiso* examines). Francesco Casetti, in his study of "cinema in the cinema" in the 1950s, identifies as a defining characteristic of the cinéphilia of the period a similar tension to the one that informs *Nuovo Cinema Paradiso*. Casseti's examination of *Bellissima* (Luchino Visconti, Italy, 1951) and *La signora senza camelie* (Michelangelo Antonioni, Italy/France, 1952) identifies two types of engagement with cinema, two types of cinéphilia remarkably similar to those displayed in Tornatore's film. Casseti also identifies a movement between the two that he sees as paradigmatic of a redefinition of cinema, "a sort of exemplary journey in the course of which the ideas about cinema current in the fifties can be put on display."[25] A way of understanding this paradigmatic shift is in terms of

> [a] slide from considering the cinema as a social phenomenon, not without its negative attributes but nevertheless rooted in popular life (*Bellissima*), to a vision increasingly centered on the individual experience of someone who would like to be, has been, and to a degree still is, part of his surroundings (8½). In this movement the cinema loses its associations of an everyday and immediately accessible presence and becomes instead an event or a ritual with all the attributes of something exceptional . . . Behind this reversal of viewpoint, however, one feature remains constant: the suggestion that cinema has to overcome a series of obstacles in order to assert itself; or rather that in order to assert itself it needs to correct some important characteristic of itself. In this sense the idea that occupies the stage is that of a cinema which achieves itself "in spite of" certain countervailing factors—in spite of the artifice of fiction, in spite of the banality of much of the content, in spite of the laughter of unappreciative spectators, in spite of the difficulties of organizing the making of a film.[26]

It seems to me that both Casetti and *Nuovo Cinema Paradiso* describe a tension inherent in European notions of cinéphilia. While in the 1950s there is an absolute polarity, in the late 1980s the hierarchical structure of the binary becomes more ambiguous, allowing the subordinate term to surface nostalgically. But such a shift in the conceptualization of cinema makes inevitable a return to issues concerning definitions of European cinema.

The European Film Revisited

IN THE OPENING chapter of this book some consideration was given to various implicit or explicit attempts to define the distinctive characteristics of European cinema and this particularly elusive category "the European film." Perhaps a slight readjustment in the way the problem was approached is required. It seems to be the case that a more promising line of inquiry might involve not the search for European specificity in cinematic texts but in the way that Europeans define their relationship to cinema. In other words, not in a cinema that captures some mysterious essence of Europeanness but in terms of a hegemonic form of European cinéphilia that permeates a number of critical and theoretical discourses as well as policy-making rationales.

What Casetti analyzes and *Nuovo Cinema Paradiso* narrates is a key moment in the formation of a specific form of cinéphilia, which in the late 1940s and early 1950s established a firm grip on European thinking about cinema. Thomas Elsaesser locates this in France in the post-war period, and more specifically in the incredible international influence of *Cahiers du cinéma*.[27] The film criticism that the film journal developed is informed by a cinéphilia that established itself as the orthodox way of approaching and relating to cinema. There are several contradictions in the project that Elsaesser lucidly identifies, two of which are particularly relevant for the present argument. While the branch of criticism that was born out of such cinéphilia was uniquely European, the object of study (and "loved object") was American:

> after the Second World War a number of French cinéphile intellectuals . . . began to apply a highly literate sensibility and a sophisticated appreciation of aesthetic problems to a body of films (roughly the Hollywood output from 1940 onwards) which on the face of it appeared impressive mainly by its quantity.[28]

In the process the critics of *Cahiers du cinéma* transformed Hollywood cinema from a much-despised form of "mindless entertainment" to a highly respectable form of art. However, the elevation of popular culture into high art constitutes a fundamental ideological contradiction of such cinéphilia:

what gave *Cahiers du Cinéma* its impact and made it known abroad was the dedication with which its contributors put the prestige of French highbrow culture behind their enthusiasm for Hollywood. With benign self-confidence they made the cinema appear in almost every respect on an equal, if not superior footing with contemporary literature, and often enough with the great art of the past.[29]

One of the implications of the project of the French critics was the establishment of an exemplary way of relating to cinema that bears the marks of seriousness and uninterrupted attentiveness formerly reserved for experiencing traditional works of art. It establishes a relationship between Europeans and cinema that accords primacy to the text and to the discovery of its artistic merit through the educated eye of the cinéphile. Such conceptualization of the viewing experience sets the genuine cinéphile apart from the crowd and excludes any interactive and interruptive relationship with the venue and the audience. It is exactly this type of cinéphilia that informs the aggressive movement away from the everyday that Casseti identifies in relation to Italian cinema. In this sense, the more "audience and venue friendly" approach of *Nuovo Cinema Paradiso* is not a mere historical accident but relates to the unfolding crisis in the coherence of hegemonic European cinéphilia.

The assertion of a confident and elitist cinéphilia in the fifties takes place at the peak of cinema's popularity in Europe and functions as a mark of distinction that separates the cinéphile from the masses safeguarding at the same time the "art" status of cinema itself. The emergence of the specialized venue of the art-house cinema is a clear manifestation of such processes of exclusion on the level of exhibition. By the late eighties, nevertheless, audiences declined so much that the very survival of cinema (in any form) was at stake—the threat was no more of surrendering cinema to the unappreciative, ignorant masses but of the masses deserting cinema. Furthermore, the highly specialized and exclusive art-house (the natural habitat of the cinéphile) part of the exhibition sector was considered to be in remarkably good shape. *The White Book of the European Exhibition Industry* notes

[t]he good health of the Art and Experimental sector, which functions as a network of its own. Even if the fact that art-houses have become the main channel for European films is to be

deplored, one notices that Europe still boasts one group of exhibitors that have suffered little from the contraction of admissions. In certain countries, this sector even shows a potential for growth.[30]

The realization of the safety of the "art" sector and the weakening of the "commercial" sector are strong contributing factors in what appears to be a change of priorities around exhibition on the level of pan-European organizations. The MEDIA Salles initiative (the branch of the MEDIA programme of the European Union that aims to understand and strengthen the European distribution and exhibition sectors) is monitoring the state of the sector and is also attempting to redefine aims and objectives. The latter involves an abandonment of some of the fundamental assumptions about the relationship between Europeans and the cinema.

Forced by the inescapable pressures of the market, the rhetoric adopted by MEDIA Salles is in marked contrast with the sensibility of an elitist and exclusive form of European cinéphilia. Not only has "popularity" rather than "quality" now become the most-desired characteristic of European films, but even the category of European film is subjected to the scrutiny of cynical pragmatism:

> An effective European film policy must seek to support significant levels of economic activity in the European film industry and not only follow a cultural objective. The culturally-driven policy risks putting European film-makers into a niche position that will always make it difficult for them to reach a significant share of the cinema-going audience. A more commercially-driven policy would also support international, big-budget film making as long as there was a significant share of activities that were undertaken in Europe, or by Europe-based film-makers. In such a world, the nationality of the producers or the origin of finance would lose its over-riding importance as criteria for qualifying for European film support.[31]

Faced with the difficulty to justify such a radical change of political will and mode of approach, the policy-makers have been forced to abandon the rhetoric of the uniqueness and self-sufficiency of European culture and identity by redefining the European film, the category that they are supposed to protect and promote:

> The question of defining the origin of a film for the purpose of devising a support system—be it a quota or a subsidy—must first ask what the policy is trying to achieve. It hardly makes sense to support only films that are 100 per cent European. The European film industry does not need to consist of films that have only European themes or stories as their basis, a European producer, a European financier, a European production crew, and are shot in Europe . . . What a European film policy needs to achieve is an increased use of European inputs into mainstream films as well as specialist films, not any increase in 100 per cent European films with small budgets and little chance of popular success.[32]

It is important to note firstly that this pragmatism openly contradicts many of the cultural and political values attached to the "idea of Europe," and secondly that such astonishing revision of the definition of "European film" surfaces in the context of exhibition practices and policies. There seems to be a discrepancy between the discourse that informs the conceptualization of European culture and identity on the level of production (as discussed in Chapter 1) and that revolving around consumption. And while the difference in terms of rhetoric might seem relevant only within an academic discourse, there are specific practical developments that place the contradictions around Europeanness firmly in the public domain by a *de facto* challenge to the hitherto hegemonic cinéphilia.

Crucial here is the recent trend towards multiplex cinemas[33] that is heralded by MEDIA Salles as responsible for the improving attendance figures.[34] The multiplex, however, is a particularly problematic venue in terms of its obvious departure from the urban viewing experience that informs elitist cinéphilia. The latter revolves around a modernist sensibility that places the cinema and the magical encounters that it offers in the context of the modern city, unlike the multiplex which signals a "movement of cinemas to the outskirts . . ." with "the center of gravity of the exhibition industry . . . shifted to the outskirts."[35]

The structural changes in the exhibition sector, the abandonment of a specifically European form of cinéphilia and the rethinking of the identity and role of European film that it entails have thrown some of the categories that this book set out to investigate into an even deeper crisis. And while such developments are introduced through dubious economic and political reasoning they have clearly destabilized the hegemonic alignment of Europeanness with art cinema and have opened up possibilities of positive evaluation of and engagement with popular forms. What the discussion of open air cinemas in Greece and cinéphilia in *Nuovo Cinema Paradiso* has brought to our attention is the necessity to re-evaluate the viewing experience so that the emphasis is shifted away from the solitary, all-absorbing engagement with the text. Indeed, some of the "mysteries" that popular European films pose for Anglo-US film criticism might disappear within a framework that places proper attention on the interactive "looking around" that informs both their textuality and the historically specific conditions of viewing.

Notes

1. Jean-Louis Baudry, "Ideological effects of the basic cinematographic apparatus," in Leo Braudy and Marshall Cohen (eds), *Film Theory and Criticism: Introductory Readings* (Oxford and New York: Oxford University Press, 1999), pp. 352–53.
2. Christian Metz, "Story/discourse: notes on two kinds of voyerism," in Bill Nichols (ed), *Movies and Methods*, vol. II (Berkeley, Los Angeles and London: University of California Press, 1985), p. 548.
3. Laura Mulvey, "Visual pleasure and narrative cinema," *Screen*, vol. 16, no. 3, 1975; the analysis of the "pleasures" of cinema is supported by a description of the viewing experience that happens in darkness and isolation.
4. John Ellis, *Visible Fictions* (London: Routledge, 1984); in a work that explores cinema-going as a social practice, and in this sense is more sensitive to difference, the description of the theatre remains unrevised: "The audience is seated in rows, separated from each other to some degree, and the image is projected in near-darkness. This induces a particular kind of mental state in the commercial cinema viewer: a concentration of psychic activity into a state of hyper-receptivity . . . Sitting still in the dark has overtones of sleep and dreaming." op. cit., p. 40.
5. Robert C. Allen, "From exhibition to reception: reflections on the audience in film history," *Screen*, vol. 34, no. 1, 1990.
6. Ibid, p. 349.
7. Christopher Wagstaff, "A forkful of westerns: industry, audiences and the Italian western," in Richard Dyer and Ginette Vincendeau (eds), *Popular European Cinema* (London: Routledge, 1992).
8. Rosie Thomas, "Indian cinema: pleasures and popularity," *Screen*, vol. 26, nos. 3–4, 1985, p. 129.
9. R. C. Allen, op. cit., p. 349.

10. David Bordwell, Janet Staiger and Kristin Thompson, *The Classical Hollywood Cinema: Film Style and Mode of Production to 1960* (London and New York: Routledge, 1985), p. 6.

11. John Caughie, "Adorno's reproach: repetition, difference and television genre," *Screen*, vol. 32, no. 2, 1991, p. 140.

12. As well as the presentation of the venues themselves—this was a wide spread indirect form of advertising for restaurants, tavernas and nightclubs.

13. Yiannis Soldatos, *History of Greek Cinema*, vol. 2 (Athens: Aigokeros, 1989), p. 193; my translation.

14. Dimitris Eleftheriotis, "Questioning totalities: constructions of masculinity in the Greek popular cinema of the 1960s," *Screen*, vol. 36, no. 3, 1995, p. 238.

15. Data taken from Soldatos, op. cit.

16. Lalitha Gopalan, "The role of the interval in the Hindi film," unpublished paper presented at the Screen Studies Conference, University of Glasgow, July 1998.

17. Karagiozis shows were a form of shadow theatre probably introduced into Greek popular culture from Turkey. They were extremely popular throughout the first half of the twentieth century and the live performances featured Karagiozis as the central hero.

18. Caughie, op. cit., pp. 135–46.

19. Data from Unesco's *Statistics on Film and Cinema 1955–1977* (Paris: Division of Statistics on Culture and Communication, Office of Statistics, 1981).

20. Giovanna Grignaffini, "Female identity and Italian cinema of the 1950s," in Giuliana Bruno and Maria Nadotti (eds), *Off Screen: Women and Film in Italy* (London: Routledge, 1988), p. 118.

21. Marcia Landy, *Italian Film* (Cambridge and New York: Cambridge University Press, 2000), pp. 344–79; Pierre Sorlin, *Italian National Cinema 1896–1996* (London and New York: Routledge, 1996), pp. 144–72.

22. Data taken from Ginette Vincendeau (ed), *Encyclopedia of European Cinema* (London: Cassell and BFI, 1995).

23. Allen defines "performance" as a key component of the reception of a film: "By this [performance] I mean the immediate social, sensory, performative context of reception. We tend to talk of films being 'screened' as if the only thing going on in a movie theatre were light being bounced off a reflective surface," op. cit., p. 352.

24. Caughie, op. cit.

25. Franco Casetti, "Cinema in the cinema in Italian films of the fifties: *Bellissima* and *La signora senza camelie*," *Screen*, vol. 33, no. 4, 1992.

26. Ibid, p. 378.

27. Thomas Elsaesser, "Two decades in another country: Hollywood and the cinéphiles," in C. W. E. Bigsby (ed), *Superculture: American Popular Culture and Europe* (London: Paul Elek, 1975).

28. Ibid, p. 200.

29. Ibid, pp. 210–11.

30. *White Book of the European Exhibition Industry*, vol. 1 (electronic publication of MEDIA Salles, 1994), "Introduction".

31. Ibid, vol. 2, Chapter 3.1.

32. Ibid, vol. 2, Chapter 3.2.

33. Defined by the *1999 European Cinema Yearbook* (MEDIA Salles, 1999) as cinemas "with ≥ 8 screens" as opposed to the "megaplex" which is a cinema "with ≥ 15 screens".

34. See the *White Book of the European Exhibition Industry*, vol. 1, op. cit.

35. Ibid, Chapter 1.3.

Bibliography

Sitney P. Adams, *Vital Crises in Italian Cinema* (Austin: University of Texas Press, 1995)

Theodor Adorno and Max Horkheimer, *Dialectic of Enlightenment* (London: Allen Lane, 1973)

Robert C. Allen, *Vaudeville and Film 1895–1915: A Study in Media Interaction* (New York: Arno Press, 1980)

———, "From exhibition to reception: reflections on the audience in film history," *Screen*, vol. 34, no. 1, 1990

——— and Douglas Gomery, *Film History: Theory and Practice* (New York: Alfred A. Knopf, 1985)

Rick Altman, *Film/Genre* (London: BFI, 1999)

Benedict Anderson, *Imagined Communities: Reflections on the Spread of Nationalism* (London and New York: Verso, 1991)

Roy Armes, *The Ambiguous Image: Narrative Style in Modern European Cinema* (London: Secker and Warbug, 1976)

———, *French Cinema* (Oxford: Oxford University Press, 1985)

———, *Third World Film Making and the West* (Berkeley: California University Press, 1987)

Bill Ashcroft, Gareth Griffiths and Helen Tiffin (eds), *The Post-Colonial Studies Reader* (London and New York: Routledge, 1995)

Richard Astle, "*Seven Beauties*: survival, Lina style," *Jump Cut*, July 1977

Jacques Attali, "Hope borne on a trade wind," *The Guardian*, 8 September 1992

Bruce A. Austin, *Immediate Seating: A Look at Movie Audiences* (Belmont CA: Wadsworth, 1989)

Guy Austin, *Contemporary French Cinema: An Introduction* (Manchester and New York: Manchester University Press, 1996)

Mikhail Bakhtin, *The Dialogic Imagination: Four Essays by M. M. Bakhtin* (Austin: University of Texas Press, 1981)

Tino Balio (ed), *The American Film Industry* (Madison: University of Wisconsin Press, 1985)

———, "The art film market in the new Hollywood," in Nowell-Smith and Steven Ricci (eds), *Hollywood and Europe: Economics, Culture, National Identity 1945–95* (London: BFI, 1998)

Charles Barr, *Ealing Studios* (London: Cameron and Tayleur, 1977)

Roland Barthes, *Camera Lucida* (London: Flamingo, 1984)

Jean Baudrillard, *Simulations* (New York: Semiotext(e), 1983)

———, *America* (London: Verso, 1988)

Jean-Louis Baudry, "Ideological effects of the basic cinematographic appa-ratus," in Leo Braudy and Marshall Cohen (eds), *Film Theory and Criticism: Introductory Readings* (Oxford and New York: Oxford University Press, 1999)

André Bazin, "The western: or the American film *par excellence*," in André Bazin, *What Is Cinema?*, vol. 2 (Berkeley: *University* of California Press, 1971)

———, "The evolution of the western," in André Bazin, *What Is Cinema?*, vol. 2 (Berkeley: University of California Press, 1971)

———, Jacques Doniol-Valcroze, Pierre Kast, Roger Leenhardt, Jacques Rivette, Eric Rohmer: "Six characters in search of *auteurs*: a discussion about the French Cinema," in Jim Hillier (ed), *Cahiers du cinéma*, vol. 1 (London: Routledge, 1985)

Peter Beicken and Robert Philip Kolker, *The Films of Wim Wenders: Cinema as Vision and Desire* (Cambridge: Cambridge University Press, 1993)

Andrew Benjamin, *Art, Mimesis and the Avant-Garde: Aspects of a Philosophy of Difference* (London: Routledge, 1991)

Tim Bergfelder, "The Nation vanishes: European co-productions and pop-ular genre," in Mette Hjort and Scott Mackenzie (eds), *Cinema and Nation* (London and New York: Routledge, 2000)

Peter Besas, *Behind the Spanish Lens: Spanish Cinema under Fascism and Democracy* (Denver: Arden Press, 1985)

Homi K. Bhabha (ed), *Nation and Narration* (Routledge: London and New York, 1990)

———, *The Location of Culture* (London and New York: Routledge, 1994)

C. W. E. Bigsby, *Superculture: American Popular Culture and Europe* (London: Paul Elek, 1975)

David Bordwell, "The art cinema as a mode of film practice," *Film Criticism*, vol. 4, no. 1, 1979

———, Janet Staiger and Kristin Thompson, *The Classical Hollywood Cinema: Film Style and Mode of Production to 1960* (London: Routledge, 1994)

David Boswell, "Health, the self and social interaction," in Robert Bocock and Kenneth Thompson, *Social and Cultural Forms of Modernity* (Cambridge: Polity Press, 1992)

Pierre Bourdieu, *Distinction: A Social Critique of the Judgement of Taste* (Cambridge: Cambridge University Press, 1986)

John Brannigan, *New Historicism and Cultural Materialism* (London: Macmillan, 1998)

Timothy Brennan, "The national longing for form" in Bhabha (ed), *Nation and Narration* (Routledge: London and New York, 1990)

Gian Piero Brunetta, "The long march of American cinema in Italy from fascism to the cold war," in David Ellwood and Rob Kroes (eds), *Hollywood in Europe: Experiences of a Cultural Hegemony* (Amsterdam: University of Amsterdam Press, 1994)

Giulian Bruno and Maria Nadotti (eds), *Off Screen: Women and Film in Italy* (London and New York: Routledge, 1988)

Kristina Brunovska Karnick and Henry Jenkins III (eds), *Classical Hollywood Comedy* (London: Routledge, 1995)

Peter Bürger, *Theory of the Avant-Garde* (Manchester: Manchester University Press, 1984)

Victor Burgin, *The End of Art Theory: Criticism and Postmodernity* (London: Macmllan, 1986)

Edward Buscombe and Roberta E. Pearson (eds), *Back in the Saddle Again: New Essays on the Western* (London: BFI, 1998)

Judith Butler, *Gender Trouble: Feminism and the Subversion of Identity* (London and New York: Routledge, 1990)

Michael Cacoyannis, "A sense of belonging: an interview with Michael Cacoyannis," *Educational Broadcasting International*, vol. 11, no. 3, September 1978

Carmel Camilleri (ed), *Difference and Cultures in Europe* (Strasbourg: Council of Europe Press, 1995)

Noel Carroll, *Mystifying Movies: Fads and Fallacies in Contemporary Film Theory* (New York: Columbia University Press, 1988)

Erica Carter, James Donald and Judith Squires (eds), *Cultural Remix: Theories of Politics and the Popular* (London; Lawrence and Wishart, 1995)

Deborah Cartmell, I. Q. Hunter, Heidi Kaye and Imelda Whelehan (eds), *Trash Aesthetics: Popular Culture and its Audience* (London: Pluto Press, 1997)

Franco Casetti, "Cinema in the cinema in Italian films of the fifties: *Bellissima* and *La signora senza camelie*," *Screen*, vol. 33, no. 4, 1992

Catalogo Bolaffi del cinema italiano 1975/76 (Torino: Giulio Bolaffi editore, 1976)

Catalogo Bolaffi del cinema italiano 1978/79 (Torino: Giulio Bolaffi editore, 1979)

John Caugie (ed), *Theories of Authorship* (London and New York: Routledge, 1988)

———, "Adorno's reproach: repetition, difference and television genre," *Screen*, vol. 32, no. 2, 1991

———, "Becoming European: art cinema, irony and identity," in Duncan Petrie (ed), *Screening Europe: Image and Identity in Contemporary European Cinema* (London: BFI, 1992)

Gurinder Chadha, "Interview with Gurinder Chadha," *Sight and Sound*, vol. 4, no. 2, February 1994

Rowena Chapman and Jonathan Rutherford (eds), *Male Order: Unwrapping Masculinity* (London: Lawrence and Wishart, 1988)

Partha Chatterjee, *Nationalist Thought and the Colonial World: A Derivative Discourse* (London: Zed Books for United Nations, 1986)

Constance Classen, *Worlds of Sense: Exploring the Senses in History and Across Cultures* (London: Routledge, 1993)

Jean-Louis Comolli, Jean Domarchi, Jean-Andre Fieschi, Pierre Kast, Andre S. Labarthe, Claude Ollier, Jacques Rivette, François Weyergans: "The misfortunes of *Muriel*," in Jim Hillier (ed), *Cahiers du cinéma*, vol. 2 (London: Routledge, 1986)

Antoine Compagnon, "Mapping the European mind," in Duncan Petrie (ed), *Screening Europe: Image and Identity in Contemporary European Cinema* (London: BFI, 1992)

Conflict or Cooperation in European Film and Television (Manchester: The European Institute for the Media, 1992), p. 25

Stephen Cornell and Douglas Hartmann, *Ethnicity and Race: Making Identities in a Changing World* (Thousand Oaks, London, New Delhi: Pine Forge Press, 1998)

Andrea Cornwall and Nancy Lindisfarne (eds), *Dislocating Masculinity: Comparative Ethnographies* (London and New York: Routledge, 1994)

Pam Cook and Mieke Bernink (eds), *The Cinema Book* (London: BFI, 1999)

Colin Crisp, *The Classic French Cinema* (Bloomington: Indiana University Press, 1997)

Stephen Crofts, "Reconceptualising national cinema/s," *Quarterly Review of Film and Video*, vol. 14, no. 3, 1993

————, "Concepts of national cinema," in John Hill and Pamela Church Gibson (eds), *The Oxford Guide to Film Studies* (Oxford: Oxford University Press, 1998)

Joao Benard da Costa, *Stories of the Cinema* (Lisbon: Imprensa Nacional— Casa da Moeda, 1991)

Martin Dale, *The Movie Game: The Film Business in Britain, Europe and America* (London: Cassell, 1997)

Angela Dalle Vacche, *The Body in the Mirror: Shapes of History in Italian Cinema* (Princetown: Princetown University Press, 1992)

Sara Delamont, *Appetites and Identities: An Introduction to the Social Anthropology of Western Europe* (London and New York: Routledge, 1995)

Celestino Deleyto, "Motherland: space, femininity, and Spanishness in *Jamón, jamón*," in Peter William Evans (ed), *Spanish Cinema: The Auteurist Tradition* (Oxford, Oxford University Press, 1999)

James Donald and Ali Rattansi (eds), *"Race," Culture and Difference* (London: SAGE, 1992)

N. P. Dubinin, "Race and contemporary genetics," in Leo Kuper (ed), *Race, Science and Society* (Paris and London: The Unesco Press and George Allen and Unwin Ltd, 1975)

David Duff (ed), *Modern Genre Theory* (Edinburgh: Longman, 2000)

Christopher Duggan and Christopher Wagstaff (eds), *Italy in the Cold War: Politics, Culture and Society* (Oxford: Berg, 1995)

Raymond Durgnat, "Review of *Fantômas*," in *Films and Filming*, vol. 15, no. 4, 1964

Richard Dyer, *Stars* (London: BFI, 1979)

———, *Heavenly Bodies: Film Stars and Society* (London: Macmillan/BFI, 1986)

———, *Now You See It: Studies on Lesbian and Gay Film* (London: Routledge, 1990)

——— and Ginette Vincendeau, "Introduction," in Richard Dyer and Ginette Vincendeau (eds), *Popular European Cinema* (London and New York: Routledge, 1992)

——— and Ginette Vincendeau (eds), *Popular European Cinema* (London and New York: Routledge, 1992)

———, *White* (London and New York: Routledge, 1997)

Umberto Eco, *Travels in Hyperreality* (London: Pelican, 1987)

———, "All for one, one for all," *The Guardian*, 11 September 1992

Gary R Edgerton, *American Film Exhibition and an Analysis of the Motion Picture Industry's Market Structure 1963–1980* (New York: Garland, 1983)

Dimitris Eleftheriotis, "Video poetics: technology, aesthetics and politics," *Screen*, vol. 36, no. 2, 1995

———, "Questioning totalities: constructions of masculinity in the popular Greek cinema of the 1960s," *Screen*, vol. 36, no. 3, 1995

John Ellis, *Visible Fictions* (London: Routledge, 1984)

Thomas Elsaesser, *New German Cinema: A History* (London: BFI/Macmillan, 1989)

———, "Two decades in another country: Hollywood and the cinephiles," in C.W.E. Bigsby, *Superculture: American Popular Culture and Europe* (London: Paul Elek, 1975)

———, "Film history and visual pleasure" in Patricia Mellencamp and Phil Rosen (eds), *Cinema Histories, Cinema Practices* (Fredrick: American Film Institute, 1984)

———, "The European art movie," *Sight and Sound*, vol. 4, no. 4, April (1994)

David Ellwood and Rob Kroes (eds), *Hollywood in Europe: Experiences of a Cultural Hegemony* (Amsterdam: University of Amsterdam Press, 1994)

European Community Audiovisual Policy (Luxembourg: Office for Official Publications of the European Communities, 1992)

European Declaration on Cultural Objectives, 4th Conference of European
Ministers responsible for Cultural Affairs, Berlin, 23–25 May 1984
Europe's Way to the Information Society: An Action Plan (Brussels, July 1994)
Peter William Evans (ed), *Spanish Cinema: The Auteurist Tradition*
(Oxford: Oxford University Press, 1999)
Wendy Everett (ed), *European Identity in Cinema* (Exeter: Intellect, 1996)
Frantz Fanon, *Black Skin, White Masks* (London: Pluto, 1986)
———, *The Wretched of the Earth* (London: Penguin, 1976)
Mike Featherstone, Scott Lash and Roland Robertson (eds), *Global
Modernities* (London: SAGE, 1995)
Steve Fenton, *Ethnicity: Racism, Class and Culture* (London: Macmillan,
1999)
Ernest Ferlita and John R. May, *The Parables of Lina Wertmüller* (New
York: Paulist Press, 1977)
Angus Finney, *The State of European Cinema: A New Dose of Reality*
(London: Cassell, 1996)
Rod Fisher, *1993: The Challenge for the Arts: Reflections on British
Culture in Europe in the Context of the Single Market and Maastricht*
(London: The Arts Council of Great Britain, 1994)
John Fiske, *Television Culture* (London and New York: Routledge, 1989)
Sandy Flitterman-Lewis, *To Desire Differently: Feminism and the French
Cinema* (Urbana: University of Illinois Press, 1990)
40 Years of Cultural Co-Operation: 1954–1994 (Strasbourg: Council of
Europe Publishing, 1997)
David Forgacs and Robert Lumley (eds), *Italian Cultural Studies* (Oxford:
Oxford University Press, 1996)
Jill Forbes, *Cinema in France: After the New Wave* (London: Macmillan,
1992)
——— and Michael Kelly (eds), *French Cultural Studies* (Oxford: Oxford
University Press, 1995)
——— and Sarah Street (eds), *European Cinema* (Basingstoke: Palgrave,
2000)
Hal Foster (ed), *Postmodern Culture* (London: Pluto, 1985)
Michel Foucault, *The Order of Things* (London: Tavistock, 1970)
———, *The Birth of the Clinic* (London: Tavistock, 1970)
———, *Discipline and Punish* (London: Penguin, 1977)
———, "What is an author," in *Language, Counter-Memory, Practice*
(Oxford: Blackwell, 1977)
———, *The History of Sexuality*, vol. 1 (London: Penguin, 1979)
———, *The Archaeology of Knowledge* (London: Tavistock, 1982)
———, *Michel Foucault: Politics, Philosophy, Culture* (New York and
London: Routledge, 1988), edited by Lawrence Kritzman
Santiago Fouz-Hernández, "All that glitters is not gold: reading Javier
Bardem's body in Bigas Luna's *Golden Balls*," in Rob Rix and Roberto

Rodriguez-Saona (eds), *Spanish Cinema: Calling the Shots* (Leeds: Trinity and All Saints, 1999)

Christopher Frayling, *Spaghetti Westerns: Cowboys and Europeans from Karl May to Sergio Leone* (London: Routledge, 1981)

Sigmund Freud, "The acquisition and control of fire," in Sigmund Freud, *The Origins of Religion* (London: Pelican, 1985)

Joseph Garncarz, "Hollywood in Germany: the role of American films in Germany, 1925–1990," in David Ellwood and Rob Kroes (eds), *Hollywood in Europe: Experiences of a Cultural Hegemony* (Amsterdam: University of Amsterdam Press, 1994)

Ernest Gellner, *Nations and Nationalism* (Oxford: Blackwell, 1983)

Henry A. Giroux, "Film and the dialectic of alienation: the paradox of Lina Wertmüller," *Film Criticism*, vol. 1, no. 1, 1976

Jean-Luc Godard, "From critic to filmmaker: Godard in interview," Jim Hillier (ed), *Cahiers du cinéma*, vol. 2 (London: Routledge, 1986)

———, "Jean-Luc Godard in conversation with Colin MacCabe," in Duncan Petrie (ed), *Screening Europe: Image and Identity in Contemporary European Cinema* (London: BFI, 1992)

Catherine Grant, "www.author.com?" *Screen*, vol. 41, no. 1, 2000

Giovanna Grignaffini, "Female identity and Italian cinema of the 1950s," in Giuliana Bruno and Maria Nadotti (eds), *Off Screen: Women and Film in Italy* (London: Routledge, 1988)

Thomas H. Guback, *The International Film Industry: Western Europe and America since 1945* (Bloomington: Indiana University Press, 1969)

———, "Hollywood's international market," in Tino Balio (ed), *The American Film Industry* (Madison: University of Wisconsin Press, 1985)

Jürgen Habermas, "The project of modernity," in Hal Foster (ed), *Postmodern Culture* (London: Pluto, 1985)

Stuart Hall, "New ethnicities," in *Black Film, British Cinema*, ICA Documents, 7 (London: Institute of Contemporary Arts, 1989), reprinted in Bill Ashcroft, Gareth Griffiths and Helen Tiffin (eds), *The Post-Colonial Studies Reader* (London and New York: Routledge, 1995)

Paul Hammond (ed), *The Shadow and its Shadow: Surrealist Writings on Cinema* (London: BFI, 1978)

Donna Haraway, "Manifesto for cyborgs: science, technology and socialist feminism in the 1980s," *Socialist Review*, no. 80, 1985

David Harvey, *The Condition of Postmodernity: An Enquiry into the Origins of Cultural Change* (Oxford: Blackwell, 1990)

Sylvia Harvey, *May '68 and Film Culture* (London: BFI, 1980)

Molly Haskell, "Swept away on a wave of sexism," *Village Voice*, 29 September 1975

Colin Haskins, Stuart McFadyen and Adam Finn, *Global Television and Film: An Introduction to the Economics of the Business* (Oxford: Oxford University Press, 1997)

Philip Hayward and Tana Wollen (eds), *Future Visions: New Technlogies of the Screen* (London: BFI, 1993)

Susan Hayward (ed), *European Cinema* (Birmingham: Aston University Press, 1985)

———, *French National Cinema* (London and New York: Routledge, 1993)

———, "State, culture and the cinema: Jack Lang's strategies for the French film industry 1981–93," *Screen*, vol. 34, no. 4, 1993

——— and Ginette Vincendeau (eds), *French Film: Texts and Contexts* (London: Routledge, 2000)

Stephen Heath, *Questions of Cinema* (London: Macmillan, 1981)

——— and Teresa de Lauretis (eds), *The Cinematic Apparatus* (London: Macmillan, 1980)

Martin Heidegger, "The age of the world picture," in *The Question Concerning Technology* (New York: Harper and Row, 1977)

Agnes Heller, "Europe: an epilogue?" in Brian Nelson, David Roberts and Walter Veit (eds), *The Idea of Europe: Problems of National and Transnational Identity* (New York and Oxford: Berg, 1992)

John Hess, "La politique des auteurs," *Jump Cut*, nos. 1 and 2, 1974

Nichola Hewitt (ed), *The Culture of Reconstruction: European Literature, Thought and Film* (London: Macmillan, 1989)

Virginia Higginbotham, *Spanish Film under Franco* (Austin: University of Texas Press, 1988)

Andrew Higson, "The concept of national cinema," *Screen*, vol. 30, no. 4, 1989

———, *Waving the Flag: Constructing a National Cinema in Britain* (Oxford: Oxford University Press, 1997)

John Hill, Martin McCloone, and Paul Hainsworth (eds), *Border Crossing: Film in Ireland, Britain and Europe* (London: BFI, 1994)

Jim Hillier (ed), *Cahiers du cinéma*, vol. 1 (London: Routledge, 1985)

——— (ed), *Cahiers du cinéma*, vol. 2 (London: Routledge, 1986)

Mette Hjort and Scott Mackenzie (eds), *Cinema and Nation* (London and New York: Routledge, 2000)

Eric Hobsbowm, *Nations and Nationalism since 1780: Programme, Myth, Reality* (Cambridge: Cambridge University Press, 1990)

John Hopewell, *Out of the Past: Spanish Cinema after Franco* (London: BFI, 1986)

John Hutchinson and Anthony Smith (eds), *Nationalism* (Oxford: Oxford University Press, 1994)

——— (eds), *Ethnicity* (Oxford: Oxford University Press, 1996)

John Hutnyk and Raminder Kaur (eds), *Travel Worlds: Journeys in Contemporary Cultural Politics* (London and New York: Zed Books, 1999)

In from the Margins: A Contribution to the Debate on Culture and Development in Europe (Strasbourg: Council of Europe Publishing, 1997)

Dina Iordanova, "Kusturica's *Underground* (1995): historical allegory or propaganda," *Historical Journal of Film, Radio and Television*, vol. 19, no. 1, 1999

Albert Jacquard, "Science and racism," in *Racism, Science and Pseudo-Science* (Paris: The Unesco Press, 1983

Diane Jacobs, "Lina Wermüller: the Italian Aristophanes?," *Film Comment*, vol. 12, no. 2, 1976

Fredric Jameson, "Postmodernism or the cultural logic of late capitalism," *New Left Review*, no. 146, 1994

———, *Postmodernism or the Cultural Logic of Late Capitalism* (Durham, NC: Duke University Press, 1990)

Ian Jarvie, "The postwar economic foreign policy of the American film industry: Europe 1945–1950," in *Film History*, vol. 4, 1990

Jean-Pierre Jeancolas, "From the Blum-Byrnes agreement to the GATT affair," in Geoffrey Nowell-Smith and Steven Ricci (eds), *Hollywood and Europe: Economics, Culture, National Identity 1945–95* (London: BFI, 1998)

Brian Jenkins and Spyros A. Sofos (eds), *Nation and Identity in Contemporary Europe* (London and New York: Routledge, 1996)

Brian Jenkins and Nigel Copsey, "Nation, nationalism and national identity in France," in Brian Jenkins and Spyros A. Sofos (eds), *Nation and Identity in Contemporary Europe* (London and New York: Routledge, 1996)

Stan Jones, "Wenders' *Paris, Texas* and the 'European way of seeing,'" in Wendy Everett (ed), *European Identity in Cinema* (Exeter: Intellect, 1996)

Barry Jordan and Rikki Morgan-Tamosunas, *Contemporary Spanish Cinema* (Manchester and New York: Manchester University Press, 1998)

Terry Jordan, *The European Culture Area: A Systematic Geography* (New York: Harper and Row, 1973)

Pauline Kael, "Seven Fatties," *New Yorker*, 17 February 1976

E. Ann Kaplan (ed), *Psychoanalysis and Cinema* (New York and London: Routledge, 1990)

———, "Problematizing cross-cultural analysis: the case of women in the recent Chinese cinema," in Chris Berry (ed), *Perspectives on Chinese Cinema* (London: BFI, 1991)

———, *Looking for the Other: Feminism, Film and the Imperial Gaze* (London and New York: Routledge, 1997)

Marsha Kinder, *Blood Cinema: The Reconstruction of National Identity in Spain* (Berkeley, Los Angeles and London: University of California Press, 1993)

——— (ed), *Refiguring Spain: Cinema, Media, Representation* (Durham: Duke University Press, 1997)

Pat Kirkham and Janet Thumim (eds), *Me Jane: Masculinity, Movies and Women* (London: Lawrence and Wishart, 1995)

Paschalis Kitromilides, *Enlightenment, Nationalism, Orthodoxy: Studies in the Culture and Political Thought of South-Eastern Europe* (Brookfield and Aldershot: VARIORUM, 1994)

Jim Kitses, *Horizons West* (London: Secker and Warburg/BFI, 1969)

Rosalind E. Krauss, *The Originality of the Avant-Garde and Other Modernist Myths* (Cambridge, Mass: MIT Press, 1986)

Frank Krutnik and Steve Neale, *Popular Film and Television Comedy* (London: Routledge, 1990)

Annette Kuhn (ed), *Alien Zone: Cultural Theory and Contemporary Science Fiction Cinema* (London and New York: Verso, 1990)

—— and Jackie Stacey (eds), *Screen Histories: A Screen Reader* (Oxford: Oxford University Press, 1998)

Raymond Kuhn, *The Media in France* (London and New York: Routledge, 1995)

Jacques Lacan, "The mirror stage as formative of the function of the I," in Jacques Lacan, *Écrits: A Selection* (London: Tavistock, 1977)

Marcia Landy, *British Genres: Cinema and Society, 1930–1960* (Princeton: Princeton University Press, 1991)

——, *Italian Film* (Cambridge: Cambridge University Press, 2000)

Jan-Erik Lane and Svante Ersson, *Politics and Society in Western Europe* (London, Thousand Oaks, New Delhi: SAGE, 1999)

George Lellis, "Fantômas," *Cinema Texas Program Notes*, vol. 5, no. 10, 1973

Pierre Leprohon, *The Italian Cinema* (London: Secker and Warbug, 1972)

Peter Lev, *The Euro-American Film* (Austin: University of Texas Press, 1993)

Mira Liehm, *Passion and Defiance: Film in Italy from 1942 to the Present* (Berkley: University of California Press, 1984)

Jean François Lyotard, *The Postmodern Condition: A Report on Knowledge (*Manchester: Manchester University Press, 1984)

——, "Presenting the unpresentable, the sublime," *Artforum*, April 1982

——, "The sublime and the avant-garde," *Artforum*, April 1984

——, "Philosophy and painting in the age of their experimentation: contribution to an idea of postmodernity," *Camera Obscura*, no. 12, 1985

Rosana Maule, "De-authorizing the *auteur*: postmodern politics of interpellation in contemporary European Cinema," in Cristina Degli-Esposti (ed), *Postmodernism in the Cinema* (Oxford: Berghahan, 1998)

Judith Mayne, *The Woman at the Keyhole: Feminism and Women's Cinema* (Urbana: Indiana University Press, 1990)

——, *Cinema and Spectatorship* (London: Routledge, 1993)

Colin MacCabe, *Godard: Images, Sounds, Politics* (London: BFI/Macmillan, 1980)

Marshal McLuhan, *Understanding Media: The Extensions of Man* (London and New York: Ark Paperworks, 1987)

Ruth McCormick, "*Swept Away,*" *Cinéaste*, Spring 1976

Media: Guide for the Audiovisual Industry (Brussels: Commission of the European Communities, 1991)

Annette Michelson, "Screen/Surface: the politics of illusionism," *Artforum*, September 1972

Mirco Melanco, "Italian cinema, since 1945: the social costs of indusrialization," *Historical Journal of Film, Radio and Television*, vol. 15, no. 3, 1995

Christian Metz, "Story/discourse: notes on two kinds of voyerism," in Bill Nichols (ed), *Movies and Methods*, vol. II (Berkeley, Los Angeles and London: University of California Press, 1985)

John J. Michalczyk, *The Italian Political Filmmakers* (London and Toronto: Associated University Presses, 1986)

Toby Miller, "The crime of Monsieur Lang: GATT, the screen and the new international division of labour," in Albert Moran (ed), *Film Policy: International, National and Regional Perspectives* (London and New York: Routledge, 1996)

Sara Mills, *Discourses of Difference: An Analysis of Women's Travel Writing and Colonialism* (London and New York, Routledge, 1991)

Vijay Mishra, "Towards a theoretical critique of Bombay cinema," *Screen*, vol. 26, nos. 3–4, 1985

Tania Modleski, "Wertmüller's women: swept away by the usual destiny," *Jump Cut*, June 1976

—— (ed), *Studies in Entertainment* (Bloomington: Indiana University Press, 1986)

Albert Moran (ed), *Film Policy: International, National and Regional Perspectives* (London and New York: Routledge, 1996)

Mario Morandi, "Italy: auteurs and after," in Geoffrey Nowell-Smith (ed), *The Oxford History of World Cinema* (London and New York: Oxford University Press, 1996)

Meaghan Morris, "Banality in cultural studies," in Patricia Mellenchamp (ed), *The Logics of Television: Essays in Cultural Criticism* (Urbana: Indiana University Press, 1990)

Jean-Luc Moullet, "La peur et stupeur," in *Cahiers du Cinéma*, no. 486, December 1984

Laura Mulvey, "Visual pleasure and narrative cinema," *Screen*, vol. 16, no. 3, 1975

——, *Visual and Other Pleasures* (London: Macmillan, 1988)

Charles Musser, "The travel genre in 1903–04: moving toward fictional narratives," *Iris*, vol. 2, no. 1, 1984

———, *The Emergence of Cinema: The American Screen to 1907* (Berkeley: University of California Press, 1990)

———, *Before the Nickelodeon: Edwin S. Porter and the Edison Manufacturing Company* (Berkeley: University of California Press, 1990)

Steve Neale, *Genre* (London: BFI, 1980)

———, "Art cinema as institution," *Screen*, vol. 22, no. 1, 1981

———, "Masculinity as spectacle," *Screen*, vol. 24, no. 6, 1983

———, *Cinema and Technology: Image, Sound, Colour* (London: Macmillan, 1985)

———, "Question of genre," *Screen*, vol. 31, no. 1, 1990

——— and Murray Smith (eds), *Contemporary Hollywood Cinema* (London and New York: Routledge, 1998)

Jan Nederveen Pieterse, "Globalization as hybridization" in Mike Featherstone, Scott Lash and Roland Robertson (eds), *Global Modernities* (London: SAGE, 1995)

Brian Nelson, David Roberts and Walter Veit (eds), *The Idea of Europe: Problems of National and Transnational Identity* (New York and Oxford: Berg, 1992)

1999 European Cinema Yearbook (MEDIA Salles, 1999)

Kim Newman, "Thirty years in another town: the history of Italian exploitation," *Films and Filming*, nos 624, 625, 626 (1986)

Geoffrey Nowell-Smith (ed), *The Oxford History of World Cinema* (London and New York: Oxford University Press, 1996)

——— with James Hay and Gianni Volpi (eds), *The Companion to Italian Cinema* (London: Cassel and BFI, 1996)

——— and Steven Ricci (eds), *Hollywood and Europe: Economics, Culture, National Identity 1945–95* (London: BFI, 1998)

Ireneusz Opacki, "Royal genres" in David Duff (ed), *Modern Genre Theory* (Edinburgh: Longman, 2000)

Umut Özkirimli, *Theories of Nationalism: A Critical Introduction* (London: Macmillan, 2000)

Sven Papcke, "Who needs European identity and what could it be?" in Brian Nelson, David Roberts and Walter Veit (eds), *The Idea of Europe: Problems of National and Transnational Identity* (New York and Oxford: Berg, 1992)

Andrew Parker, Mary Russo, Dorris Sommer and Patricia Yaeger (eds), *Nationalisms and Sexualities* (New York and London: Routledge, 1992)

Rebecca Pauly, *The Transparent Illusion: Image and Ideology in French Text and Film* (New York: Peter Lange, 1993)

V. F. Perkins, "The Atlantic divide" in Richard Dyer and Ginette Vincendeau (eds), *Popular European Cinema* (London and New York: Routledge, 1992)

Duncan Petrie (ed), *Screening Europe: Image and Identity in Contemporary European Cinema* (London: BFI, 1992)

Roberto Poppi, *Dizionario del cinema italiano: i registi* (Rome, Gremese Editore, 1993)

—— and Mario Pecorari, *Dizionario del cinema italiano: i film*, vol. 1–4 (Rome: Gremese Editore, 1996)

Mary Louise Pratt, *Imperial Eyes: Travel Writing and Transculturation* (London and New York: Routledge, 1992)

Jose Rabasa, *Inventing A-M-E-R-I-C-A: Spanish Historiography and the Formation of Eurocentricism* (Norman, Oklahoma and London: University of Oklahoma Press, 1993)

Ernest Renan, "Qu'est-ce qu'une nation," published with translation and annotation by Martin Thom in Homi K. Bhabha (ed), *Nation and Narration* (Routledge: London and New York, 1990)

Brooks Riley, "Lina Wertmüller: the sophists' Norman Lear?" *Film Comment*, vol. 12, no. 2, 1976

Rob Rix and Roberto Rodriguez-Saona (eds), *Spanish Cinema: Calling the Shots* (Leeds: Trinity and All Saints, 1999)

Philip Rosen, "History, textuality, nation: Kracauer, Bürch, and some problems in the study of national cinemas," *Iris*, vol. 2, no.2, 1984

——, "Nation and anti-nation: concepts of national cinema in the 'new' media era," *Diaspora*, 5:3 (1996)

Kathleen Rowe, *The Unruly Woman: Gender and the Genres of Laughter* (Austin, University of Texas Press, 1995)

Tony Ryans, "*Underground*: Review," in *Sight and Sound*, vol. 6, no. 3, March 1996

Edward W. Saïd, *Orientalism* (Harmondsworth: Penguin, 1976)

——, *Culture and Imperialism* (London: Vintage, 1993)

Saskia Sassen, *Cities in a World Economy* (Thousand Oaks, London and New Delhi: Pine Forge Press, 1994)

Paddy Scannel, Philip Schlesinger and Colin Sparks (eds), *Culture and Power: A Media, Culture and Society Reader* (London: SAGE, 1992)

Tassilo Schneider, "Finding a new *Heimat* in the Wild West: Karl May and the German western of the 1960s," in Edward Buscombe and Roberta E. Pearson (eds), *Back in the Saddle Again: New Essays on the Western* (London: BFI, 1998)

Steve Seidman, *Comedian Comedy: A Tradition in the Hollywood Film* (Ann Arbor: UMI Research Press, 1981)

Rob Shields, *Places on the Margin: Alternative Geographies of Modernity* (London and New York: Routledge, 1992)

Ella Shohat and Robert Stam, "The cinema after Babel: language, difference, power," *Screen*, vol. 26, no. 3–4, 1985

——, *Unthinking Eurocentricism: Multiculturalism and the Media* (London and New York: Routledge, 1994)

Pamela Shurmer-Smith and Kevin Hannam, *Worlds of Desire, Realms of Power: A Cultural Geography* (London: Edward Arnold, 1994)

Kaja Silverman, *Male Subjectivity at the Margins* (New York and London: Routledge, 1992)

Barry Smart, "Europe today and the postmodern paradox," in Brian Nelson, David Roberts and Walter Veit (eds), *The Idea of Europe: Problems of National and Transnational Identity* (New York and Oxford: Berg, 1992)

Anthony Smith, *National Identity* (London: Penguin, 1991)

——, "Speaking in tongues: words and images as vehicles for the cultures of Europe," in Rod Fisher, *1993: The Challenge for the Arts: Reflections on British Culture in Europe in the Context of the Single Market and Maastricht* (London: The Arts Council of Great Britain, 1994)

Paul Julien Smith, *Vision Machines: Cinema, Literature and Sexuality in Spain and Cuba 1983–1993* (London: Verso, 1996)

Edward Soja, *Postmodern Geographies* (London: Verso, 1989)

Tytti Soila, Astrid Söderberg Widding and Gunnar Iversen, *Nordic National Cinemas* (London and New York: Routledge, 1998)

Yiannis Soldatos, *Istoria tou Ellinikou Kinimatografou (History of Greek Cinema)*, vol. 1. (Athens: Aigokeros, 1988)

——, *History of Greek Cinema*, vol. 2 (Athens: Aigokeros, 1989)

Pierre Sorlin, *European Cinemas, European Societies* (London: Routledge, 1991)

——, *Italian National Cinema 1896–1996* (London and New York: Routledge, 1996)

Specificities and Universality: Problems of Identities (Strasbourg: Council of Europe Press, 1995)

Gayatri Chakravorty Spivak, *In Other Worlds: Essays in Cultural Politics* (London: Routledge, 1988)

Annabelle Sreberny-Mohammadi, Dwayne Winseck, Jim McKenna and Oliver Boyd-Barrett (eds), *Media in Global Context: A Reader* (London: Arnold, 1997)

Statistics on Film and Cinema 1955–1977 (Paris: Unesco, 1981)

Jackie Stacey, *Star Gazing: Hollywood Cinema and Female Spectatorship* (London: Routledge, 1994)

Sarah Street, *British National Cinema* (London and New York: Routledge, 1997)

Richard Taylor, Nancy Wood, Julian Graffy and Dina Iordanova (eds), *The BFI Companion to Eastern European and Russian Cinema* (London: BFI, 2000)

Rosie Thomas, "Indian cinema–pleasures and popularity," *Screen*, vol. 26, nos. 3–4, 1985

Kristin Thompson, *Exporting Entertainment: America in the World Film Market 1907–1934* (London: BFI, 1985)

Jane Tompkins, *West of Everything: The Inner Life of Westerns* (Oxford and New York: Oxford University Press, 1992)

Jean-Paul Torok, "La cadavre exquis," *Positif*, July 1961

François Truffaut, "A certain tendency of the French cinema," reprinted and translated in Bill Nichols (ed), *Movies and Methods*, vol. 1 (Berkeley London: University of California Press, 1976)

Andrew Tudor, *Theories of Film* (London: BFI/Secher and Warburg, 1974)

Jon Tuska, *The American West in Film: Critical Approaches to the Western* (Westport and London: Greenwood Press, 1985)

Ravi Vasudevan, "Addressing the spectator of a 'third world' national cinema: the Bombay 'social' film of the 1940s and 1950s," *Screen*, vol. 36, no. 4, 1995

Ginette Vincendeau, "France 1945–65 and Hollywood: the *policier* as inter-national text," *Screen*, vol. 33, no.1 (1992)

——— (ed), *Encyclopaedia of European Cinema* (London: Cassell and BFI, 1995)

———, *The Companion to French Cinema* (London: Cassell/BFI, 1996)

———, "Issues in European cinema," in John Hill and Pamela Church Gibson (eds), *The Oxford Guide to Film Studies* (Oxford: Oxford University Press, 1998)

Johann Gotfried von Herder, *Ideen zur Philosophie der Geschichte der Menschheit* (Darmstadt: Melzer, 1966)

Christopher Wagstaff, "A forkful of westerns: industry, audiences and the Italian western," in Richard Dyer and Ginette Vincendeau (eds), *Popular European Cinema* (London and New York: Routledge, 1992)

———, "Cinema" in David Forgacs and Robert Lumley (eds), *Italian Cultural Studies* (Oxford: Oxford University Press, 1996)

———, "Italian genre films in the world market," in Nowell-Smith and Steven Ricci (eds), *Hollywood and Europe: Economics, Culture, National Identity 1945–95* (London: BFI, 1998)

——— and Christopher Duggan (eds), "Italy in the post-war international cinema market," in *Italy in the Cold War: Politics, Culture and Society* (Oxford: Berg, 1995)

Malcolm Walters, *Globalization* (London and New York: Routledge, 1995)

Thomas E. Wartenberg, *Unlikely Couples: Movie Romance as Social Criticism* (Oxford and Boulder: Westview Press, 1999)

Thomas Weisser, *Spaghetti Westerns: The Good, The Bad, The Violent* (London:McFarland, 1992)

White Book of the European Exhibition Industry, vols 1 and 2 (electronic publication of MEDIA Salles, 1994)

White Paper on Growth, Competitiveness, and Employment (Brussels, December 1993)

Raymond Williams, *Keywords: A Vocabulary of Culture and Society* (London: Fontana Press, 1988)

R. T. Witcombe, *The New Italian Cinema* (New York: Oxford University Press, 1982)

Janet Wolff, *The Social Production of Art* (London: Macmillan, 1981)

————, *Aesthetics and the Sociology of Art* (London: George Allen and Unwin, 1983)

Peter Wollen, *Signs and Meaning in the Cinema* (London: BFI, 1998)

Will Wright, *Sixguns and Society: A Structural Study of the Western* (Berkeley: University of California Press, 1975)

Esther Yau, "*Yellow Earth*: Western analysis and a non-Western text," in Chris Berry (ed), *Perspectives on Chinese Cinema* (London: BFI, 1991)

R. J. C. Young, *Colonial Desire: Hybridity in Theory, Culture and Race* (London: Routledge, 1995)

Index